The Perennial Philosophy

Series

World Wisdom
The Library of Perennial Philosophy

The Library of Perennial Philosophy is dedicated to the exposition of the timeless Truth underlying the diverse religions. This Truth, often referred to as the *Sophia Perennis*—or Perennial Wisdom—finds its expression in the revealed Scriptures as well as in the writings of the great sages and the artistic creations of the traditional worlds.

The Way and the Mountain appears as one of our selections in the Perennial Philosophy series.

The Perennial Philosophy Series

In the beginning of the twentieth century, a school of thought arose which has focused on the enunciation and explanation of the Perennial Philosophy. Deeply rooted in the sense of the sacred, the writings of its leading exponents establish an indispensable foundation for understanding the timeless Truth and spiritual practices which live in the heart of all religions. Some of these titles are companion volumes to the Treasures of the World's Religions series, which allows a comparison of the writings of the great sages of the past with the perennialist authors of our time.

Wayside message: *Om Mani Padme Hum*

The Way and the Mountain
Tibet, Buddhism, and Tradition

by
Marco Pallis
(Thubden Tendzin)

Edited & Introduced by
Joseph A. Fitzgerald

Foreword by
Harry Oldmeadow

Appreciation by
Paul Goble

World Wisdom

The Way and the Mountain:
Tibet, Buddhism, and Tradition, Marco Pallis (Thubden Tendzin)
© 2008 World Wisdom, INC.

Library of Congress Cataloging-in-Publication Data

Pallis, Marco, 1895-1989.
  The way and the mountain : Tibet, Buddhism, and tradition / by Marco
Pallis (Thubden Tendzin) ; edited & introduced by Joseph A. Fitzgerald ;
foreword by Harry Oldmeadow ; appreciation by Paul Goble.
     p. cm.
Includes bibliographical references and index.
  ISBN 978-1-933316-53-6 (pbk. : alk. paper) 1. Buddhism–China–Tibet.
2. Tibet (China)–Religion. I. Fitzgerald, Joseph A., 1977- II. Title.
BQ7612.P35 2008
294.3'923–dc22

                                        2007050288

Printed on acid-free paper in Canada

For information address World Wisdom, INC.
P.O. Box 2682, Bloomington, Indiana 47402-2682
www.worldwisdom.com

Cover: Taktshang Goemba (Tiger's Nest Monastery), Bhutan
Photograph by Joseph A. Fitzgerald

Table of Contents

The "Great Black One," a defender of the *dharma*

Foreword

The recent history of Tibet exemplifies the fate of traditional civilizations in the modern world. Behind the snowy ramparts of the Himalayas, Tibet had stood as one of the last bastions of a way of life which properly deserved to be called traditional—one directed, in the first place, not to a godless ideal of material "progress" but to the spiritual welfare of its people, a culture which, in T.S. Eliot's phrase, was an incarnation of the religious outlook which informed it. In a sense, Tibet served as a haven for all those principles and ideals, all those aspirations of the human spirit, which were elsewhere being trampled underfoot by the forces of modernity. That the invasion of Tibet and the destruction of its religious culture should be carried out by its neighbor in the name of a profane Western ideology is one of the most bitter ironies of recent history. Let us not mince words: the systematic subversion of Tibet's religious heritage, the slaughter of its monks and nuns, the sacking of the monasteries, the unceasing violation of human rights, the cynical "population policy" to make Tibetans a minority in their own land, and the desecration of the environment, make the Chinese occupation an imperial vandalism no less appalling than that of the Western powers in so many different parts of the globe in the preceding century.

There are those who make much of the various social abuses and corruptions which, as the present Dalai Lama has conceded, were to be found in Tibet on the eve of the Chinese invasion, as if these could in any measure justify the monstrous brutalities which were to follow. On the other hand, there is nothing to be gained from that sentimental romanticism and nostalgia for the exotic which paints traditional Tibet as a pristine Utopia. Marco Pallis did not fall into either trap.

In an Appendix to *Peaks and Lamas* and in his Foreword to Chögyam Trungpa's *Born in Tibet* he acknowledged various ills in traditional Tibet and situated them in the proper context. Pallis was well aware of the following admonition of Frithjof Schuon, whose writings proved such an inspiration for his own work:

> When the modern world is contrasted with traditional civilizations, it is not simply a question of seeking the good things and the bad things on one side or the other; good and evil are everywhere, so that it is essentially a question of knowing on which side the more important good and on which side the lesser evil is to be found. If someone says that such and such a good exists outside tradition, the answer is: no doubt, but one must choose the most important good, and it is necessarily represented by tradition; and if someone says that in tradition there exists such and such an evil, the answer is: no doubt, but one must choose the lesser evil, and again it is tradition that embodies it. It is illogical to prefer an evil which involves some benefits to a good which involves some evils.[1]

No one with any sense of proportion can for a moment doubt that the good in Tibet's traditional civilization far outweighed the bad, and that something infinitely precious and irreplaceable was destroyed forever by the invading juggernaut.

The peculiar character of Tibetan civilization stemmed from the creative fusion of the indigenous shamanistic tradition of Bön-po with the *Mahayana* Buddhism brought to Tibet by Padmasambhava and the monks of India. From this spiritual intercourse sprang forth the *Vajrayana*, that luminous form of Buddhism which expressed the religious genius of the Tibetan people and which seemed to draw its inspiration from the austere and awesome beauty of Tibet's majestic

[1] *Light on the Ancient Worlds* (London: Perennial Books, 1966), p. 42.

peaks and vast plateaus. Here, preserved in the monastic lineages and in the customs and institutions of the people, was to be found a spiritual treasury of almost incomparable beauty and richness. We need think no further than the ideal of the Bodhisattva and its resplendent iconography, of Chenrezig, Tara, and Manjushri, of Milarepa, of the long line of Dalai Lamas who embody the ideal of Wisdom-Compassion which lies at the very heart of the tradition.

Marco Pallis was one of a small group of Westerners who had the privilege of experiencing the traditional culture of Tibet in its eventide, visiting the Himalayan regions in 1923, 1933, 1936, and 1947. He was drawn there by his love of mountaineering and, no doubt, by impulses which at the time he himself could only sense as through a glass darkly. So profound was the impact of his early visits that by the mid-1930s Pallis had become a committed *dharma*-practitioner and an initiated member of one of the Tibetan orders. Thenceforth he was to be one of the most eloquent witnesses of the calamity which afflicted his spiritual homeland, one of a small handful of Westerners who alerted the rest of the world to the magnitude of the tragedy which was unfolding in Tibet. He also devoted himself to the explication of Tibetan religious and cultural forms which were still so little understood in the West. At a time when all too many of the Western cognoscenti hailed Buddhism as a kind of rational and humanistic psychology, Pallis' writings served as an implacable reminder of the Transcendent which is the fountainhead of all integral religious traditions and without which all the doings of mortals are nothing. He also exposed counterfeit forms of "Tibetan esotericism," such as the bizarre concoctions conjured up by "Lobsang Rampa" (one Cyril Hoskin). In explaining the doctrines of the *Vajrayana*, some of them arcane, Pallis was aided by the peerless metaphysical works of the great perennialists—René Guénon, Ananda Coomaraswamy, and Frithjof Schuon. These enabled him to discern the universal significance of beliefs and practices which, at first glance, seemed

strange and alien to untutored Western eyes. (Among Pallis'
many other achievements were fine translations of works by
both Guénon and Schuon.)

Pallis was not a prodigious writer. His essential *oeuvre*
comprises three books: the present volume, first published in
1960, the more widely-known *Peaks and Lamas* (1939), and *A
Buddhist Spectrum* (1980). *Peaks and Lamas*, recounting Pallis'
early sojourns in Western Tibet and the Himalayan kingdoms,
is a captivating work and one of the most distinguished works
of the genre. *A Buddhist Spectrum* gathers together several
essays from his later years, irradiated by a gentle but clear-
eyed wisdom that was the fruit of his long years of study,
spiritual practice, and first-hand experience. In reviewing *A
Buddhist Spectrum* Huston Smith remarked, "For insight, and
the beauty insight requires if it is to be effective, I find no writer on Buddhism surpassing him." This was high praise indeed
from the doyen of contemporary comparative religionists,
but amply justified. These are indeed works to cherish. But,
assuredly, Pallis' master work is *The Way and the Mountain*,
focusing on the Tibetan tradition but situating it in the wider
context of the perennial wisdom and the spiritual life which
it entails. Pallis had no interest in research for its own sake,
nor in any purely theoretical understanding of doctrine: his
work was always attuned to the demands of the spiritual life
itself. The essays to be found within these covers should be
of interest not only to those on the Buddhist path but to all
spiritual wayfarers.

There have been other Westerners whose writings are, to
varying degrees, marked by acute metaphysical discernment,
wide-ranging erudition, imaginative sympathy, and a heartfelt
love for Tibet and its people, although none have so pre-
eminently combined these qualities as Pallis. One might mention not only Frithjof Schuon, whose few essays on Tibetan
subjects are worth more than many shelves of orientalist
studies, but figures such as Giuseppi Tucci, Lama Anagarika
Govinda (formerly Ernst Hoffman), Hugh Richardson, David

Snellgrove, and Arnaud Desjardins. Nor should we forget the path-breaking labors of pioneers such as W.Y. Evans-Wentz and the redoubtable Alexandra David-Neel, or indeed of the first Tibetologists, those intrepid Jesuit scholars of the seventeenth and early eighteenth centuries. Then, too, there are the burgeoning works and teachings of the Tibetan diaspora, not least from the Dalai Lama himself, which keep alive at least some aspects of the tradition. But Marco Pallis, visiting Tibet at a fateful moment in its history, and gifted with a rare metaphysical intelligence, had a singular role to play, testifying to the deepest significance of Tibet and its fate for the dark times in which we live. His works poignantly recall the beautiful and priceless treasures which have been so shamelessly destroyed. However, *The Way and the Mountain* is far more than an elegy; it is also an affirmation of that inviolable Spirit which cannot be destroyed.

Harry Oldmeadow

View of a *chorten* with the Potala Palace in the background, Lhasa, Tibet

Introduction[1]

In the Tibet we visited . . . the whole landscape was as if suffused by the message of the Buddha's Dharma; it came to one with the air one breathed, birds seemed to sing of it, mountain streams hummed its refrain as they bubbled across the stones, a dharmic perfume seemed to rise from every flower. . . . The India of King Ashoka's time must have been something like this; to find it in mid-twentieth century anywhere was something of a wonder.[2]

I never felt that I was among strangers; rather was it a return to a long-lost home.[3]

A lama once explained to Thubden Tendzin (or Marco Pallis), that he showed "unmistakable signs" of having been a Tibetan in some previous existence. Pallis warns us not to take his friend the lama's utterance too literally, but whatever be the case regarding his past, "I can at least say this about the next life: had I the choice, I should be well content to be reborn as a Tibetan."[4] Some would say that Pallis did not

---

[1] Biographical information is taken primarily from the published writings and private correspondence of Marco Pallis; from the memoirs of his niece, Dominie Nicholls, entitled *Quite a Lot* (privately published in 2002); from Harry Oldmeadow's *Journeys East* (Bloomington, IN: World Wisdom, 2004); from the obituary of Marco Pallis written by his friend and pupil Peter Talbot-Wilcox (published June 1989, *The Independent*, London); from an unpublished biographical note by William Stoddart; and from interviews conducted with longtime friends of Pallis, including Catherine Schuon, Paul Goble, Christopher James (5th Lord Northbourne), and Rama P. Coomaraswamy.

[2] Marco Pallis, *A Buddhist Spectrum* (Bloomington, IN: World Wisdom, 2003), p. 113.

[3] Marco Pallis, *Peaks and Lamas* (Washington, D.C.: Shoemaker & Hoard, 2005), p. 202.

[4] Ibid.

have to wait for a future life to become, in his heart, a true son of Tibet.

In 1895, Marco Alexander Pallis was born in Liverpool, England, the youngest son of wealthy and cosmopolitan Greek parents. He was his mother's favorite child—different, more sensitive than his other siblings—and from an early age was interested in religion. While studying at the exclusive all-boys school Harrow, he asked the chaplain to give him special bible lessons. As a young man studying at Liverpool University he became deeply attracted to Roman Catholicism, though this met with strong disapproval from his Greek Orthodox parents. While Pallis' life seemingly began far removed from the land of Chenrezig, *Vajrayana*, and Tantra, there was one exception: his parents, who had lived in India for several years, decorated the house in which the young Marco was raised with works of Indian and Oriental craftsmanship. For an artistic and receptive youth, it was a subtle first beckoning from the East.

Still young during the Great War, Pallis, after having briefly aided the Salvation Army in Serbo-Croatia, enlisted in the British Army. His first commission was in 1916 as an army interpreter in Macedonia. Malaria and a severe inflammation of his right eye cut short his Macedonian service. After a forced, lengthy convalescence in Malta, Pallis applied and was accepted to the Grenadier Guards. He first received basic training, then advanced training as a machine-gunner. In 1918, as a second lieutenant, he was sent to fight in the trenches of the Western Front. During the battle of Cambrai, in a charge that killed his captain and first lieutenant, Pallis was shot through the knee; for Pallis the war was over.

Following the war, in addition to family duties, Pallis occupied himself with what were then his two loves: mountaineering and music. He climbed and explored whenever and wherever he could, and this despite the fact that doctors had told him that he might never walk on his injured knee again.[5] He went on expeditions to the Arctic, Switzerland, and the Dolomites, while Snowdonia, the Peak District, and the Scottish Highlands provided him with opportunities closer to home. At the same time Pallis studied music under Arnold Dolmetsch, the distinguished reviver of early English music, composer, and performer.[6] Under Dolmetsch's influence,[7] Pallis soon discovered a love of early music—in particular chamber music of the sixteenth and seventeenth centuries—and for the viola da gamba. Even while climbing in the region of the Satlej-Ganges watershed, he and his musically-minded friends did not fail to bring their instruments.

His love of mountains was destined to help guide Pallis to his third—ultimately all-encompassing—love: Tibet and its civilization. In 1923, for purposes of climbing, Pallis visited Tibet for the first time. He returned to the Himalayas for a more prolonged climbing expedition in 1933 and again in 1936.[8] His best-selling book *Peaks and Lamas* describes these latter treks and the transformation that he underwent. From being an outsider, sympathetic but merely looking on,

---

[5] According to one of his Himalayan climbing partners, "Pallis hides a good deal of determination behind his mild manner" (F. Spencer Chapman, *Helvellyn to Himalaya: Including an Account of the First Ascent of Chomolhari* [London: The Travel Book Club, 1941], p. 84).

[6] Arnold Dolmetsch (1858-1940), was a true pioneer in his field. His circle of friends and collaborators extended to many of the major literary and artistic figures of the late nineteenth century and early twentieth century, including William Morris, George Bernard Shaw, Ezra Pound, and W.B Yeats.

[7] Dolmetsch also influenced Pallis intellectually, through pointing the way to the writings of the traditionalist metaphysician and critic of the modern world René Guénon, and the great Indologist and historian of sacred art Ananda K. Coomaraswamy. These authors helped Pallis to see the indispensable role tradition plays in perpetuating the transcendent and foundational ideals of a civilization. This understanding of tradition *per se*, was to inform Pallis' later writings on Tibet and its traditions.

[8] The expeditions Pallis led are cited today by dozens of books on the history of Himalayan mountaineering, although for Pallis their import was more spiritual than technical or physical.

he penetrated ever deeper into the heart of Tibetan life. He discarded his western clothes in favor of Tibetan dress, and furthered his study of the Tibetan language, culture, and religion. Often staying in monasteries, he received his religious education directly from lamas from within the living tradition.[9] The Second World War[10] prevented further travels until 1947, when, in what proved to be a last-minute opportunity, he and his friend Richard Nicholson were able to visit Tibet a final time before the coming Chinese invasion. Already a practicing Buddhist since 1936, while in Shigatse, Tibet, Pallis was initiated into one of the orders; he was fifty-two years old. By the time he left Tibet, one could say that Marco Pallis—now Thubden Tendzin—had completed the inward journey to his spiritual home. He continued to be a faithful practitioner of Tibetan Buddhism—and a tireless advocate for Tibet—until his death some forty-three years later.

The overthrow of independent Tibet by the Communist Chinese marked one of the saddest events in Pallis' life. In response, Pallis did what he could, mostly through his writ-

---

[9] Arnaud Desjardins, the French writer and filmmaker, tells of a story which confirms—if confirmation is needed—the authority of Pallis' sources. In the early 1960s, guided by the Dalai Lama's personal interpreter, Desjardins met and interviewed many of the most respected Tibetan spiritual leaders, now in exile. "I remember a conversation, one evening in Sikkim, when the question which arose was of Westerners who had really come near enough to *tantrayana* to understand something more than words and formulas. One such person, of whom those present spoke with the greatest regard and deference, was repeatedly referred to in this conversation by the English word 'Tradition.' 'Tradition' had spent some time with such-and-such a guru; 'Tradition' has visited such-and-such a monastery. And all of a sudden it became apparent to me that this Mr. 'Tradition' was Marco Pallis (under his Tibetan name of Thubden Tendzin). . . ." (Arnaud Desjardins, *The Message of the Tibetans* [London: Stuart & Watkins, 1969], p. 20). Among the great teachers that Pallis met was the saintly abbot of Lachhen.

[10] Under the influence of Buddhism, Pallis was a conscientious objector during the Second World War; for alternate service he became a police officer in Liverpool.

ings, which helped to raise public awareness of the wonder that was Tibet. It must have also given Pallis much pleasure to be able to help members of the Tibetan diaspora in England. On multiple occasions, Pallis opened up his London flat to house visiting Tibetans. He offered his help through other ways as well, such as with the young Chögyam Trungpa. Pallis traveled with and encouraged Trungpa, who had just arrived in England, and had not yet garnered the world renown he was soon to achieve.[11] Some years later, Pallis was asked to write the foreword to Trungpa's first, seminal book, *Born in Tibet*. In his acknowledgement, Trungpa offers Pallis his "grateful thanks" for the "great help" that Pallis gave in bringing the book to completion. He goes on to say that "Mr. Pallis when consenting to write the foreword, devoted many weeks to the work of finally putting the book in order."[12]

At the same time that Pallis was writing about Buddhism and religion in general, he was continuing with his musical career. He taught viol at the Royal Academy of Music, and reconstituted *The English Consort of Viols*, an ensemble he had first formed in the 1930s. It was one of the first professional performing groups dedicated to the preservation of early English music. They made three records[13] and performed on several concert tours in England and abroad. When on a tour to the United States in 1964, Pallis had the opportunity to meet with Thomas Merton at the Abbey of Gethsemane in Kentucky. "Yesterday Marco Pallis was here. . . . I was glad

[11] For more on the relationship between Trungpa and Pallis, see Pallis' article "Discovering the Interior Life," published in *The Sword of Gnosis: Metaphysics, Cosmology, Tradition, Symbolism* (New York, NY: Penguin, 1974), also included in this volume.

[12] Chögyam Trungpa, *Born in Tibet* (Boston, MA: Shambhala, 2000), p. 15.

[13] *The Music of Their Royal Courts* (Saga Records, London, 1967); *To Us a Child. . .* (Abbey "Pan" Records, Eynsham, Oxford, 1968); and *Music with her Silver Sound. . .* (Decca "Turnabout/Vox" Records, London, 1971).

to meet him."[14] They spoke of Zen, Shiva, and the plight of Tibet. It was their first face-to-face encounter, although the two knew each other from prior correspondence and from an acquaintance with each other's published writings. One reads from Merton's journal before they met: "Yesterday, quiet—sunny day—spent all possible time in the woods reading and meditating. Marco Pallis' wonderful book *Peaks and Lamas* was one."[15]

Pallis described "tradition" as being the *leitmotif* of his writing. He wrote from the perspective of what has come to be called the traditionalist or perennialist school of comparative religion founded by René Guénon, Ananda K. Coomaraswamy, and Frithjof Schuon, each of whom he knew personally.[16] As a traditionalist, Pallis assumed the "transcendent unity of religions" (the title of Schuon's landmark 1948 book) and it was in part this understanding that gave Pallis insight into the innermost nature of the spiritual tradition of Tibet, his chosen love.

Marco Pallis published three books devoted primarily to tradition, Buddhism, and Tibet: *Peaks and Lamas* (1939); *The Way and the Mountain* (1960); and *A Buddhist Spectrum* (1980).[17] Several of Pallis' articles are featured in Jacob

---

[14] Thomas Merton, *Dancing in the Water of Life: Seeking Peace in the Hermitage (The Journals of Thomas Merton, Volume 5: 1963-1965)* (New York, NY: HarperSanFrancisco, 1998), p. 157.

[15] Thomas Merton, *A Search for Solitude: Pursuing the Monk's True Life (The Journals of Thomas Merton, Volume 3: 1952-1960)* (New York, NY: HarperSanFrancisco, 1996), p. 279.

[16] Pallis traveled in India with Coomaraswamy's son Rama, who later also became a writer, and knew the elder Coomaraswamy through lengthy correspondence. Pallis corresponded with both Guénon and Schuon and was able in 1946 to visit Guénon at his home in Cairo; Pallis met with Schuon, either in Pallis' flat in London or in Schuon's home in Lausanne, nearly every year for over thirty years.

[17] With the publication of the present edition of *The Way and the Mountain*, all of Pallis' works are now in print: *Peaks and Lamas* is published by

Needleman's *The Sword of Gnosis* published by Penguin;[18] he was also a regular contributor to the English journal *Studies in Comparative Religion*. After his final journey to Tibet— while living in Kalimpong, India[19]—Pallis wrote a short book in the Tibetan language addressing the dangers posed to Tibet by the encroachment of modern culture. In addition to penning his own writings, Pallis translated Buddhist texts into Greek, and translated works of fellow traditionalist writers René Guénon and Frithjof Schuon from French into English. Some of Pallis' own works were translated into French and Spanish. Since the publication of his first book, sixty-six years ago, generations of scholars and students have turned to Pallis for insight into Buddhism and Tibet. His ground-breaking work is cited by such writers as Heinrich Harrer, Heinrich Zimmer, Joseph Campbell, Thomas Merton, Robert Aitken, and Huston Smith. In Huston Smith's judgment: "For insight, and the beauty insight requires if it is to be effective, I find no writer on Buddhism surpassing him."

Shoemaker & Hoard (Washington, D.C., 2005); *A Buddhist Spectrum* is published by World Wisdom (Bloomington, IN, 2003).

[18] Jacob Needleman, *The Sword of Gnosis: Metaphysics, Cosmology, Tradition, Symbolism* (New York, NY: Penguin, 1974).

[19] After his 1947 journey to Tibet, Pallis lived in Kalimpong for several years, returning to England in 1952. Kalimpong was then a center of literary and cultural activity, as well as a refuge for those who were being forced to leave Tibet, including the tutor of the Dalai Lama, Heinrich Harrer, who, immediately upon his arrival in Kalimpong, began to write his *Seven Years in Tibet*. Pallis formed many lasting relationships during this time, including an acquaintance with the then queen of Bhutan and her family, with whom he later visited in England, and with Heinrich Harrer, with whom Pallis later collaborated in exposing the fraudulent writer Lobsang Rampa. While in Kalimpong, Pallis also, met with the Dalai Lama's Great Royal Mother, and he developed a close relationship with the elderly abbot of the nearby Tharpa Choling monastery.

A brief but informative glimpse into Pallis' domestic life in Kalimpong is provided to us by Urgyen Sangharakshita (born Dennis Lingwood):

Pallis' musical career was no less accomplished. The Royal Academy, in recognition of a lifetime of contribution to the field of early music, awarded Pallis with an Honorary Fellowship. He continued composing and playing, adding to this certain scholarly articles of a musical nature. His article "The Instrumentation of English Viol Consort" was published when he was seventy-five. At age eighty-nine his *String Quartet in F#* was published and his *Nocturne de l'Ephemere* was performed at the Queen Elizabeth Hall in London; his niece writes that "he was able to go on stage to accept the applause which he did with his customary modesty."[20] When he died two weeks short of his ninety-fifth birthday (his vegetarian diet perhaps contributing to his long and active life), he was working on a project that brought together his twin loves of music and Tibet: an opera based on the life of Mila Repa.

Pallis' niece recounts a fascinating story:

> Marco mentioned that once, emerging from the underground in South Kensington, a saffron clad monk had walked up to him holding a piece of paper and had asked,

"The bungalow was situated at the top of a flight of irregular stone steps, and what with trees looming up behind and shrubs pressing in on either side it was a sufficiently quiet and secluded place. Here Thubden La, as he liked to be called, lived with his friend Richard Nicholson, otherwise known as Thubden Shedub, the companion of the travels recorded in *Peaks and Lamas*. As lunch was not quite ready, he showed me around the place. Tibetan painted scrolls hung on the walls, and the polished wooden floors were covered with Tibetan rugs. There were silver butter-lamps on the altar, and massive copper teapots on the sideboard, all gleaming in the shuttered semi-darkness. In one room I could just make out the unfamiliar shape of a harpsichord" (Sangharakshita (D.P.E. Lingwood), *Facing Mount Kanchenjunga: An English Buddhist in the Eastern Himalayas* [Glasgow: Windhorse Publications, 1991], p. 173).

[20] Dominie Nicholls, *Quite a Lot* (privately published, 2002), ch. 12.

in Tibetan, to be directed to the address written thereon. Marco was able and delighted to do so. It didn't seem to strike him as in the least odd that the monk had singled out probably the only Tibetan speaker in that London rush hour throng.[21]

But is it so strange that a Tibetan monk should single Pallis out of a crowd? A fellow countryman most often knows one of his own.

Marco Pallis "retired to the Heavenly Fields" on June 5th, 1989.

Joseph A. Fitzgerald

Above left to right: Marco Pallis, Phiroz Mehta; *below left to right*:
Ven. Lama Akong, Ven. Lama Rechung, Ven. Lama Trungpa

Lelft to right: the Queen of Buthan, her sister Miss Tashi Dorje, Marco Pallis,
Urgyen Sangharakshita, and Mrs Christmas Humphreys, London, 1965

Appreciation
Remembering Marco Pallis

It must seem unusual to write nothing about Marco Pallis' literary works in an appreciation to one of his books, but not being a scholar, and quite unqualified, I can instead write something about Marco Pallis the man, as I knew him from childhood. Although these are personal anecdotes, I do not mean them to be about myself, but rather to illuminate something about the author of this book.

My mother, Elizabeth Goble, and Marco Pallis knew each other when they were young and living in Liverpool, England. If my mother ever told me how they met, I have since forgotten. So it is that memory fades from generation to generation. Although I must have met Marco and his lifelong friend, Richard Nicholson, many times, my first memory was when they came one evening to show us the photographs of their expedition to the Himalayas. I must have been four or five years old in 1937 or '38. My brother and I were sat up in our beds, chairs brought in for the grownups, the curtains closed, and the black and white pictures projected on the wall. In those days there was no television and I had never been to a movie theatre, never before seen projected pictures, and so the event is memorable. When all the slides were shown, my brother and I were each asked to pick out our favorite picture. I chose one of yaks standing with packs on their backs ready to travel. Some weeks later we each received our chosen photograph, enlarged and nicely matted and framed. Subsequently many of those photographs appeared in Marco's book, *Peaks and Lamas*.

I was eight years old in 1941 when we all went to Liverpool and stayed for a few days in Marco's enormous house in Fullwood Park. I remember there was one floor, possibly two, quite empty of any furniture. The garden was an overgrown wilderness with a chicken run, because during World War II everyone kept hens, and Marco and Richard being vegetarians, needed the eggs. However, I doubt that many eggs were ever laid because occasionally, amidst the ranks of stinging nettles and brambles, one would catch a glimpse of a superannuated hen, too old to lay eggs any longer, but given the space and food to live out its old age.

After World War II, in 1947, my parents were able to buy, with Marco's generous help, a large rambling house and workshops on the outskirts of Oxford, where my father established his harpsichord building business. For several years Marco and Richard lived in part of the house. Everything was to do with music. Marco had a small Handel organ, and both he and Richard, my mother too, played the viols, and were founder members of the English Consort of Viols. My father and brother were in the workshops making harpsichords, clavichords, and spinets. Design, construction, woods, art, and music were the usual topics of conversation around the dining table; interesting times for a teenager growing up.

During those years Marco lent me a precious old violin, *Gasparo da Salo*. It was kept in the most beautiful velvet lined case. Marco told me that when I could play a Bach sonata the violin would be mine, but I never reached that level. Marco encouraged many musicians by buying them precious instruments that they could never have afforded. The viola da gamba that my mother played in the Consort of Viols was a *Barak Norman* (1600s), on permanent loan from Marco. He was generous in many ways, also helping his friend of early Liverpool days, Aristide Messinesi, teacher and master weaver, to set up a workshop in Kalimpong, India.

After I came out of the army in 1954 nobody knew what to do with me because all I was interested in seemed to lead nowhere as far as a career was concerned. Being a feckless youth, Marco and Richard, and my parents decided that I should live in their house at Egerton Terrace in

Knightsbridge, London, to work at Harrods. I lived there for
eighteen months on the fourth floor. Although they lived on
a most exclusive street, they lived simply: one telephone on
the ground floor, no radio or television, no gadgets in the
kitchen, just a gas stove, very ordinary crockery and cutlery,
a small dining table, and three chairs. The rest of the house
was, in a similar way, sparsely but tastefully furnished; upright
rather than easy chairs. On the top floor, next to my room,
was their meditation room, for they were both Buddhists,
with a *tanka* hanging above a low painted and carved table, a
bowl of rice, a Tibetan inscription, and a small carpet.

In those days I was a smoker, and looking back I wonder
why he put up with the smell. In his quiet way he let it be
known that he disapproved of smoking and so bought the
most ordinary of ashtrays from Woolworths! He once told
me, which I either did not take in at the time, or did not wish
to, that it was never good in life to rely upon anything outside oneself. In fact whenever Marco wanted to put me right
about something, he would always preface it by saying: "I
hope you do not mind me saying, but. . . ." He could correct
without ever causing a person to get angry or depressed, and
his advice was always good and memorable. I believe many
people came to Marco for advice on different things. He had
a special way of seeing to the core of the matter, and the ability to explain and advise in a wonderfully clear manner. Now,
years later, whenever I have a problem I still ask: "Now what
would Marco have advised? How would he explain it?"

There was an occasion when I must have grumbled to
Marco that I did not have the right conditions to work. He
told me that I should never wait, nor grumble that conditions
were not perfect, because they never would be. He told me
how in Tibet he visited a known painter of sacred pictures:
the man had one small corner of the kitchen area of a one
room house in which several generations were living. When
the painter was at work, he was totally alone, nothing disturb-
ing him, creating beautiful paintings—and that I should be

like that painter. I never saw Marco angry or depressed or heard him say unkind words about other people. If he found a fault it might be mentioned in an amusing way. He used to joke about Richard getting up late, telling me how in the Himalayas he would usually have to take down the tent to wake him!

Living in Marco's house was always stimulating: many interesting people visited; there was often music, or there were evenings of interesting discussions, sitting in the garden under the old acacia tree, drinking coffee and admiring Richard's flower garden. There were evenings at Covent Garden for Wagner operas, sitting in the best stall seats, wearing evening clothes because Marco felt it important that one always be dressed correctly. There were long walks in the country, for both were great walkers. And there were frequent meals at Italian or Indian curry restaurants. I never saw Marco drink or eat except that he would first dip a fingertip into his cup and touch it over the rim; or at the edge of his plate he would squash a grain of rice or leave a crumb of bread. It was his unobtrusive offering which most people would never have noticed.

The first essay in this book, *The Way and the Mountain*, he wrote initially for his Liverpool mountaineering colleagues, but it was published later for all of us to read. This essay can be a pattern upon which we can base our lives. He was the kindest of men. He never married and I think, and hope, I was a little like a son to him. I was always too young, but now with age, I so much miss his thoughtfulness. It never crossed my mind that one day I would have the privilege to write something in one of his books. And Marco wrote many books and articles, all on sacred subjects, and as a wise man he integrated these things into his life.

Paul Goble
Black Hills

Author's Preface

The nine essays forming the present collection, though composed at intervals and in answer to particular requests, are connected into one whole by the presence of a common theme towards which each separate essay stands in the relation of a descant. "Tradition" is the name of this theme: already it had provided the *leitmotif* for another work by the same author, *Peaks and Lamas* (Cassell, London, 1939; Alfred Knopf, New York, 1949) telling the story of how access was gained, across the varying episodes of Himalayan travel, to a traditional world, still complete and vigorous, that of Buddhism in its Tibetan branch. A farther journey, following the enforced delay of the war years, took the author and one companion, Richard Nicholson, (in 1947) into the very heart of that same world, independent Tibet as it then was: this time participation was full from the outset in a manner that allowed one to co-ordinate and clarify many previous impressions and, where necessary, to revise them. The present book is, in many senses, an outcome of that experience.

It will already be apparent to the reader that by tradition more is meant than just custom long established, even if current usage has tended to restrict it in this way. Here the word will always be given its transcendent, which is also its normal, connotation without any attempt being made, however, to pin it down to a particular set of concepts, if only because tradition, being formless and supra-personal in its essence, escapes exact definition in terms of human speech or thought. All that can usefully be said of it at the moment is that wherever a complete tradition exists this will entail the presence of four things, namely: a source of inspiration or, to use a more concrete term, of Revelation; a current of influence or Grace issuing forth from that source and transmitted without interruption through a variety of channels; a way of "verification" which, when faithfully followed, will lead the human subject to successive positions where he is able to "actualize" the truths that Revelation communicates; finally there is the formal embodiment of tradition in the doctrines, arts, sciences and other elements that together go to determine the character of a normal civilization.

Quite evidently, the first two of these four elements lie outside any possibility of corruption; the third element, though likewise incorruptible in its principle, can yet be lost from view through human neglect of the opportunities and means it provides; as for the fourth element, traditional form, this will necessarily be exposed to the vicissitudes affecting all forms as such, since who says manifestation in form also says limited and conditioned, and this in its turn spells subjection to the triple fatality of changefulness, decrepitude and eventual death. Only the divine Suchness is unborn and therefore also undying, limitless and therefore not limiting, free and therefore the seat of Deliverance. The voice of tradition is the invitation to that freedom whispered in the ear of existential bondage; whatever echoes that message in any degree or at any remove may properly be called traditional; anything that fails to do so, on the other hand, is untraditional and humanistic, and this reproach will apply whatever may be the nature of the apparent achievements, within the world, to which that thing has given impetus.

One possible question by readers must be answered in advance, though it is of more topical interest: seeing that several sections of this book treat of matters concerning the Tibetan tradition, it may well be asked how far the things described here are likely to survive now that Tibet has fallen under the domination of men, who, to say the least of it, are not given to tenderness in regard either to traditional institutions or to the feelings of those who would wish to conserve them. It would be surprising if its Sino-Marxist overlords did not try to remodel Tibet according to the accepted totalitar-

ian pattern, though, for the sake of political window-dress-
ing, the ambiguous word "autonomy" may still continue to
be utilized from time to time. Certainly Tibetan spirituality
is facing pressure the severity of which it would be folly to
minimize; nevertheless it would be a mistake to prejudge the
final result which depends on complex factors, some of which
still remain obscure.

The physical menace, however, persists. Even as we write,
signs are not wanting that the aggressors, after their initial
failure to bend the will to freedom of the Tibetans, are thinking more and more on the lines of their gradual swamping
by Chinese settlers; a deadly weapon this, which a fearsome
overpopulation places in the hands of China's present masters and one moreover which, because it need not necessarily
involve an actual breaking of heads, will be labeled "peaceful" by the priest and levite of this world: with the Tibetan
name itself once reduced to a memory the whisperings of
conscience will doubtless be comfortably stilled.

There must be scandal in this world, the Bible has said it:
is this to be the end of the matter, the only kind of comfort
anyone dare offer the sturdy, freedom-loving, religious people of Tibet fallen among thieves and crying out for help?

In conclusion, something perhaps ought to be said about
the choice of subject matter for inclusion in the present volume; it will doubtless be noticed by some that material has
been drawn from many different traditional currents besides
the one to which the author himself is affiliated. Should this
cause surprise, the answer is that the book is not in fact meant
to serve readers of one orientation only; rather is there a wish
to be read in such manner that anyone spiritually intent may
find here something for his need, were it only "extrinsic and
probable proof" (to borrow a phrase of St. Thomas Aquinas)
confirming him in the course indicated by his own tradition; if looking in the mirror of another form of spirituality
serves to deepen understanding of one's own, that already
is great gain. As for those whose traditional home is still in

the seeking, the best that can be offered them is to bring to their notice some of the criteria wherewith to discriminate between what is truly traditional—one need not keep off the word "orthodox"—and a pseudo-mystical sectarianism such as readily proliferates on the denatured soil of materialist frustration; with its claims being advertised on all sides, it offers a continual lure to the insufficiently informed. And most of all is it important, in things of the spirit, to distinguish what belongs to essence from what, being of a derivative or contingent order, is like a key giving access to a sanctuary, not to be mistaken for the treasure to be had within, after turning that key.

The author founds his hopes especially on the fact that none of the essays figuring here would have seen light of day had it not been for a request, pressing enough to be accounted "a sign", made by some individual or, in one or two instances, by a group; it takes that much to push the pen into the reluctant hand of one who mostly feels happier when passing a bow across the strings of a viol. What has once proved its usefulness to a known person may well do so again to others yet unknown. It is in this hope that *The Way and the Mountain* and the chapters to follow are offered under their new and enhanced form to his eventual readers by

Marco Pallis

Symbol of the *Kalachakra*, the Wheel of Time; the seven intertwined letters standing for the seven words of the *Kalachakra mantra*

The Wayside Stupa at Bod Karbu; its tiers are the Way's stages; superimposed, they make the Mountain

1

The Way and the Mountain

Among the several clubs existing in this country for the encouragement of the sport of mountaineering there is one, centered in Liverpool, with which the present writer is united by the close ties of membership and of shared adventure both on home crags and in the greater ranges abroad. That certain knowledge is to be picked up on the hills which elsewhere is hard to come by, under the conditions of ever increasing sophistication that modern urban life imposes, is a commonplace for those who have sought peace of mind as well as bodily health among the mountains; for the writer, as for some others, this experience extended itself to the point of opening the door, not only of unspoiled Nature, but also of the traditional world in one of its most intact forms, that of Tibetan Buddhism, truly a far-flung wayfaring. That is why, when asked to contribute an article to the Club Journal in 1945, two years before going out to Tibet, the idea came to him to write about the metaphysical implications which the name of the club itself carries. The founders who chose it can hardly have suspected, guided as they were by considerations of a temporary and topical kind, that in deciding to christen their club "The Wayfarers" they had actually attached to it a name that enshrines one of the most ancient and significant symbolisms of mankind.

It is this symbolism, or rather a few of its more elementary applications, which provides the subject for the present study; however, lest the motives for introducing it here should be misinterpreted, it must be stated at once that they are entirely unconnected with archaeology, anthropology or any kindred pursuits. Nor do they enter into the study of what is often patronizingly referred to as "folklore" (a word which, however, can be given a much more profound sense, corresponding to its original meaning)—there exist more profitable pastimes than making "collections" of fairy tales, or rather it is our whole modern conception of what underlies a "fairy tale" that has gone wide of the mark, since we are able to conceive it only in terms of the picturesque, the romantic and the curious, products all three of our own sophistication and utterly foreign to the ways of thinking of the real "folk". For us the traditional opening phrase "once upon a time" has come to mean "not in reality" whereas those by whom and for whom the fairy tales were originally told received it in an exactly contrary sense, as meaning "at no specifiable time" because everywhere and ever presently real. The fairy tales, far from having been designed for the entertainment of children or of the childishly immature minds of those whom we, in our arrogance, and ignorance, miscall "primitive" and "backward peoples", are simply part of a symbolic language, not only intelligible but also of profound significance for those who are capable of receiving its message "as a little child". In view of the common misconceptions on the subject it would seem advisable, before embarking on a more detailed discussion of a particular set of symbols, those of "wayfaring", to say something first on the subject of symbolism in general, its nature and its uses, for in modern practice even the word itself has been emptied of the greater part of its meaning.

Were an average person in Europe or America today to be asked what he understands by a "symbol" he would probably answer—if indeed the word conveyed anything at all to his mind—that it was a figurative representation of an idea, "picturesque" in the literal sense of the word, that is to say an imaginative rhetorical device designed to supplement, but only in quite a secondary sense, the otherwise sufficient resources of common speech; he would therefore regard it as something purely decorative and superfluous, an arbitrary rather than a necessary means of expression. Few are those who still see in symbolism what it is pre-eminently, namely, a means perfectly adapted for the communication of truths otherwise inexpressible because they are of such a fundamental character as to defy the analytical and roundabout methods of ordinary language, being indeed in their essence only attainable by a direct act of intellectual recognition such as lies beyond the powers of discursive thought; for the latter, unlike the true Intelligence, is by its nature indirect and relative, capable, that is to say, of finding out something about things, and of relating them to other things, but never of knowing things as they are in themselves. Ordinary human speech, being itself a rational construction, is ill-fitted to handle knowledge which, by reason of its universal character, precludes analysis and escapes relativity; such a purpose requires the use of other means, calculated to evoke an idea immediately as in a single flash unblurred by more or less clumsy attempts to discuss or explain.

Nevertheless, whatever is expected to serve this purpose must, in the first place, be taken from that world in which the human being is actually abiding (which in this case happens to be the world of physical appearances), since no one is able to set out on a journey, to start "wayfaring", except from the point where he is actually situated at the time—this may sound like a truism, but it is a truth of which the wider implications are only too often missed. Applying the general principle to the case in point, it therefore follows that the means to be used in suggesting the idea not only may, but must, be derived from the world to which the being concerned belongs. In other words, something to be found in a lower (i.e., limited and relative) order of reality—such as, for instance, the world of physical existence we have just mentioned—is presented in a manner calculated to make it the vehicle of an idea of a superior order; this being possible in virtue of the connection between all the various orders in a universe wherein no absolute state of separation is admissible. Thus whatever is contingent, superficial and confined corresponds, in some degree, to that which is free, profound and universal and which indeed is its ultimate source of reality, being reflected in it as far as its own possibilities will allow; and moreover it is this correspondence which allows the former to be used as a "support" for the conceiving of the latter, that is to say, used "symbolically". It seems hardly necessary to point out that everything enjoying any kind of existence whatsoever must therefore have its symbolical aspect, which actually constitutes its most profound reality; those who see in symbolism nothing better than an invention of the poets miss the point, unless indeed they are prepared to take the word "invention" in its primitive sense of "a finding" of something that is already and always there to be found—one might also say a "discovery" or even a "revelation". Moreover they would also have to restore to the words "poet" and "poetry" that fuller meaning which they bore for the ancients but which now survives in their etymology alone—for, in Greek, "poiesis" is actually derived from "poiein" = "to do" or "make", and poetry is fundamentally nothing other than "doing" or "making", or what we should nowadays call "an act of creation". In that sense, it is the supreme Poet who, by symbols, constructs the worlds, and in so far as he conforms to that eternal model every true artist may justly call himself a poet.

Furthermore, even an elementary acquaintance with traditional art all over the world—ranging from the antique relics of Ur of the Chaldees and Tutankhamen, through the sublime creations of Gothic architecture or Chinese painting, down to quite simple domestic objects still in use among African and Polynesian tribes—will reveal the fact not only that every object, whatever its nature, is regarded from a twofold point of view, physical and metaphysical, as an object of contingent utility and ultimate significance, but also that every feature entering into its construction, as well as the whole craft of making it, is itself symbolical, being intimately related to the underlying symbolism of the object as well as to its practical uses regarded as a whole; most of the features that we call "decorative" are so in a secondary sense only, their primary appeal being not aesthetic but intellectual. The divorce between utilitarian and significant—otherwise the decay of the sense of symbolism—is the invariable mark of cultures in process of decay—sometimes even described as "progressive"—whereas for normal mankind, for the man around whom the fairy tales are being enacted daily, such a splitting up into compartments is unthinkable, and every function of his life is but the acting of yet another part in the symbolical play that is existence.

Symbolism, within its human confines and apart from its most universal sense, is best described as a traditional Algebra serving for the expression of ideas of the universal order. Additional investigation reveals the fact that there are a variety of different ways of symbolizing the same idea. It is also a matter of historical observation that men usually have preferred to take, as symbols of the highest to which they could aspire, those things which were most directly and intimately bound up with their daily life, because it was those things which appeared most real to them in their earthly existence, consequently providing the most appropriate symbolical links with that transcendent and unconditional reality of which their own relative reality was a translation in conditioned mode.

Thus for hunting peoples, such as the Red Indians, the pursuit of truth quite naturally appears as the Grand Chase. In order that they may keep themselves perpetually reminded of this theme, it is in its turn allowed to overflow into the practice of the daily hunting which serves as its "support" so that the hunting itself is treated as a ritual—a "mystery play" in which the hunter and his quarry both correctly play their allotted parts. Similarly all weapons or other implements used in this service are themselves fashioned so as to be symbolically suggestive of their double purpose. So also for the warrior peoples, their natural symbolical dialect is drawn from the practice of war; in this connection one might mention the Japanese Samurai, the Bedouins and the Knightly Orders of

Mediaeval Europe. For them the typical representation of the process of Self-perfection is the "holy war" or "crusade", in which the external enemy corresponds, at one level of reality, with the internal enemies at another, those far more formidable foemen who carry on civil war within the soul, all of whom must in turn be overcome and slain. Similar examples can be multiplied almost indefinitely, as one passes from one form of civilization to another. Therefore it should surprise nobody that there is a metaphysical doctrine of wayfaring and also one of climbing, each carrying with it its appropriate symbolism.

In this chapter it is proposed to examine some aspects of a particular symbol of world-wide significance, the one that the title of "The Wayfarers" unwittingly enshrines; that symbol is the Way, and this is moreover often considered in correlation with another symbol of like importance, the Mountain. Firstly, let us enumerate a few examples chosen out of the long catalogue of traditional allusions to the Way as symbolizing the destiny of Man and its fulfillment.

Starting with the Far East we find that the Way, *Tao,* has actually given its name to a whole body of tradition, commonly known as Taoism; though it would be more accurate to say that this is the name for one side of the Chinese tradition, of which the other side is represented by Confucianism, the latter being concerned with the social applications of the traditional teaching, while the former is of a purely intellectual character and deals with principles.

The *Tao Te Ching,* the fundamental scripture of this tradition, has sometimes been translated as "The Book of the Way and of Virtue", but this should be regarded rather as a derivative meaning, for the underlying idea is "The Book of the Principle and Its Activity". But it is no accident that a word symbolizing the ultimate and utterly indefinable Principle is also, in human parlance, called the Way; since if the passage of the wayfarer along his appointed way is an imitation on the earthly plane of the Activity of Heaven (to use a Chinese term) upon the cosmic plane, the Way itself is indefinable apart from the wayfarer. Without a way there can be no wayfaring but it is the wayfarer's presence in it which in effect makes it possible to speak of a way at all. The "realizing" of the Way is therefore, for the wayfarer, nothing other than the "pilgrimage of his own Self" (as an Indian sage once described it) and it is the unseen Way which itself makes its own various stages and incidents real according to their kind and degree.

In China the symbolism of the Way is far from being confined to one tradition; for we find it again figuring prominently in the Buddhist doctrine. Buddhism, though Indian in origin, is now but slightly represented in its parent country; it has made its principal home in the Far East and adjoining regions like Burma, Siam and Tibet. In this tradition the idea of the Way is put into close correlation with another symbol, that of the Goal; the latter represents the attainment of the state of a Buddha, meaning one who is "awake", having been roused from the drowsy state of ignorance and illusion in which beings spend their lives, in order to become aware of the one and only reality. In Buddhist writings much attention is devoted to the consideration of various stages which have to be traversed by the wayfarer seeking the Goal; the present writer formerly possessed a Tibetan scroll-painting actually entitled "Stages in the Way" and there is also a well-known Tibetan book of the same name, as well as another bearing the title "A Lamp for the Way"; both of these works occupy an important place in the education of a lama. Moreover the Buddhist tradition, in the form that it assumes in China, Japan and Tibet is generally known as the *Mahayana* or Great Way, along which all beings without exception are led towards Enlightenment. The Tibetans also make an important distinction between the indirect route followed by the ordinary run of men, stage by stage, and the "direct path" or "short cut" which is the way of the saints whose concentration on the Goal is such that no obstacle is able to delay their arrival.

This idea of the "short cut" may be compared with a very similar one to be found, this time, in Christianity, namely the symbol of the "narrow way" leading into the Kingdom of Heaven. There is besides a more general allusion contained in the words of Christ Himself when He said "I am the Way"; it would be impossible to find a more telling example than this.

To the doctrine of the Way must also be referred the many descriptions of symbolic journeys which play so prominent a part in the traditional lore of almost every people. To mention only a few; we have the Homecoming of Odysseus and the story of the Argonauts sailing in search of the Golden Fleece (which is evidently equivalent to the Goal), only here the Way is represented as leading not overland but across the seas, as is only natural in the tradition of a pre-eminently seafaring people like the ancient Hellenes whose minds such a symbolism would impress with peculiar vividness. The various dangers and monsters encountered in the course of the voyage are relatable to the stages of Self-Knowledge.

In both the above-mentioned legends an important episode occurs in the form of a passage through a narrow strait (and again one should remember the "narrow way" and the "strait gate" of the Gospel), a passage which entails the avoidance of two extremes. In the case of Jason, we have the *Symplegades* or Clapping Rocks (geographically identified with the entrance to the Black Sea) that kept alternately opening and closing to the great danger of any ship adventuring between them. In the *Odyssey*, on the other hand, the sides of the straits (here represented by those of Messina) are guarded respectively by the monsters Scylla and Charybdis, ever ready to prey upon the crews of ships sailing too close inshore on the one or the other side. Symbols conceived after this pattern commonly refer to the oppositions arising out of any dualism that fails to be resolved by reference to the unity of a superior principle, the most typical example being that of "me" and "other", containing as it does the ultimate root of all conflicts. Since the journey invariably is a quest for Unity, the escape from dangers lurking on either side of the strait represents the avoidance of both the poles which together constitute the opposition; in this connection one might recall the words of the Buddha when He said: "I teach you a Middle Way", that is to say one which, to use our nautical symbolism once again, "steers clear" of both Scylla and Charybdis.

The foregoing examples should be sufficient to give an inkling of what is implied by the symbolism of Wayfaring. We must now pass on to the consideration of a complementary symbolism, that of the Mountain. Here we have an almost bewildering wealth of examples to draw upon. Sacred mountains, symbolizing the exaltation of Divinity, are to be found in every corner of the globe. The Grecian Olympus will be the first to spring to mind, only here it is important to expose the common error of thinking that the ancients believed their gods to be physically resident on the actual Mount Olympus, that glorious peak which some of us who were out in the Balkans during the 1914-18 war remember having seen reflecting the sunset beyond the Gulf of Salonika. Such a supposition really reverses the symbolical relationship: the true Olympus is only discernible by those "who have eyes to see", and it can only be scaled by a true wayfarer, while the earthly mountains that have been given that name (for there are several of them) are themselves so called in order to turn them into reminders, or symbols, of the heavenly Olympus. The taking of such a symbolism too literally by the ignorant, among whom many professional scholars must be included, is but an example of how a doctrine can degenerate in times of decay into a "superstition", by the literal survival of its symbols after their deeper meaning has been lost sight of.

The way to the Mountain is nowhere and everywhere; it therefore cannot be specified in rational language, but it becomes immediately apparent to those who have earned that knowledge by paying the required price. That price is the renunciation or denial of self in its separative individual sense, in order to realize true Selfhood in the universal sense. Middle English possessed a most concise and expressive term for this sacrificial abandonment: it called it "self-noughting" (which is the same as Self-knowing), and this it is which furnishes the principal theme for many a Gospel and for all the fairy tales. Whatever other elements may be found therein are accessory to this one and only end, and therefore come under the heading of means.

The idea of an inherent invisibility of the Way such as only will yield to true insight is brought out with particular emphasis in another tradition centered round a mountain, that of the Holy Grail; the legend, rendered familiar to us by Richard Wagner's setting of it, is Celtic in origin but passed over later into Christianity. In this story the mountain is significantly named Monsalvat or Mount of Salvation on which is situated the castle of the Grail guarded by its dedicated knights. Behind the mountain lies the factitious paradise of the magician Klingsor, himself a renegade knight, thus illustrating the fact that every lie or error arises through the perversion of some aspect of the truth. Moreover, the word "error" itself contains an implicit tribute to the Way, since its original meaning in Latin is "wandering", as judged by reference to the standard of wayfaring when unswervingly conducted.

It is noteworthy that Parsifal's attainment of the Grail (which was identified with the chalice in which angels received the Precious Blood of the Crucified Christ) involved three distinct phases: firstly, as a simple-minded youth, taken for a fool by the world, he roamed about in apparently aimless fashion and came upon Monsalvat as if by accident. This symbolism is intended to convey the truth that every being, whether aware of it or not, is born a potential wayfarer, and that his true destiny is to realize all that is implied in such a status by searching for and ultimately arriving at the Goal. Secondly, Parsifal was allowed to enter the temple and actually set eyes on the Grail itself because he asked the right question which alone could evoke the right answer—"What is the Grail?"; here we see the symbolism of "initiation", the conscious election to the life of wayfaring with a view to discovering the Goal; thirdly, before Parsifal was fitted to take over the Kingship of the Grail he had not only to subdue Klingsor and dispel the illusions out of which his magic garden was constructed, but also to spend some years journeying through the world, this time, however, in full awareness of what the life of a wayfarer really means, as contrasted with the pale reflection of it that he had previously, and half-unconsciously, experienced.

It would be impossible in a small space to enumerate one half of the mountain peaks that are traditionally associated with this kind of symbolism; some mention should however be made of the practice of going on a pilgrimage to a sacred mountain, since the ritual act assuming such a form is one in which the ideas of the Way and the Mountain are closely linked together. In quite a general sense, the rite of pilgrimage is always an imitation of the Way, while the place of pilgrimage itself, whether this be some natural landmark, or a shrine, represents the Goal. Pilgrimage to Mecca for the Moslem or to Jerusalem for the Jew are well-known examples.

Many pilgrim routes exist in which the center in question takes the form of a mountain; one of the most famous of these, a familiar feature in Japanese art, is the conical summit of the volcanic Mount Fuji up the slopes of which thousands of pilgrims make their way annually to the edge of the crater. Among pilgrim ways having this character there is one, however, which, to the mountaineer, is more than ordinarily suggestive, and that is the track leading across the main Himalayan chain to the Kailas, a high peak situated in Tibet near the sources of the rivers Brahmaputra and Satlej. This mountain is particularly sacred to both Hindus and Buddhists. The former regard it as the symbolical abode of Shiva, which is the name attached to the divine function of Transformation, or passage beyond individual forms and their distinction into the indistinction of formless Knowledge. The long and arduous journey through the mountains of Garhwal, with their indescribably glorious scenery, is well calculated to awaken, in the mind of one coming from the plains, an aspiration to enter that supreme and inward Way which is thus outwardly prefigured.

On arrival at the foot of the Kailas, after crossing the last and highest of the passes, the pilgrim makes a solemn circuit round the mountain in a clockwise direction, fixing his attention meanwhile upon the Divine Name to which the mountain is dedicated; his success in making of this earthly counterpart a means for the realizing of the unearthly journey of which it is the image will depend upon his own intellectual capacity and on his skill in concentration. This circumambulation or "girdle-traverse" occupies several days and also involves the crossing of a number of subsidiary passes. Similarly, Buddhist pilgrims from all over Tibet visit the Kailas; among the Tibetans it goes by the name of the Mountain of Precious Snow. In passing, it might also be mentioned that if members of Everest expeditions have sometimes claimed particular holiness for their chosen peak, this can only be said to hold good in quite a general sense, in so far as all perpetual snow is looked upon as holy in Tibet, so that the chief snow-mountain of any and every district serves the same purpose locally that the Kailas serves in a larger way for the entire region.

It will have been noticed, in the examples just given, that in the one case, that of Mount Fuji, the pilgrimage involves an actual ascent, whereas, in the others, the mountain is simply treated as a whole. The former case, however, might well be regarded as the one in which the rite of mountain pilgrimage is carried nearest to its logical conclusion, since it is the focal point towards which all the ridges and slopes of the mountain converge and in which their diverse tendencies are finally unified, namely the summit, which most perfectly typifies the Goal, in which all separate and individual ways go to lose themselves in the end, this being an indispensable condition for finding themselves, as the Christian Gospel has declared; and this brings us to the consideration of the most profound and fundamental of all the ideas connected with mountain symbolism, that of the Universal Axis.

In the Hindu and Buddhist cosmology, which however can be paralleled in many other traditional forms, the center of the Universe is marked by a symbolical mountain known as Mount Meru. If each degree or mode of existence be regarded as occupying a horizontal plane, higher or lower in proportion to the presence or absence of limitative conditions, or, if you will, by the relatively greater or smaller degree of freedom enjoyed on that level, it will be apparent that they will one and all be graded in relation to a vertical axis running through the center of each of them and thus associating them in a common synthesis. The path of the axis, in an ascending direction, therefore indicates the path of escape from the massive compression and diffuseness of the base towards the concentration and unrestricted freedom of the apex, and it is here that we find the twin symbolisms of the Way and the Mountain merging into one.

As long as we spoke of a Way and its stages only, or even of such a Way as leading to a center occupied by a mountain, the mental picture conveyed was based on the flat, with or without ups and downs, since it is in the nature of paths to seek the level and to thread their way along the bottom of valleys; but as soon as one has introduced the conception of a mountain consisting of tiers centered on the axis and gradually narrowing towards the summit, it becomes evident that the Way is nothing different from the ascent of the Mountain itself, and that the stages of the former and the superimposed levels of the latter are one and the same thing. Moreover one is immediately brought back to the distinction made by the Tibetans between the "short cut" or "direct route" of the saints and the indirect road followed by the generality of mankind; for it is obvious that the only really direct route is the one coinciding with the axis itself, compared with which

13

all the other ways up a mountain, however steep and severe, must necessarily be indirect. This also goes to prove that the theory according to which a climb will be valid in proportion to its directness rests on no arbitrary fanaticism of a few purists but rather upon a metaphysical truth that far transcends the practice of a favorite sport. Moreover, even ordinary reason tells us that no one in his senses would step to one side on a climb if a hold were available in the direct line; every deviation from that line is dictated by the presence of some obstacle and by the climber's own inability to surmount it.

The doctrine of the Axial Peak, with all that this implies, can be taken for granted in every case where there is question of a sacred mountain, whatever particular form the idea may assume in this or that place or tradition. The Chinese, in particular, have made a free use of this symbolism, and the Mountain of the Axis, rising boldly out of the middle of the swirling Sea of Possibilities, invariably forms the central feature of the border of the ritual robes worn by the Emperor in his capacity as mediator before Heaven on behalf of his people: what its Axis is for the World, the ruler should be for his own subjects. Part of such a robe has been reproduced to illustrate the present chapter.

There are, of course, many obvious reasons why mountain climbing should lend itself to a symbolism of the Way and the Goal; for one thing, going uphill involves, on the physical plane, more persistent effort than most other forms of activity and effort is inseparable from wayfaring on every plane. But there are also a number of less self-evident points that deserve attention: in order to consider them in logical sequence the best thing is to take the phases of our climb, now assimilated to the Way, in their natural succession, while carrying on a running commentary intended to bring out their symbolical implications.

First of all, we come to the cairn that indicates the starting-point at the foot of the climb. Cairns marking various spots of particular significance are among the most ancient and widely distributed monuments of human art; and the derivation of the word itself will suggest a reason. The primitive sense of the Celtic *carn* is "horn" (actually the same root) and the word is secondarily applied to any horn-like eminence, especially to mountain tops—one has only to think of Carnedd, Carn Dearg, Y Garn and many others. The miniature cairn built of a pile of stones was used by the Celts and other peoples in order to mark sites of burial; the profound reasons for this practice are clear, since the cairn is itself an emblem of the Mountain of the Axis and fashioned on its model; it stands there to serve as a perpetual reminder to the quick and the dead alike that the true Way, the direct route up the climb, must follow the axis, and that until the Goal has been attained by Knowledge, wayfaring must needs continue in this and other worlds.

In Tibet, for example, on reaching any high point occupied by a cairn, such as the crest of a pass, the traveler adds his stone to the pile with the ritual exclamation "the gods are victorious, all the devils are defeated," thus re-affirming his self-dedication in the Way; for in the larger sense the gods correspond to the higher possibilities of his being, and the devils to all those inferior tendencies that would drag him back and downward and that must be mastered and recalled to order if the Supreme Climb is ever to be completed.

The cairn is therefore the true image of the mountain pivot of the universe and provides, as it were, a preliminary vision of that which is presently to be realized. The building of a cairn "correctly" is indeed a ritual of the highest moment, whether this takes place at the foot or "gate" of the Way or, on completion of the ascent, upon the summit, where it symbolizes the "holy of holies", that is to say the Goal. In their outward form however the two cairns are indistinguishable so that, in one sense, whoever has contemplated the one with the "single eye" of understanding has likewise beheld the other. By this means the essential identity of the Way and the Goal is established and any ultimate contradiction repudiated as between Alpha and Omega, the beginning and the end, the Principle and that which manifests It. It is the supreme affirmation of Unity by the recognition and worship of the Cause in the effect. The two cairns are therefore one and the same symbol and their identity is more truly "real" than any apparent separation wrought by time and space.

From the moment of starting up the climb every movement is necessarily ordered with a view to "realizing" the summit; under no circumstances can any other feature afford more than a relative and passing interest, so that it may be said, without exaggeration, that the summit "embraces" the entire space of the mountain, but without being itself a part of it, since a point by definition occupies no space whatsoever. It has been said earlier that the ideal climb follows the axis without any deviation; in actual practice, however, and setting aside the exceptional case of those whose path is the "direct" one, the route involves a number of movements to the right or left, the most extreme example of which is offered by the traverse; every path but one involves an oblique movement of some kind, or, if a ridge be in question, the passage over a number of minor obstacles in the form of rocky "gendarmes" or even subsidiary summits. Where such a summit is important enough to require a prolonged effort it is then not entirely illegitimate to regard it as a provisional goal and to refer to it as such—always provided one does not forget that it is a goal and not *the* Goal. In so far as it assumes the form of a peak, it too, like its predecessor the cairn, can be regarded as an adequate symbol of the true summit; in so far as it marks a definite point on the climb, it is one of the "stages" in the Way. But woe to him who, after having reached the top of one of these secondary eminences, lingers there through letting himself imagine that he has accomplished something final; for then it immediately turns from an aid into a hindrance, from a stage into a barrier, from an open into a closed door, from a symbol into an "idol". This indeed is the essence of that "idolatry" against which all the traditions are continually inveighing; nothing can be called an idol in itself, but any-thing, even down to "good works" and "service", can become one if it is for a moment allowed to assert its own independence of the Principle and thus enter into rivalry with it.

There are many subsidiary aspects of mountain symbolism which, though meriting discussion, cannot find a place in the present chapter. One exception may however be made in favor of the first really important stage on the Way, the one that bounds the wayfarer's horizon immediately after he has set out, and which, on the Mountain, may well be likened to a prominent though lesser peak on the main ridge, which must be climbed before the true summit actually springs into unobstructed view; for up till that moment the latter remains half-veiled by the mists of ignorance and its presence has been sensed by inference from the trend of the slopes rather than by any direct observation.

The first clear view-point, therefore, corresponds to the stage we are now about to consider, which has variously been called the "primordial" or "adamic" state, or the state of "true man". All the traditions are agreed in teaching that, for the wayfarer, though the starting-point on his journey must necessarily be found somewhere in his present stage of individual human existence, yet in a larger sense, his human status is something to be won back, having been impaired as the result of a fall sustained at a time when he was actually residing at the height of that first peak which he now has to re-climb so laboriously. In other words, that peak corresponds to the realizing of the full possibilities of human individuality, short of which the description of the wayfarer as "human" is something in the nature of a courtesy title bereft of its deeper reality.

For a detailed description of this first important stage of wayfaring one cannot do better than turn to the Italian poet Dante, whose *Divine Comedy* is largely developed around this theme. In the second part of his journey through "the three worlds" the poet describes the ascent of the Hill of Purgatory, on the top of which he situates the "terrestrial paradise", which is precisely the condition of "true man" (as the Chinese call it) or Adam before the Fall, following the Biblical symbolism. From that point the traveler is able to step forth into the Celestial regions, representing states of the being higher than the human, and which do not for the moment concern us.

It will be remembered that the "terrestrial paradise" or Garden of Eden was described in Genesis as disposed around a central tree, known as the Tree of Life. Now this tree is simply an alternative symbol of the Axis; among similar examples one might mention the Sacred Oak of the Druids, the World Ash-tree of the Scandinavians and the Lime-tree of the ancient Germans. Adam and Eve, or in other words humanity in its truly normal state, dwell in the garden near the Tree, that is to say they lead a life in which the Contemplative Intelligence is always directed towards the one essential Truth, excluding all competition, while the various faculties of indirect knowledge and action are grouped around it in their proper order, each occupying the place that belongs to it in virtue both of its possibilities and its limitations. Such a condition of inward harmony is automatically reflected in the outward peace symbolized by the garden in which all kinds of creatures, including Man himself, dwell together in friendship. The Fall, when it occurs, is ascribed to the tasting of the forbidden fruit of the Tree of Knowledge of Good and Evil; that is to say, the formerly single eye begins to see double, and unity gives place to dualism, or polarization into contraries. From that moment harmony is destroyed and now Man, at war with himself, finds himself likewise vowed to conflict with everything else around him, while peace lingers on only as a more or less blurred memory in the back of his consciousness, causing him to feel perpetually discontented with his present state and thus inspiring him to seek the path of return to the lost paradise, or, following our mountain symbolism, to climb up the Hill of Purgatory. As for the main summit of the Mountain, its recollection has by then grown so dim that its existence has largely to be taken on trust, as a matter of "faith".

It is to this symbolism of the "primordial state" that should logically be attached all those movements that take the form of a cultivation of the simple life or of a flight from the artificiality and distraction of the city, and which might well include, among accessory aids to realization, both way-faring and mountaineering as we know them. Many forms of art have quite consciously drawn their inspiration from this source. Chinese landscape painting provides a notable example. Moreover it is the same doctrine that is able to offer a consistent basis for all kindred movements such as those having for their aim the protection of animals and plants and the preservation of natural beauties, as against their abuse and profanation by the sophisticated and commercial-minded. In the love and championship of wild Nature and of solitude one must recognize a distant echo of the original harmony in which Man, instead of acting like a tyrant and exploiter, was on the contrary the acknowledged protector and ruler of his fellow-creatures and their spokesman with the celestial Powers; in fact, like the Chinese Emperor mentioned before, he himself played the part of the axis for them, and this in virtue of his own firm adherence to the axial position which kept his wayfaring ever on the line of the "direct route".

"Fallen" man, on the other hand, lacks this sureness of judgment, for he regards all things in a disconnected way and this often leads him to act in an inconsistent and self-defeating manner; seizing on one aspect of a question, he is only too apt, in his enthusiasm, to turn it into an idol, that is to say to abstract it from the whole by losing sight of its relativity and treating it as a self-contained reality. When this happens, the results actually achieved are often diametrically opposed to his avowed intentions; how easy it is, by too self-centered a wooing and too acquisitive an embrace, to smother the very object of our love! Thus the mountaineer, seeking escape from the dirt and turmoil of the town, but lacking time and grudging trouble, may try to bring his beloved peaks within too easy reach by an indiscriminate demand for transport facilities or by promoting the wholesale erection of huts in which his ingrained habits, which he is unable to shake off altogether, may also lead him to install all kinds of superfluous apparatus, thus re-introducing that very element of artificiality against which he was minded to react: and soon commercialism lurking round the corner will step in and take a hand and Nature will be natural only in name.

The author was once asked by a young explorer just back from the South American forest how to account for the overwhelming sense of awe experienced there as nowhere else in the world, a joy that hurt almost beyond enduring; the author himself had had the same experience in the high temperate forests of the Himalaya and, when still very young, in the tropical rain-forest of Guiana. At the time a straight answer was not forthcoming, but later it became plain: primeval forest, as indeed all Nature in her truly pristine state, is something intrinsically *sacred,* it has the specific quality of wholeness, holiness—for the Red Indians, as we know, this was their ever open Bible in which to read the signs, better Scripture than this they never wanted. When a man of unhardened heart is placed as it were by chance, as that explorer was, in touch with primeval Nature, there springs up in him an instant, an insistent recollection of his own true homeland; by that inescapable humbling of all in him that is not spirit, the wind of liberation is felt to blow.

This holiness of Nature is a fragile thing: it wilts in proportion as her own virginal purity is tampered with, her modesty pried into, her austere exuberance "tamed", as the brutal saying goes. "Avoid tampering" is a spiritual maxim the Taoist sages made into the keynote of their teaching; the world's busybodies have gone on neglecting it to their own and our great peril. Under the continual measuring and delving and lumping together which now has reached its climax, the face of the Great Mother is becoming so disfigured that soon it may be unrecognizable, with all its eminences "conquered", its furrowing dales "brought under discipline of a map" (as another blasphemy hath it), its underwater—sky even—contaminated, the whole so blotched and flayed and carved up and reshuffled that only the all-seeing Intellectual Eye will still be able, across the wreckage of a dishallowed world, to perceive the Motherly Presence there where she subsists, unenhanced as undiminished by the variegated issue of her womb, in the eternal actuality of Divine Intellect Itself.

If the accumulated pressure of historical fatality (which some call "progress") now seems to be closing in upon this matricidal, suicidal modern world of ours, let this not be the cause of overmuch concern (advice easily given, but how hard to follow!), for this process men undergo with such mixed feelings dates back to the beginning, to that first slide from Eden. Rather should it be borne in mind that every way, to be such, must run in both directions, every slope will have its up and its down. If one end be called Heaven and the other Hell, then to walk the Way is itself a hill of purgatory and when the pilgrim-climber feels it growing steep and narrow, and not broad and easy, he may take comfort—he knows he is not straying off his route.

All that remains now is to speak of the summit of the Mountain; other intermediate stages can be taken for granted, since once the primordial state has been regained, once the Hill of Purgatory has been climbed, the path to the Goal henceforth lies clear before the wayfarer; the summit once plainly seen, its attraction is irresistible.

Mention of the word "attraction" in this context moves us to draw particular attention to a question which is really of the first importance, but which might otherwise escape notice. Until now the standpoint which we have all along taken up has been that of "free-will", that is to say we have treated the wayfarer as if he were the active agent throughout, the Goal being simply regarded as the term of his aspiration and effort; this, however, gives but one half of the picture and not the most important half, so that it is now necessary to consider the other and complementary point of view, that of "grace". Once we have spoken of the attraction exerted upon the wayfarer by the summit, their respective parts are reversed and now it is the latter which reveals itself as the essentially active power, while in the case of the former, his initiative, from being seemingly absolute, now is seen to be relative, since it is both evoked and sustained by the idea of the summit, failing which it could not even come into existence. Indeed, not a step would be taken but for this incentive, which conditions both the form of the climb and its direction; apart from the "actionless activity" of the summit the whole route would be devoid of meaning.

After this last digression, only the final step need concern us, but here Man must frankly confess his impotence, for nothing that he can say will fit the occasion; only he who has attained the summit and made himself one with it knows the solution of the mystery, for as between any stage or step, even the most exalted, and the supreme realization there is an absolute discontinuity which it would be idle to try and bridge by word or thought. So long as there yet exists a step to be taken there are alternatives and hence there are possibilities of comparison, but at the summit all alternative routes become one; every distinction between them, and therefore every opposition, is spontaneously reconciled. The summit itself not only occupies no space, although the whole mountain is virtually contained in it, but it is also outside time and all succession, and only the "eternal present" reigns there. It is utterly inexpressible in its uniqueness; silent is the Knower of the Summit and the whole Universe strains its ears to catch the accents of his speechless eloquence.

Those who have had the patience to follow this argument along its winding course may perhaps by now have formed the opinion that, besides other things, it may also contain, by implication, an answer to the question, so frequently, and fruitlessly, debated—"Why do we climb?" If the explanations offered by moralists and advocates of "pure sport" alike have proved on the whole unsatisfying, this has largely been because the question itself was badly put in the first instance. Let us think back for a moment to the legend of Parsifal previously mentioned; it will be remembered that he received the right answer only because he knew how to frame the question itself aright. Concerning the Grail, Parsifal did not inquire "Why?" but "What is the Grail?" "Why?" by its very form, requires a rational solution and Reason, by definition, is concerned with the relation of things to one another, as the Latin word *ratio,* from which it is derived, plainly testifies, a meaning which has been preserved in mathematics; things in their essence Reason is impotent to touch. The Grail, which is the same as the Goal and the Summit of the Mountain, transcends all relativities and therefore escapes all rationalizing. It must be known immediately or not at all; ultimately all roundabout approaches must rejoin the direct route, of which they are but translations in discursive mode, or they will not arrive.

In the controversies alluded to above, it is somewhat paradoxical that those who apparently take up the more earnest standpoint are usually the ones who have gone widest of the mark, while their lighthearted opponents, those who are out to repudiate any serious purpose in mountaineering, have come closer to the true answer, though both parties alike have fallen victims to the unsuitable form of the question put. The former are right in their contention that unless climbing can, somehow or other, be integrated in the Way, in wayfaring, it must come under the heading of waywardness, of error. But in seeking their justification in some moral purpose, one related to the social order, they neither find it possible to make their case fit the facts nor have they avoided giving their argument an almost priggish sound which was hardly their intention.

Their opponents on the other hand, those who put the case in favor of pure sport exclusively of all other motives, have failed in that they have been inclined to abstract their conception from the whole, thus establishing an irreducible opposition between responsible work and duty as they saw them, and certain other things, apparently lightly undertaken, which they called sport. The fact is that they too, in spite of their protestations, have tended to confine their point of view to the social or moral order, in which they do not differ from their adversaries, and as they were not able to fit climbing into it—for after all climbing is not a social occupation, springing as it does rather from a wish to react against social pressures—they simply were content to call it "a sport" leaving the question at issue to answer itself. The course of the controversy indeed has been in many ways typical of all oppositions; it was a factor derived from an underlying community of outlook that really was answerable for the apparent divergence—it is like pole that repels like, and the fiercest conflicts are always those that occur between persons whose points of view are similar, leading them to pursue similar ends and thus engaging them in competition. It is rather in the recognition and fostering of formal differences that lies the way towards peace.

The solution to any opposition, whatever its nature, should always be sought in the knowledge of some unifying principle to which both its terms alike can be referred because it lies beyond their distinction. This is true even on the relative plane, just as all the ridges and faces of the Mountain are resolved in the unity of the summit, on the universal plane. The Hindus, who have had the happiest knack of suggesting ideas while avoiding the danger of attempting over-exact verbal definitions, here also can help us to get clear of the horns of our dilemma. Their wise men have always steadfastly refused to entertain such a question as "Why was the world created?" for the same reasons as were given above. All that they have been content to say on the subject is that Creation is the "Divine Sport".

The essence of a sport, as opposed to the idea of work, is the element of freedom, or in other words, the absence of coactive necessity. The moment we admit a specifiable reason impelling us to do something we tacitly recognize the existence of some law that thus imposes the need for the action. But Divinity admits of no law whatsoever, for who says law says limitation by some extraneous power, which in the case of Divinity would land one in an absurd contradiction. Therefore in describing Creation symbolically as "God's Sport", we are, as far as language allows, affirming the divine freedom from all limitation. That is why a sport, taken in the traditional sense, after excluding all such motives as personal or national competition and other similar irrelevancies that might vitiate its purity, can be regarded as a mirror of the godlike liberty and, for us, a possible means towards its eventual knowledge. On the other hand the true workman, artist or poet, that is to say he who does anything whatsoever that needs to be done, is himself an imitator of the creative art, so that in his work the free element is present as well as the element of necessity, wherefore he too can justly claim for his own work, if correctly done, that "this service is perfect freedom". Thus at the summit, the spot where all oppositions are finally laid to rest, sport and work likewise find themselves reconciled.

In conclusion, we must return once again to our original symbolism of the Way and the Mountain. It will be remembered that at the outset we had pictured the Way as a road with stages, therefore as following the valleys. Later, we reconsidered it as an ascent of the mountain, its stages becoming levels superimposed on one another, while the original direction of the valley is now represented by the traverse round the mountain at a particular level, for example the human individual level. It will perhaps be noticed that these two conceptions, that of the mountain axis and that of the valley or traverse, together go to form a Cross. The axis itself, passing as it does through each level at its central point, may truly be said to be productive of it, since the level or stage in question is nothing but an indefinite development of possibilities entirely contained within that point: thus in the fullest sense, the realization of the Axis, the direct route, is the realization of the mountain in its totality and beyond. "Once upon a time" as the fairy tale would say, "there was a wayfarer called Polestar. He reached the Summit and in him the Way and the Mountain were made one so that he sang with Isaiah 'every valley shall be exalted and every mountain and hill shall be made low'. He was a Knower of the Cross and his was the peace thereof."

A lay monk on the left, a novice monk on the right, Bhutan

Tibetan harvest

2
The Active Life
What it is and what it is not

The title and subject-matter of the present essay has been chosen, not because Action is to be regarded as the most important element in the life of beings or as coincident with the full extent of their possibilities, but simply because it is, for many of us, the chief vehicle of realization at the present moment. We are largely engaged in leading the Active Life, at least in intention, and it is therefore of immediate and practical consequence for us to discover something of its nature and to be made aware of the conditions governing it, and perhaps most important of all, to recognize what are its limitations, so that while profiting by the Life of Action in the greatest possible degree we may at the same time be saved from a common delusion which takes the form of expecting from it certain benefits that lie outside its resources. But even if we do come to recognize the existence of those limits and succeed in catching a glimpse of the realms beyond them, we shall still be compelled, if we intend to penetrate to those regions, to take our present situation in the world of Action as a starting-point, since it is evident—or perhaps not always quite so evident—that a person can only set out on a journey from the place where he actually is situated and not from elsewhere.

When this essay was originally composed, it was designed to be read to a small group of people who used to meet regularly once a week for the common study of questions having a bearing, direct or indirect, on certain personal issues raised for them by the war; it formed the last item of a special program of talks given in the autumn of 1943 and the author was at some pains to make it link on to the subjects of previous talks. For example, the first evening of the series was taken up with the need for a doctrine; it is the traditional doctrine of the Active Life that is now about to be presented to the reader. Another of the talks took for its title "Man, God and the land"; man's proper use of the land plainly enters into the Active Life, while all that concerns man's knowledge of God is on the contrary the subject of what has usually been known as the Contemplative Life. The reason for this is obvious, since man is not capable of *doing* anything to God, who is beyond his reach as far as Action and its effects are concerned. It is only through Knowledge, through a direct and indissoluble identification, that he can fully respond to the Divine Grace, the Activity of Heaven as the Chinese call it, and it is this supreme Knowledge together with the methods dispositive to its acquisition, methods which differ from those of the Active Life, which go to make up the Contemplative Life. The aim of these methods is to train the being to keep its gaze constantly fixed on its Transcendent Cause, without so much as a flicker of distraction, so that the springing up of Knowledge may take place without the slightest interference from outside; such a centering of the attention upon a single point might be compared to the action of the fine tip of a silversmith's punch focusing the whole power of his hammer-blow upon one chosen spot. This state of "one-pointedness", as it has been called, constitutes an essential condition for perfect contemplation; outwardly the being is quiet, with mind withdrawn from all the separate objects of sense around it; its gaze is "turned inward"—to use a common Tibetan expression—and wholly absorbed in the vision; but that apparent stillness, which the ignorant mistake for inactivity, actually represents the most real and intense state of activity conceivable, for it is indistinguishable from the Activity of Heaven itself. Compared with it, the efforts of the Active Life in the more restricted sense of the word, activities outwardly turned and directed towards the environment of the being and which are visible by reason of their very dispersion, are of quite a subordinate character. If we use the same word "activity" in both cases, this is only in virtue of the interconnection of all the constituent elements of existence, whereby the lower, relatively bound and limited orders reflect in varying degrees the reality of the one unfettered and universal order, on which all lesser realities depend. Indeed did they not do so they would be bereft of any reality whatsoever and their existence would be nothing but a pure fiction, that is to say an impossibility.

It is with this reflected activity, commonly called Action, that a great part of this essay will be taken up, for the reasons given at the beginning. It might be added that the present study will not be unconnected with the subject of another of the talks in the same series, when one of the members of the group presented the theory of work and vocation; for this again is a theme that relates to the Active Life, which is taken up with either a making or a doing—the member in question was chiefly concerned with the former. It might also be pointed out that the whole of the ethical and social provinces similarly fall under the heading of the Active Life, outside of which they are meaningless.

Before actually proceeding with our attempted exposition, however, it is necessary to offer a word of warning. The doctrine that is about to be considered is not "original" and it does not form part of any "system of philosophy". In a previous passage the adjective "traditional" was applied to it expressly in order to make it clear that the individual who utters the commentary was in no sense its inventor. It is a doctrine on the nature and use of Action that has been common to all traditional civilizations, whether ancient or modern, Eastern or Western, and it is the impossibility of ascribing it to any particular human originator which makes it worth hearing about; the author's private opinions might be interesting to himself perhaps, but they are of small importance to others. Moreover a subject like the present one is not to be looked upon as something that does not concern the ordinary man; it is not a theme for a contest of wits such as might arise in the course of an academic dinner-party; either its knowledge has a genuine purpose, or else it is no more than an empty form of self-indulgence.

The truth is that no theoretical exposition is of the slightest moment to anyone except as a preparatory step with a view to an eventual realization by the being that has assimilated it. As for the "theory" itself, (which has nothing to do with those working hypotheses resting on statistical generalizations which have now come to bear that name), it is but the Greek word for "vision"—something to be contemplated—and refers to those preliminary and then gradually sharpening views of the yet distant goal vouchsafed to the pilgrim, without which he would have no incentive either to set out or to continue on his journey. By theory the gate is opened that gives access to the Way, and theory is likewise the name given to the vista of successive visions, merging imperceptibly into one another, which draw the traveler on step by step from comparative ignorance through many intermediate stages of partial knowledge, towards the end of all journeyings.

The most important point to grasp about the traditional conception of a complete doctrine is that it is always to be regarded as potentially "effective", in the fullest possible sense, and its theoretical exposition must be accompanied by the appropriate methods for realizing it; which is neatly expressed by a favorite saying of the Tibetan lamas that Wisdom (pertaining to theory) and Method (pertaining to realization) are eternal partners and can never be divorced. It is on the strength of this association that the various traditions, especially the Eastern ones, have been at such pains to stress the essential part to be played by the *guru* or Spiritual Master, a personal guide who, in virtue of his own place in a regular line of succession going back to a more-than-human origin, is qualified to "initiate" others into the method he himself has followed, adapting it, as occasion may require, to each disciple's individual character and powers. The relationship so established between them is of the most intimate kind, often described as a "spiritual paternity" on the one hand and a "spiritual filiation" on the other, expressions which again translate the idea of the transmission of something that transcends the individual order. The influence of the master, whose function makes of him an embodiment of tradition as well as a mouthpiece of the theory, will embrace all that might in any way affect the pupil's proficiency, action being no exception, since one of the commonest obstacles in the way of spiritual development is the existence, in greater or lesser measure, of a contradiction between the outward and inward life of the being. The former must be brought to order in such a way that no sense of strain persists between the two; or rather the outward activities, in so far as these are necessary, which to some extent applies to most beings if not to all, should be so ordered and directed as to form part of the method itself, furnishing it with many of its natural appliances. That is why this conception of the teacher and his function has by no means been confined to the transmittal of obviously contemplative disciplines, but has also embraced all the active arts, from government downwards.

Given that the indissoluble wedlock of the pair Wisdom-Method has been fully recognized, the entire conception of what really constitutes Knowledge will be seen to be founded upon the idea of effective realization. It is this possibility of an immediate verification which clearly distinguishes true Knowledge from the various special sciences dealing, by methods necessarily roundabout, with the unnumbered separate "facts" apparent to the senses—their authority can at best only be a derived one, in so far as they are able to be effectively linked to the transcendent Knowledge as auxiliary means. It is only through an abuse of language, corresponding to an advanced state of scientific decadence, that the bare word "knowledge" has come to be loosely applied to the heterogeneous and disconnected results of such studies, for which the word "information" would be a more accurate term.

Information about things, when pursued with reasonable aims and not, as so often happens, as part of an idle and pretentious academic hobby, comes within the province of the Life of Action, in conformity with the "practical" character of the objects kept in view by the sciences in question. The same applies to "scholarship", "research", "philosophy" and indeed to whatever can be codified in a system and expounded in classrooms, no less than to more outdoor or obviously manual activities; the fact that certain professions are comparatively sedentary in no wise authorizes us to regard them as a halfway house to contemplation, though many people seem to suffer from such a delusion. It must be repeated— Knowledge, in the full and unrestricted sense given to it by the sacred doctrines of both East and West, excluding as it does all methods of indirect investigation, is not *about* things but *of* That on which our very being depends. Ultimately the only way to know is to be—on the highest planes of reference any distinction between the two disappears, as has been recognized by all the traditional teachers; and it was the same doctrine that found an echo in Aristotle when he declared that "the soul is all that it knows". Once this idea has been properly grasped, it will be found to carry the most far-reaching implications, which will have their repercussions in every sphere of existence.

One additional remark is still needed and it is this: one must remember that in every idea, whether it be profound or comparatively superficial, the idea itself greatly surpasses in scope all possible forms of its expression. Even the most faultless exposition is bound, by definition, to leave out far more than it includes; moreover what it omits is really the kernel of the kernel, the very essence of the idea, which is incommunicable by its nature and can only be seized by those "who have ears to hear", that is by means of a direct intellectual assimilation, accomplished in loneliness. Therefore even if someone should succeed in presenting the doctrine without distortion—and that would be no small feat and one truly deserving of the epithet "original"—even then, the listener or reader must make every allowance for the inexpressible, which is the one all-important factor.

Enough has now been said for the reader to have gained a certain insight into the relation of Action to Knowledge, even though the foregoing remarks have in great part been concerned with the latter, while the theme that gives its title to this chapter has remained rather in the background. This postponement need not occasion any surprise, however, since it is reasons arising out of the inherent instability of Action in comparison with Knowledge which thus impose the need for "situating" the former in regard to the latter, whereas the converse does not hold good. Whatever is contingent, transitory and limited in its scope can only be "valued" in terms of something that escapes those limitations; failure to put things into their proper perspective through attempting to consider the life of Action independently would, almost literally, have been to build upon the sand, and this is perhaps the most profound of the lessons contained in the Gospel story of the two men who set out to build their houses, the one upon sand and the other upon rock. Those who allow their horizon to be bounded by Action and put their entire trust in it for the accomplishing even of quite worldly, let alone other-worldly, ends might well take warning from this aspect of the parable, so persistently overlooked. If both the world and the way of living which they are so laboriously engaged in organizing seem to disintegrate as fast as they are put together, the results are only what are to be expected from any attempt to use one of the chief weapons borrowed from the armory of Method—for that is all that Action amounts to—independently of Wisdom.

The ultimate identification of "knowing" with "being" carries with it the corollary that the fruits of Knowledge are one and the same thing as the Knowledge itself and thus constitute a permanent acquisition for the knower; wherein they differ from the fruits of Action which cannot but be ulterior to the act that produced them, whether that act was undertaken with some specific purpose in view or in response to an outside stimulus, as a reaction; but in either case the result of the action will involve someone or something besides the agent himself, though that other might of course form part of his own person. It follows from this that the things that have been obtained through one action are equally liable to be lost as a result of a different action, since, in themselves, they remain separate and therefore separable. The Hindus put it concisely when they say that "Action is always separated from its fruits"; whereas Knowledge, once realized, is there for ever.

All this contributes to showing that there is a fundamental irreciprocity of relation between Action and Knowledge in favor of the latter, which is enshrined in the formal statement that "Knowledge is superior to Action"; from which it also follows that if two constituents of any order of existence are respectively attached to Knowledge and Action, the two must stand towards one another in a similar relationship. It seems hardly necessary to point out that this principle will apply to the Contemplative and Active Lives as a whole. Other and more particular applications of it can also be made to the various faculties constituent of a single being, according to whether it is Knowledge or Action that uses this or that faculty for its vehicle—it is therefore unquestionably the faculty of inward understanding, the "single eye" of Contemplation or the transcendent Intellect (to give that word the meaning it bore in Christian usage and which later misuse has perverted) that must be the guide and ruler, with the rational mind and the senses and bodily limbs carrying out their indirectly active tasks in the light it transmits to them. Otherwise one really has no right to speak of a normal human life at all; and, in passing, it might be mentioned that all the traditions are agreed that the Active Life is pre-eminently an instrument adapted for the restoration of the being to this condition of normality, usually known as the "primordial state" or state of Adam before his fall; after that point has been reached the importance of externally active disciplines is much diminished. Again, turning to the social order, it is a similar principle that governs the much misunderstood institution of the Hindu "castes" and the analogous institutions to be found in other civilizations, the hierarchy of different social functions being determined according to the degree in which they involve participation in the two chief factors now under discussion. Although in any traditional way of life the pre-eminent position of Contemplation remains beyond dispute, individuals and even whole races will be found to differ considerably in their capacity for it—apart from more or less exceptional cases—some kinds of temperament being inclined more in the direction of Action and others contrariwise. Stability and harmony consist in giving the fullest effect to these differences; it is only after the individual point of view itself has been superseded in favor of an attitude in which knowledge of the Universal is the sole concern that these distinctions lose their force and meaning, with a consequent shedding of duties, rights and other social ties. Lastly, it is again the same principle that underlies the complementary conceptions of the Spiritual Authority and Temporal Power, as acknowledged in Christendom, and that has likewise decided which of them shall always have the final say.

We have now reached the point where we can usefully begin to be more explicit about what is meant by the "Active Life" itself—for though it is too early to attempt any very complete definition, it is at least possible to arrive at some working approximation, which will gradually take clearer shape as we advance deeper into our subject. Moreover we shall attain to a truer understanding if we rely more upon the suggestive power of symbols than upon any formula of a systematic and therefore exclusive character; such attempts at an exact verbal definition are usually unsatisfactory and are best avoided. There are many aspects of the subject to which no one could hope to do justice in the course of a short survey; at times we shall have to content ourselves with a bare outline, leaving details to be filled in on some subsequent occasion, while at other times we shall go no further than just pushing a door ajar simply in order to give some slight inkling of possibilities that lie beyond it, but without trying to explore them for fear of too many complicated digressions. A subject like this is positively inexhaustible and the present essay cannot hope to provide much more than a rather sketchy introduction to it.

Traditionally, the Active Life is distinguished from, and therefore delimited by, two other Lives existing respectively above and below it, namely the Contemplative Life (which we have mentioned already) and the Life of Pleasure. In modern times the sharp distinction between these three attitudes in the face of Existence has been blurred through the name "Active Life" being often applied loosely so as to include both the second and third-named in one and the same category; to which one might add that the transcendent character of the Contemplative Life first came to be doubted, and then denied, with the result that its influence has almost vanished as a positive factor in human affairs, at least in the West. The reason for both the above-mentioned changes of valuation resides in the fact that modern thought has tended to restrict its conception of reality to the realm of relativity, or in other words to the natural world, wherein movement and change appear to reign supreme. Thus, wherever movement was apparent, as occurs in both the Active Life and the Life of Pleasure alike (though, as we shall see later on, the nature of their activities differs in certain important respects), it was supposed that activity without any further qualification was to be found, whereas where outward movement was not observable people were led to impute inactivity in a purely negative sense. The difference between the two attitudes of mind which we have just been comparing, and which might conveniently be labeled the traditional and anti-traditional outlooks, lies in the fact that the first-named derives the lesser reality of the changing and moving world from a principle or "sufficient cause" residing in the universal realm, which is by its nature the seat of the changeless and the uncompounded, while the second of the two mentalities attempts to place all reality in the realm of change. The difference of these two ways of looking at things is of fundamental importance, as affecting not only general ideas but even the minutest details of daily life; for whereas the traditional outlook fosters a habit of always looking to the cause rather than to the effect in all orders, and not least in the order of the changing world itself, the anti-traditional attitude encourages precisely the contrary tendency, namely the paying of more attention to applications than to principles, to effects than to causes, to symptoms rather than to the disease—and still less to health—to the absence of open warfare rather than to the things that make for peace. This mental habit, which is all the more dangerous in that it is largely unconscious, lies at the root of most of our troubles, and so long as it is prevalent among us we shall be condemned to remain the dreamers that we are, instead of the men of awareness that we might be.

The first requisite, therefore, is for one's ideas to be clarified—hence the need for a doctrine; continual worrying about acts before one's general outlook has been reduced to some degree of order is an unpractical policy, since it is one's ideas, or the lack of them—one's knowledge or ignorance, what one is or is not—that will condition one's acts; though these acts will in their turn serve to reinforce this or that tendency, ploughing certain furrows deeper and filling up others, thus providing a firmer "support" to knowledge or, alternatively, interposing a more insurmountable obstacle in its path.

It is above all this state of dependence upon a corresponding knowledge that gives to an act such importance as it possesses, and the effectiveness of all symbolism rests upon this correspondence between different orders of reality. An act, when viewed by itself, is just an isolated occurrence devoid of significance and the whole multitude of such acts when regarded separatively, that is to say apart from their causes, amounts to little more than an unresolvable chaos; but these same acts, taken as "symbols" or "signs" able to reveal something more fundamental and real than their mere appearance, then become an effective means of understanding. In this way whatever is situated in a lower or more limited order of existence can always be utilized as a means of approach to that higher order which its relative reality mirrors. Through the effect we are put in mind of the cause, through the act the idea is suggested, through the exercise of the Active Life in its entirety we are disposed towards the Contemplative Life. Meister Eckhart, one of the brightest stars of Christian knowledge, expressed this truth by saying that "any flea as it is in God is higher than the highest of the angels as he is in himself"—that is to say, anything that forms part of the manifested world, whether being or occurrence, exalted or lowly, if regarded in isolation is worthless, but if referred to its principle, that is to say to its "sufficient cause", is of supreme moment. Thus, almost inadvertently, we have stumbled into awareness of one of the most important characteristics of the Active Life—perhaps the most important—namely that it provides a means of reference to the life of Knowledge, the Contemplative Life: and what is true of the whole also holds good of the parts—every act or fact or distinct being, all human conduct or the entire Universe itself, are but signs, that can only be rightly interpreted and made use of by being referred back to their principle. There is no question of denying the reality of their appearance, as an appearance; but an appearance must be the appearance of something and the essential question to ask is "what is that reality of which these things are appearances?" In the answer to that question will be found the key to Knowledge.

The function of the Active Life which we are at present considering is illustrated, to take one example among others to be found in the Gospels, by the words of Christ when He spoke of "giving a cup of water in my Name"—for the act to be effective it must be performed not for its own sake, but in the name of the All-giver and in imitation, on the relative plane, of the archetype of All-giving on the universal plane. No less important, the act of taking must be ordered according to the model set by the gesture of the All-taker, a truth which is remembered in those places where Tradition still holds sway, though ignored by the fashionable school of altruists, whose name betrays their obsession with the notion of "other" and, therefore, inevitably, with the correlative notion of "I" and "mine". Once the idea has been firmly grasped that the entire Life of Action, for all its wide and varied range of possibilities, is yet essentially dependent and therefore limited, the temptation to single out certain particular spheres of activity, as if they were privileged to stand alone, will with all the more reason lose its power over us. The mind will, for instance, no longer be so inclined to over-stress questions affecting social relationships nor yet to toy with such catchwords as "virtue is its own reward" or "art for art's sake", so dear to our pseudo-intellectuals, who allow themselves to be taken in by the specious disinterestedness expressed by these high-sounding phrases. A statement of this kind could only be valid if the activity referred to were absolutely independent and real in its own right, carrying within itself its own principle or "sufficient cause", and for this to be true it would have to be all-embracing, unlimited in every respect, which would amount to making it identical with the Infinite Itself. It is not possible to admit a plurality of self-suffing but limited entities, for they will inevitably limit one another and this precludes their self-sufficiency. Such a suggestion lands one in an absurdity, which is however disguised by the rhetorical appeal of the phrase, a purely sentimental deception. Action on the relative plane has no other justification than its dependence on a superior principle, which it helps the being to realize, thus earning its only possible reward. Therefore Christ's words "in My Name" include both the cause and the aim of giving the cup of water; the phrase must however not merely be taken in the momentary and literal sense of a formal citing of the Holy Name when about to perform the act, though this ritual form might sometimes usefully be employed to inaugurate the operation. Nor is the forging of a purely mental and rational link sufficient. There is much more to it than that, for the reference to the Divine Name must involve a real integration of the act in the idea, an ordering which must moreover continue to be operative throughout the action, otherwise that action will become defective to the extent that this is omitted. At the same time it must not be thought that an ascription to the principle need necessarily be conscious in the ordinary sense of the word; when it has become second nature to such an extent that it embraces every kind of action without the agent requiring to set in motion any conscious effort of will, the mastery of this pre-eminent art will be complete. To sum up—regarded separately, Action and its fruits only serve as a net that entangles attention, diverting it from the quest of the one and only source of truth; but viewed in the light of their principle, as effects depending on a cause, that selfsame Action and its fruits lose their power to restrict and instead become a powerful means promoting realization. This doctrine, together with the appropriate methods for applying it, is known in India as *karma-marga*, the "Way of Works", and it forms the subject of what is perhaps the most extraordinary of the doctrinal books composed in Sanskrit, the *Bhagavad Gita* or Song of the Lord.

There is still another way of expressing this aspect of the doctrine, which consists in saying that in the Active Life when fully integrated, all acts without exception are ritual in character. The object of any rite is to establish communication with a higher reality, and, as we have seen, every act, whatever its nature, is capable of such ritualization, not least those daily acts which we are inclined to regard as insignificant just because they are so familiar but which are really most intimately bound up with the existence of the being, acts such as eating, washing or sexual intercourse, as well as those arts of making things which minister to men's material needs or the husbandry on which they depend for their livelihood. It will be found that in a fully traditional society these are just the acts that tend to be ritualized in the highest degree and it is interesting to note that the Indian word for action, *karma*, is also used, in a more technical sense, to denote ritual action as such, the difference in the use of an identical word depending only on the angle from which the act is viewed. From the general point of view of the Active Life every act must be a rite, that is, it must be performed "in My Name", while from the general point of view of rites they must be made to embrace every kind of action. Thus it will be seen that we are dealing with two aspects of one and the same thing and that the distinction between acts and rites, though a convenience for purposes of discussion, disappears in the final analysis. In such a conception of the Active Life those more specialized acts, designed for what we now call "a religious purpose", have their place, but they by no means monopolize the ritual field and in the highest state of understanding cannot be isolated even logically. Under such circumstances life attains its maximum coherence and it is impossible to recognize distinctions, and still less oppositions, between spiritual and physical or sacred and secular.

As against the view of life that we have just outlined, wherever a civilization has to a greater or less extent accepted a division of interest as if between two independent worlds, which might respectively be called "sacred" and "profane,"—a state of affairs which, though now widely prevalent, is abnormal in the extreme if judged from the standpoint of humanity viewed as a whole both in space and time—one may be sure that in an intellectual sense a serious degeneration has taken place. At an advanced stage of this process—which shows, incidentally, the utter fallacy inherent in any hypothesis of "progress" as commonly entertained—the ritual element, if it survives at all, becomes restricted to a few specific and isolated practices and occasions, while the rest of life, including most of the vital functions, is "profaned", that is to say *abandoned to itself.* When this happens it is certain that the day of dissolution is not far off and the words of Christ concerning "the abomination of desolation standing in the holy places" apply with full force; for the "holy places" are all the possible functions of existence, and Jerusalem and Bethlehem are here with us in this room at this moment and always.

It is worth recapitulating some of the important general conclusions about the Active Life at which we have arrived so far:

(1) It is not self-sufficing, but it is a means.

(2) It can only be effective in proportion as it remains undetached from its principle; or, if the same idea be considered from the complementary point of view, every action must be "ritualized", that is to say referred to its principle throughout its performance, otherwise that action will constitute not an aid but an obstacle.

(3) The principle on which the Active Life is dependent resides in the Contemplative Life; its goal is likewise to be found there, the two being identical.

It will now be convenient to retrace one or two steps in order to state our thesis in a slightly different way with the object of throwing certain aspects of it into still sharper relief. Contemplation and Action can be described as the twofold activity, inward and outward, of any being: or again, the first may be said to pertain to universal principles, while the second has to be exercised in the relative world of becoming or Nature, and is concerned with the interaction of the being and the rest of the universe around it. The first-named, therefore, is largely taken up with the life of the being regarded in the first person and with the answer that must be given to the question "who or what am I?"; while the second, the Active Life, is made up of the relationship between that same being which we have just called "I" and all that falls under the general heading of "others".

In the Christian Gospel these two terms will be found to be respectively connected with the two fundamental propositions of the Christian Life, "thou shalt love the Lord thy God with all thy heart and with all thy strength"—this is Contemplation—and "thou shalt love thy neighbor as thyself"—taking the word "neighbor" in its widest sense as including all the other beings that form the remainder of the Universe after abstracting from it one particular being. The classical symbol of these two lives is to be found in the story of Mary and Martha, and for anyone whose mind still harbors a lingering doubt on the subject of the true relationship of the two lives in question Christ's own comment should settle the matter once and for all.

Where then does the third life come in, which we called the "Life of Pleasure"?—for some may be thinking that it has been forgotten. This life is one that is governed by the feelings of attraction and repulsion, by pleasure and its complement—displeasure or pain. In it Action is also to be found, but it is Action pursued exclusively for the purpose of procuring for the being those things which it likes and of avoiding those things which it dislikes. All the traditions agree that only the Contemplative and Active lives can be considered truly human and that the Life of Pleasure is ruled out as subhuman. This teaching must, however, on no account become inverted in our minds, after the fashion of puritanism, so that we begin to attribute to pleasure or pain, and to the senses which register their presence, a fixed character as if they were harmful things in themselves. It is when they are wholly unreferred that they turn into agents of bondage; otherwise, like everything else when duly referred to its principle, they can render good service as subordinate means of realization. Thus pleasure, though unsought, becomes, in the words of St. Thomas Aquinas, "that which perfects the operation", crowning the work of the artist; and pain itself is capable of becoming the instrument of sacrifice (a ritual instrument therefore), the cross which the being must take up in order to follow in the footsteps of the Sublime Victim.

The confusion which has occurred in contemporary usage between the sub-human life of Pleasure-Pain and the Active Life in its true sense has arisen, as was pointed out before, through the mental habit of associating activity with the appearance of movement and change exclusively; this error has been developed to such a pitch that the supremely concentrated activity of the being poised in contemplation is often actually mistaken for inertia or sloth and labeled as such. Meanwhile the Life of Pleasure, in which the behavior of the being is entirely conditioned by the impulses of the senses, a state which is not one of activity but actually of the utmost passivity despite any appearance to the contrary, is accepted as quite normal. Frenzied movement, so easily stimulated in an attempt to overtake a happiness that always seems to elude us just round the corner, or all the various practices in which people indulge simply in order to rid themselves of a boredom which will fatally reappear after each fresh kind of drug has been tried and found wanting, are mistaken for genuine activity simply because of the wide range of displacement to which they give rise. One must remember that convulsive movements are often very violent (for example, a man struggling in the water—applying this simile at all levels, not only at the physical level), yet such movements do not deserve to be called "active" because the being is really responding passively, a cork swept along with the tide. If the seas are stormy the cork moves up and down wildly, if the water is calm the cork seems almost motionless, but in both cases one is witnessing an essentially passive phenomenon, for it is the waves that are the active factor as compared with the cork. For the ocean let us substitute the continually shifting pressure of the environment upon the being, communicated to it through the medium of the senses in the form of pleasure or pain, and we have an adequate picture of the Life of Pleasure.

It would also be possible to give this life another name and call it the Passionate Life. It is no accident that there exists an affinity between the words "passive" and "passion" derived from their common Latin root meaning "to suffer". For all the paroxysms of energy to which it can give rise, passion is nevertheless, in its innermost nature, as its name betrays, something suffered by the being, something done to it, rather than an activity exercised by it. In short, passion is but a provoker of action, by way of compensation or reaction, and in no wise a truly active influence as people usually imagine it to be—what is misleading is the impression received through the senses of the observer, which the mind is apt to misinterpret in proportion to the degree of movement displayed. Conversely, that dispassion which is one of the clearest signs of self-mastery, but which so annoys the partisan and the sentimentalist, who accuses its possessors of coldness, indifference or of "escapism"—to use a word borrowed from the contemporary jargon—is, as its name likewise indicates, a state that is negative of passivity and consequently affirmative of activity in the highest degree.

The Life of Pleasure consists of nothing else but a residue left over from an emptying of the Active Life through the abstraction of its superior principle which normally should order it from within; an impoverishment which, wherever it has occurred, arose in the first place from an overvaluing of the Active Life itself, in comparison with the Contemplative Life that provides it with its sanction; for there is no surer way of corrupting a thing than by inviting it to occupy a higher place in the hierarchy of values than naturally belongs to it in virtue of its possibilities. Pushed by human adulation on to an impossible pedestal, it tries in vain to stretch its own limitations and disintegrates in the process.

Once the principal focus of attention has been allowed to shift away from Contemplation to the side of Action, it is only natural that the tendency to seek in the latter a remedy for every kind of ill should be progressively re-enforced; and with such a tendency the development of the means of action is also bound to keep pace, for the human mind is exuberantly ingenious, so that whatever engages its interest is almost certain to prosper, at least after a fashion, while other things from which it has been withdrawn will as certainly perish from want of care. Furthermore one of the manifold effects issuing out of the incessant multiplication of practical appliances of every kind is a restricting, even to the point of their virtual suppression, of such conditions as solitude, silence and the like, conditions commonly associated with the survival of Nature in an untamed state, but which also, though in a more relative way, enter into the question of the tempo of social existence itself. In either case, however, the more unfamiliar such conditions become, the greater the probability that they will, whenever they are experienced, be productive of a sense of disquiet and even fear, leading to a deliberate attempt to abolish them; and since these are among the conditions that are known to favor the growth of a habit of meditation and inward recollection, their extinction, apart from all other possible disadvantages, amounts to depriving mankind of some of its most effective aids in cultivating the contemplative art, with the further result that it is delivered more irremediably than ever into the power of Action and of its uncontrollable boon-companion, Reaction. If the forms that these two are liable to assume include many of a peculiarly violent and destructive kind, involving the loss of much that seemed precious beyond replacement, it is nevertheless idle to give oneself over to lamentation on that score, at least so long as one persists in following the same course as before under the dictate of the blind feelings of resentment aroused by the tangible results of the antecedent action, hideous and cruel though these results may often be.

The key to the understanding of a situation of this nature, with all the frightful but still quite typical symptoms it presents, is to be sought in the original denial of the supremacy of Knowledge over Action. This repudiation, as it is pushed further and further towards the remotest stages of its fulfillment, is also certain to bring with it an attempt to rearrange the world in a manner more in accordance with the new valuation and especially to remodel Man himself and his ways of living and acting, under the compulsion of a relentless logic that will not suffer elements inconsistent with one another to continue side by side for any length of time.

It would be possible to discover other and still more profound reasons why Man, whether normal or wayward, is impelled to take the rest of the world along with him on whatever path he may choose to follow, as is implied in such statements as "Man has been made in the divine image", and "Man is the measure of all things". It is the dominant position which he has been called upon to occupy in the earthly sphere which confers on him the power of acting towards his fellow-creatures situated at the same level of existence either as their ruler and mediator or as a tyrant and exploiter. It is only to be expected that Man, once he is engaged in civil war with his own higher self, likewise finds himself committed to strife with his human neighbors and with all his surroundings—and this notwithstanding some fitful yearnings after order and inward contentment, yearnings that might well strike the mind of an impartial observer as being like a sudden welling-up of ancient memories inherited from a time when this state of conflict did not exist. Nor is it any more surprising that beings so afflicted should seek to drown their discomfort by drinking ever deeper of the cup of distraction, the cloying draught of the Life of Pleasure, with its persistently bitter aftertaste of unslaked desire, well calculated to drive the being from action to action in an endless round of attempted acquisition and divestment.

Just as the contemplative influence over men's activities leaves an unmistakable stamp of its presence on everything they do or make, so, conversely, are the signs of its absence equally recognizable. The instruments designed to minister to the Life of Pleasure, whether as forms of activity or as objects invented for that purpose, are in their own way just as characteristic as their traditional counterparts. To a dispassionate eye, the shadow cast by a thing is almost as revealing as the sight of the thing itself, and no less indicative of the existence of the light. A fact that must be faced, even though it is apt to prove an extremely uncomfortable one, is that whatever admits, whether explicitly or merely by tacit implication, that the Life of Pleasure is an adequate human life, whatever stops short at providing for the needs of Man as if he were a being whom the Life of Pleasure is or might be sufficient to satisfy, is itself ascribable to that same Life of Pleasure. This is true not only of those luxuries which men usually call "enjoyments" and which furnish the professional moral censor with his favorite targets, but also, and not less so, of many activities which are commonly supposed to serve "humanitarian" purposes, including much that passes under the name of "public service" and even a good deal of activity actually labeled as "religious". Similar considerations apply to social institutions of every kind, to the conception both of "education" and "standards of living", to the products of human manufacture, to arts and sciences and indeed to anything, whether private or public, that can conceivably be described as human activity. All turns on the fundamental conception of the being and its constitution, from which its various needs are necessarily derived; a man's own picture of himself contains the touchstone by which he may distinguish one kind of activity from another outwardly similar, leading to their respective inclusion in the Active Life or in the Life of Pleasure. No judgment of Action is possible except by reference to the Contemplative principle; even if the latter be not formally denied, to leave it out of account amounts to a virtual disavowal.

So far it might appear that we have been content to treat of acts as if each one of them would come, automatically, under one of two headings labeled respectively "normal" and "profane". Such a simplification, though convenient for purposes of discussion, has its dangers, since it can only too easily give rise to a radical dualism of the type associated with the words "spiritual" and "material", such as has dominated Western European thought for several centuries. On reflection, however, it will become apparent that many of the actions which men perform do not in practice fall unequivocally into one or other of our two main categories either in respect of their conception or of their execution, but partake of a mixed character, into which some elements of normal activity may enter, diluted, to a greater or lesser extent, by the presence of by-products derived from the Life of Pleasure. It is the particular task of discriminative Reason, as the accessory of the superior Intelligence, to make unrelenting inquisition for the detection of these compromises, welcoming any genuine activity wherever it happens to be found and exposing the insufficiency of whatever falls short.

Another obvious deduction from the same general premises is that no act can ever be regarded as endowed with a "neutral" character, or "harmless" as the saying goes—there should, strictly speaking, exist an equivalent word "goodless" and its absence is rather significant because it shows on which side the scales tend to be weighted. The belief in a neutral realm occupying an intermediate position between two other realms, regarded as self-contained and designated respectively as "good" and "evil", is largely an unconscious expedient for evading some of the more awkward dilemmas created by the habit of reading a moral, that is to say a prevailingly social, issue into every conceivable occurrence and situation, as is liable to happen in times when intelligence is at a discount and sentimentality has become all-invading, which is why this convenient neutral domain tends to grow more and more inclusive. It is largely the people who attach exclusive importance to moral judgments who supply it with its contents because they are thus enabled to countenance in others, and even to accept for themselves, many things that they might otherwise feel impelled to condemn as not conducive to those moral satisfactions for which they are always craving. Moreover, the need to remove as much as possible out of the range of the moral point of view becomes all the more imperative from the fact that sentimental morality, whether professing to be religious or merely abstract, tends to place an almost pathetic reliance on violence as the only really effective means of attaining its objectives; violence, at least in the usual sense of the word, being nothing else but an intensified form of Action, released and driven by ungovernable sentiment. But for his department of neutrality, the sentimentalist, through his indulgence in what may well be termed "moral gluttony", would be vowed to ceaseless warfare, and indeed he comes very close to that state as it is. It is not the rationally-minded person, still less the man with a contemplative bent, who flies readily to the use of violence; for moderation is the usual companion of impartial criticism, while in the second case there is in addition the fact that the main center of attraction lies elsewhere than on the moving surface of events; so that, as between him and his more passionate colleague, the differences in their respective points of view, if translated into action, are likely to be productive of policies no less markedly contrasted.

Together with its equally colorless inhabitant, the so-called "common man", this realm of supposedly neutral activities represents one of the subtlest, as well as one of the most frequent disguises assumed by the Life of Pleasure, one of those in which the spirit of passivity and negation is carried to its maximum. But, even while stripping off that disguise in order to expose the real nature of any given action, it must still clearly be borne in mind that Action itself is devoid of any absolute character by definition, since it can only be exercised within the confines of the relative world; so that in speaking of the perfection or imperfection of an act one can mean it in a relative sense only. This, once again, invalidates all attempts to bestow an absolute authority upon a moral code, for that also plainly comes within the province of the Active Life and cannot avoid sharing in its relativity. Ethics, like any other constituent of that life, do provide a salutary, and indeed at most stages an indispensable, instrument for restoring and maintaining order in the little kingdom of human individuality. If they are given exaggerated and independent value by the mind however, ethics, no less than other things, will point the way into a blind alley: for neither deeds, however meritorious, nor facts, however interesting or useful, nor indeed any of the dual fruits of the Tree of the Knowledge of Good and Evil, are to be reckoned as "food for the soul" in Plato's sense, the kind of nourishment on which, as he said, "the soul can grow wings" for its final flight. What is demanded is something more; to be perfect "even as your Father in heaven is perfect". Even stopping short of this idea of transcendent perfection, which is the proper object of the Contemplative Life, the adjective "perfect" may however, without undue impropriety, be applied in a relative way to an act simply in order to show that it conforms, to the limits of its inherent possibilities, to the conditions appropriate to such an act. Nevertheless, if those conditions were to be regarded as limiting it in an absolute sense—which is impossible, since to say "absolute limit" is to utter a contradiction in terms—the act would be devoid of any reality whatsoever and could never exist at all.

Consequently that which within the limits of Action is an act is also more than an act in virtue of its dependence on a principle which transcends those limits. Thus the act, in its function of a "support" for the realization of something residing outside its relative limitations, that is to say the act in its symbolical capacity, is able to serve a purpose far exceeding the possibilities of the same act considered in itself. No component of the Universe, whether a being or a happening, forms a completely watertight compartment, and it is this possibility of communication which alone enables beings to aspire to the Knowledge which otherwise would be forever closed to them. It is this same possibility of communication which constitutes Tradition in its essence.

Below the level of the perfect act, as we have defined it, all remaining acts suffer from a greater or lesser degree of defectiveness, which can easily be proved by recalling a few of the conditions that a competently conceived and executed act must fulfil. It must be necessary, that is, performed in view of a genuinely necessary end—it goes without saying that an arbitrary or luxurious attribution of necessity in no wise fulfils the condition in question—and it must be skillfully ordered for its purpose. It must exclude all irrelevancy, and lastly it must throughout the whole cycle of its manifestation be referred to its principle, through a full use of its symbolical or ritual possibilities. The doctrine of Islam contains a particularly apt formula to describe such an act: "It must be all that it should be and nothing else besides". Comment would seem superfluous, and this formula may well be left to each person as a suitable theme for meditation in order that he may extract for himself the secret of its manifold applications. Whoever tries to apply it as an invariable test to the various actions of his day-to-day life will soon discover in it potentialities of self-discipline that are as numberless as they are severe. That single sentence contains the most complete and concise theory of Action conceivable, and he who succeeds in applying it consistently and intelligently can be sure of realizing the highest possibilities of the Active Life. He will do more than that, since one who sails forth on this course may well awake one day to the discovery that the wind that "bloweth where it listeth" has carried him whither he did not even dream at the outset; for at the end of it all must come release, according to the universal law that only he "who shall lose his life shall find it", the Active Life being no exception to the rule. In the last extremity, after it has yielded all those things of which it is capable, it too must be denied, suffering death in the sacrificial fire of pure Contemplation which is both its principle and its end, *alpha* and *omega*. This death to Action is the ultimate fulfillment of the Active Life: outside this purpose the pursuit of any activity is but agitation, an aimless strewing by the wayside.

Additional note on ritual action

Someone to whom the foregoing chapter was shown has raised a question of considerable practical importance at the present time, one which, however, because of its contingent character failed to find a natural place in the main text where it would have created too much of a digression. Did not the virtual equating of rites and acts when correctly accomplished, he asked, entail the danger of causing people to neglect or despise ritual activities in their more specific sense, as enjoined by the various religions upon their adherents? Certainly the last thing one would wish to do is to depreciate the value of ritual action against the background of an otherwise profane-minded society, for without it even the most elementary spirituality would find it hard to survive, so that the mere fact that such a danger has troubled the thoughts of one qualified person is sufficient reason for trying to counter it to the best of one's ability.

Therefore one would answer his objection as follows: the assimilating, under normal conditions of traditional life, of acts to rites, as being re-enactments here below of divinely executed prototypes, in no wise authorizes one to exchange the emphasis, as between the two, by saying that rites, as such, amount to mere acts and no more, for it is the ritual principle, as it were, which will justify the act, and not vice versa: any inference to the contrary could only be drawn by one already imbued with a profane outlook, such as could hardly exist in the midst of a world still fully traditional; and were it ever to arise there sporadically, it would certainly receive no kind of recognition or indulgence.

However, seeing that we are now living in a world where on the one hand the value of ritual action has been largely called in question and where, on the other, the distinction of rites and acts is felt in an extreme degree, it is quite proper and in accordance with prudence for one to take up the standpoint of that distinction; in which case rites will appear, among all other forms of activity, as the highest possible, one might say as human action *par excellence,* this being moreover transcendent in relation to other forms of action in proportion to their degree of dissociation from the operative spiritual principle, or, put the other way, in proportion to the degree of ignorance affecting both the intention behind them and the manner of their execution. In such a context, assuredly, the principial indistinction of rites and acts disappears in favor of their distinction carried in fact to the highest power—for such is the penalty of admitting the profane point of view at all.

Under the conditions prevailing today, especially in the West, ritual action in the above sense, and more particularly rites having a sacrificial character, such as the Christian Eucharist for instance, are of extreme importance if only because the action in question alone continues to fulfil the normal conditions of the Active Life, those to which all actions whatsoever should by rights conform; indeed it is no paradox to say that in this sphere as in others it is the normal that has become rare, while abnormality abounds, the criteria of what is or is not normal being in no wise quantitative ones. For the many people compelled by circumstances to give their time to profane activities, despite any wish of their own, the sacramental rites in which they participate constitute for them almost the only firm support of the sacred influence of their tradition, and it is only when taking part in these rites that their acts are able to be disengaged altogether from profane influences such as, in everything else, have come to attach themselves to the activities of men. That is why, in judging a Christian's mode of living, for instance, it is not quite far-fetched to count it more in his favor that he "goes to church" than that he "does good". Whoever wishes to recapture the true spirit of the Active Life under present circumstances has no other choice but to set out from the accomplishment of those few ritual acts that still, in essence as in their finality and form, possess the character of normal acts.

Sri Anandamayi Ma (1896-1982), a Hindu saint

3

On Crossing Religious Frontiers

Among the many phenomena of an unprecedented character to which modern civilization has given rise there is one that calls for particular attention at the present time inasmuch as it affects the religious outlook of men in a very vital, if hitherto unaccustomed, manner. Indeed it is not too much to say that every religiously inclined person whose mind is open to fresh impressions is, or soon will be, compelled to face the issue raised by this cause, and this holds good whatever may be the trend of his personal conclusions, whether these have been formed, that is to say, in the light of a traditional orthodoxy or under influences of a more aberrant kind.

In previous ages, and even until quite recently, contacts between different religions, though continually occurring as a result of geographical proximity, military invasion and other similar causes, partook, generally speaking, of an "accidental" character, while the greater number of those who were attached to the various traditional forms continued to think and believe much as if their own tradition constituted an enclosed world, one in which the ideas of those dwelling outside the form in question could safely be ignored. Inter-traditional exchanges did of course nevertheless take place from time to time, and sometimes at a very high intellectual level; such occasions must however count as relatively exceptional when regarded from the standpoint of average traditional conformity, as can still be observed, for instance, in many parts of Asia, where differing forms of traditional life, despite mingling of populations, have continued over long periods to flow along entirely separate channels in a state surprisingly uninfluenced by the ideas of their neighbors.

When it comes to defining the attitude of one religion towards another in a more specific sense, a difference is observable between those that have sprung from the great Semitic stem, including Christianity, and most others, inasmuch as the former have tended to exclude from their point of view the possibility that spirituality, for different sections of humanity, might assume different forms; whereas in the second case, for which the Indian traditions provide the type, a plurality of spiritual paths, at the level of form, is taken for granted without any fear that doing so might carry with it implications damaging to one's own tradition. It is but normal for that tradition to represent for its adherents "the highest *Dharma*", but this is a very different thing from claiming for it the status of the one and only revealed way, all the rest being written off as mere errors or, at best, as "natural religion", that is to say as part-inventions of the human mind trying to meet its own unsatisfied aspirations to the best of its limited ability. Thus where the Christian, for instance, has hitherto but grudgingly recognized (against all the weight of evidence) the presence of an authentic spirituality in other religions and, when he did so, has tended to regard it as a purely subjective phenomenon, his opposite number in the Hindu, Buddhist or Far Eastern tradition has been prepared to accept at their face value, in forms other than his own, manifestations of Grace extending even to the occurrence there of Divine Incarnations, *Avataras*: moreover this attitude goes generally with a less individualistic point of view regarding human affairs, as also with less anthropomorphic views regarding the Divinity.

This Eastern openness of mind, which anybody who has come into intimate contact with Orientals still living traditionally will be able to substantiate, deserves somewhat closer study in the present instance, if only because it does not, as some might suppose, indicate any kind of doctrinal laxity: in fact the reverse is true, inasmuch as this attitude of practical tolerance is itself an expression of traditional orthodoxy, not of its absence. Behind it lies the clear distinction which, in the more purely metaphysical traditions, is made between the formal order in all its extension and the formless Truth, unique seat of liberty and therefore of liberation: the claims of the latter alone are treated as absolute; those of the former being recognized as relative, but valid at their own level. It is in virtue of this conviction that the Eastern devotee is able to accept, according to need, the discipline of a form yet without losing sight of the transcendence of "non-form", comprising as it does the ultimate goal to which forms themselves are but so many stepping-stones. It may be added that the tolerant outlook resulting from such knowledge is at the antipodes of the attitude of the "freethinker", as we have come to call him in unconscious irony, whose vaunted disregard of religious forms springs not from an ability to get beyond them, but rather from accepting to remain bound, as it were, on their hither side.

Turning once again to the West, while it cannot be denied that in more recent times the idea of religious toleration has found general acceptance there as part of the "liberal" creed now in vogue, it must at the same time be remembered that this otherwise welcome development has to a great extent gone hand in hand with a religious indifference such as often amounts to a quasi-dogmatic skepticism, a fact which in a religious sense can scarcely be counted as unmixed gain.

This skepticism in regard to religious values, which has by now become almost instinctive with contemporary man to the point of affecting the whole background of his thought and action, negative factor though it is, has nevertheless had one important repercussion within the sphere of religious thought itself, by causing people to review certain claims to exclusive validity which had hitherto been simply taken for granted; hence the great and increasing interest taken in the doctrinal expressions of other, and especially Eastern, traditions, with the inevitable comparisons resulting from such studies. Thus the question of the spiritual value of "foreign" forms, as well as of the attitude that one should take up towards them, has become a burning one in a world where, if on the one hand everything is laid open to discussion and even doubt, on the other hand, under the quantitative conception of knowledge which now passes for "scientific", everything is grist to the mill of research, including the religious phenomena associated with every section of humanity known to have ever existed either in time or space. It is not lack of information which will hamper a would-be inquirer, but rather its bewildering excess.

An army of translators has made available in printed form the sacred writings of every tradition and their work has been supplemented by that of the ethnologists, so that a mass of factual evidence has accumulated which, however profanely it may be interpreted, cannot but have a powerful effect on all who choose to become acquainted with its contents. Nor must one overlook the parallel results of collecting the artistic products of every possible civilization, including the tribal ones: for the arts have everywhere served as a vehicle for a spiritual message according to one or other traditional pattern, and the internal consistency of the artistic language, wherever an authentically traditional life prevails, goes together with an extreme differentiation versus other forms, the power to convey universal truth being in fact proportional to formal strictness as regards the means of expression. This observation harbors no paradox, being itself an expression of the relationship uniting form as such to the formless Truth, in the sense given above, a relationship on which all true symbolism depends for its efficacy: in any case there are some truths which speak to us more freely through visual or musical forms than through the spoken or written word, if only because the immediacy of their appeal places them outside the scope of the rational mind and its subterfuges. If this flood of information presents some serious disadvantages by reason of the mental voracity it both feeds and excites, it must at least be admitted that the evidences it supplies are difficult to explain away on purely conventional lines, as in the past.

Indeed it is a most case-hardened heart that is still prepared to interpret religious phenomena of almost identical character as being somehow more than they appear in one favored case and, in all other cases, less than they appear. The cruder missionary type may still cling to this position, but here at home, in the beleaguered castle of religion with hostile forces swarming round about, the very absurdity of such a view, in the light of now common knowledge, makes such a position hardly tenable.

Thus we have to deal with a situation where a kind of indiscriminate pooling of the fruits of spiritual creativeness is taking place, admittedly at a rather superficial level, but where at the same time the very traditions which have provided the material for such an exchange are all alike threatened with disintegration under pressure of the modern humanistic teaching, for which the focus of attention, by definition, is human interest restricted to the narrowest and most external sphere, with consequent withdrawal of that same attention from whatever can by any stretch be regarded as "otherworldly".

It is from the interplay of the two factors described above that there has arisen what is, in some ways, the most unprecedented feature of the situation, namely the emergence of the idea, almost unthinkable in antiquity, of what might be termed "inter-traditional co-operation", on a quasi-corporate as well as individual basis, between representatives of different religions, a co-operation such as could only take place on reasonably equal terms of mutual respect, itself implying at least a partial recognition of a common spiritual factor underlying all the forms concerned and escaping their formal limitations—this with a view to countering a danger, world-wide in its scope, that threatens all without distinction, a danger moreover which hereditary dissensions among the religions themselves can only make worse.

"The house of spirituality", so it has been argued more than once, "has hitherto been divided against itself, and this it is which prevents religious influences from playing their proper part in solving the crisis through which mankind is passing at present, one which, if a remedy be not quickly forthcoming, may well result in the physical and intellectual suicide of mankind. Therefore this is not the time to harp on old divisions but rather to lay stress on those things which are to be found on both sides of the religious frontiers and in this way the spiritual forces of the world will be able to make themselves felt before it is too late". However one may view such an argument, it must at least be admitted that there is an appearance of rough-and-ready logic behind it. How far that logic is able to carry one is however another matter, calling for the most careful examination of the conditions, favorable or restrictive, under which even the best intentions to co-operate could be expected to yield the desired results.

For a start, it is worth calling to mind a few actual examples of attempts to establish contacts as envisaged in the foregoing paragraph, though without seeking to assess their value in positive or negative terms: in fact many such attempts have been vowed to futility from the start, for a variety of reasons, but this is beside the point, as far as the present discussion is concerned, our aim being, not to support or oppose this or that movement, but merely to investigate a state of mind which has arisen in our time, of which all these activities, whatever may be said for or against them, are but cases in point. Among movements of this kind might be mentioned the one promoted by the late Sir Francis Younghusband under the name of the Congress of Faiths, as well as its American predecessor the so-called Parliament of Religions. More lately in Oxford one has had a most convinced and active promoter of such co-operation in the person of the late Mr. H. N. Spalding whose endowments in the field of university education both here and elsewhere, backed up by his own unremitting labors carried out in the face of failing health down to the last moments of his life, testified to his faith in the existence of a common spirituality at the basis of all the great religions and able even at the eleventh hour, as he always believed, to heal the deadly disease from which mankind is suffering. Again, one has read of conferences in North Africa attended by Muslims and Catholics, where a common faith in God and His Revelation as well as a common focus of opposition in the aggressive forces of militant atheism has served to draw together, under suitable safeguards, two old-time antagonists: the above represent but a few examples chosen at random from a list that is lengthening with every year that passes.[1]

Turning in quite another direction, account must be taken of the work of a number of writers of exceptional eminence who have taken their stand on both the fundamental unity and the universality of traditional knowledge as exem-

---

[1] Some mention ought perhaps to be made of the serial broadcasts by speakers representing the various religions of the world which, in this country, have become a frequent and popular feature. Some of these lectures have been excellent as far as they went, others less so, for it is an undeniable fact that persons affected by antitraditional tendencies are as a rule more given to publicizing their opinions than their more orthodox neighbors; heresy has always tended to be vociferous where true knowledge, as the Taoist sages so pertinently teach, is content to lie low and bide its time. Of quite unusual excellence (to quote a single example) was a talk given by the abbot of Ampleforth to mark the centenary of his abbey, one in which most of the principal religions were referred to in sympathetic terms, each being given credit for some particular quality characterizing its point of view. No one could suspect the reverend speaker of intending anything contrary to Catholic orthodoxy; yet it is fair to say that words like his would not have come easily from the mouth of a Christian prelate of but two generations ago. In its way, this is a sign of the times that cannot be dismissed as devoid of wider importance.

Highly significant, too, are the stirring words uttered by Pope Pius XI when dispatching his Apostolic Delegate to Libya: "Do not think you are going among infidels. Muslims attain to Salvation. The ways of Providence are infinite." By these words the traditional doctrine, far from being contravened, received a precise expression, one that displayed its truth, as it were, in a fresh dimension. (Quotation is from *L'Ultima*, Anno VIII, Florence 1954).

plified in the great religions despite all their differences of form, men like A. K. Coomaraswamy and René Guénon—to mention two of the principal names.[2] Neither of these writers was in any sense an eclectic and each tradition was, for him, something integral to be accepted on its own terms and expounded accordingly, failing which a claim to recognize a common principle in virtue of these very distinctions would be lacking in objective reality. A patchwork of beautiful citations drawn from all manner of traditional sources but so selected as to agree with the opinions, not to say the prejudices, of a particular author will no more constitute a "perennial philosophy" than an assemblage of the most expressive words out of half a dozen languages will add up to a super-language combining all their best qualities minus the drawbacks. The impotence of the eclectic approach to any subject springs from the fact that every form, to be such, must needs imply an exclusive as well as an inclusive aspect, the two jointly serving to express the limits that define the form in question. Thus whatever belongs in any sense to the formal order—as for instance any doctrinal expression, any language, or indeed any thought—will entail certain incompatibilities extending to qualities as well as to defects. In their formal aspects the oppositions between the various religions are not without some justification, though human prejudice and misrepresentation have often both aggravated and distorted their character; these oppositions cannot in any case be resolved

---

[2] The author cannot refrain from mentioning another work by a fellow-writer which, because of its originality as well as its clarity and beauty of expression, deserves more attention than it has received hitherto: this book is *The Richest Vein* by Gai Eaton (Faber & Faber, 1949; Sophia Perennis et Universalis [2nd ed.], 1995) and its author was a young officer just released from the Forces after the last war who, as the result of private reading and, as far as one can tell, without any direct traditional contacts at the time, has voiced the idea of traditional unity in virtue of, and not in opposition to, diversity of form. To one unfamiliar with the subject this book provides a useful introduction.

by merely brushing them aside. What is, however, important to remember is that no opposition can be regarded as irreducible in an absolute sense (to treat it as such would be to turn it into a kind of independent divinity, an idolatrous act therefore) and the whole metaphysical problem consists in knowing the point where such a reconciliation of opposites can be brought about without evasion or any ill-judged compromise.

Among Orientals, other than Muslims,[3] for reasons that have already been explained in part, the idea of a "transcendent unity of religions" finds easy acceptance as shown, for instance, by the exceptional veneration paid to the person of Christ by many sincere Hindus and, in similar fashion, to the Prophet of Islam: this is especially true of those who follow the *bhaktic* way, the way to Union through Love, for whom an attitude of extreme receptiveness versus other forms is almost a commonplace: perhaps the most notable example during recent times of a *bhaktic* Saint who took up this standpoint was Sri Ramakrishna Paramahamsa, the great Bengali teacher of the second half of the nineteenth century, inasmuch as his appreciation of non-Hindu forms went beyond a merely theoretical approach, for the Saint in question actually *lived* both Islam and Christianity during certain periods of his life and thus was able to "verify" their essential agreement with his own Hinduism at a level where differences ascribable to form

---

[3] This is a statement that wants qualifying: for though Islam, under its more external aspects, occupies a position not dissimilar to that of Christianity, with much the same exclusiveness towards other doctrinal forms, this attitude is compensated by the existence in the Islamic tradition of an "internal dimension" represented by the Sufi Orders, whose point of view, though in no wise opposed to the teachings of ordinary faith at the individual level, gives to those teachings a deeper as well as a more ample scope, thus approximating in effect to the point of view of more purely metaphysical traditions such as the Hindu *Vedanta* and *Mahayana* Buddhism. It is this influence exerted at the heart of Islam which has given to the latter, despite its fiercer aspects, a certain elasticity in the presence of other traditions which historical Christianity has not displayed to an equal extent.

ceased to apply. In our own time and at a somewhat more external level the name of Mahatma Gandhi also requires to be mentioned, for whom belief in a common source of inspiration for all the great religions was one of his deepest convictions. By a strange paradox it was his own reaction against anything savoring of religious bigotry which led Gandhi into recommending that the new India should proclaim itself a "secular state", a phrase which, if it means anything at all, countenances the possibility of an effective functioning *minus* any acknowledgment of the Presence of God or of Man's dependence upon the divine Providence. It seems a pity that in this matter the constitutional pattern set by modernist Europe should have been hastily copied largely on sentimental grounds, instead of trying to find some solution more in accordance with the common mind of India, which despite all the profane upsurge of the times is still largely dominated by spiritual values. One asks whether it would not have been better to declare the newly constituted state to be religiously "all embracing" (thus excluding all parochialism) instead of "secular" which is a purely privative term and one that suffers from an inherently blasphemous flavor that no excuses can disguise.[4]

Through the foregoing discussion, sketchy though it has necessarily been in view of the much ground to be covered, it is hoped that sufficient evidence is now forthcoming to enable the reader to "situate" the problem of effective communication between religions by showing that every such

---

[4] It must not be supposed that we are trying to champion some kind of artificially combined religious form, a would-be esperanto of the Spirit: all that the term "all-embracing" might be expected to indicate is a primary recognition of religion as the indispensable mainspring of all valid activity, even political (which also was an article of faith with the Mahatma) and, secondly, the congruent rights of all the existing traditional forms. Admittedly, there is a certain looseness in such a constitutional provision, but it would have served the purpose.

exchange, be it even confined to the realm of thought, will involve some application of the larger principle governing the relation between "forms" and "beyond forms", letter and Spirit. Admitting that individual existence will always imply the presence of the former though without prejudice to the ultimate supremacy of the latter (as containing the transcendent source of authority from which all lesser faculties derive), it is obvious that at any point short of the supreme Enlightenment a certain degree of "tension" will be felt as between those two factors (so long, that is to say, as they are regarded through the spectacles of a more or less persistent dualism), and indeed all spiritual attitudes, all ascetic method, all *yogic* skill will be determined by the angle from which that tension is envisaged; the question of how much emphasis is to be laid in given circumstances upon individual and formal or supra-formal and universal elements respectively is a matter of "spiritual opportunism", varying in obedience to changing needs.

Where reliance upon formal elements is pronounced (even in a manner that is well-founded), bridging the gap to another form becomes correspondingly hard. This is the source of the Christian's habitual hesitations when faced with any evidence of a spirituality unclothed in the specifically Christian form, for his own outlook has been so powerfully molded according to a historical perspective on the basis of certain facts (and every fact belongs by definition to the world of forms) that he finds any act of transposition to another viewpoint exceptionally perilous: not that Christianity excludes such a transposition in itself, since those same historic facts upon which Christian faith reposes are, in virtue of their symbolism, realizable also on the universal plane where they provide the key to intellections far exceeding anything that a purely individual view is able to embrace. The danger to a faith relying too exclusively upon the factual element is this, namely that it leaves the minds of those concerned peculiarly vulnerable if, with or without good reason, serious doubt comes to be cast on the particular facts in which they put all their trust, as for instance the historicity of certain past events. When this happens, panic supervenes, and the flight from tradition easily becomes a rout. The modern world and its irreligiousness is the revenge of the Spirit upon those who attached to the formal elements of their tradition (important though these certainly are) that absolute character that belongs to the unembodied and total Truth. These people have been, as it were, abandoned to the facts they idolized; for that is what the profane point of view essentially consists of, namely an indefinite fragmentation of reality with no hope of unifying the consequent and ever-shifting oppositions.

If this is the burden of Western man, whose mind always shows the impress of its Christian formation even when believing itself to have shaken loose from its effects, the Oriental, for his part, is threatened by somewhat different dangers. For him questions of form do not, as we have seen, present any great difficulty and that is why he as a rule shows himself more venturesome in going forth to meet ideas issuing from unfamiliar traditions, without a corresponding risk of losing hold on his own. Moreover, having been schooled all his life in the thought that all forms are ephemeral—even the most hallowed—and that every separate fact is but another facet of the Cosmic Illusion, *Maya*, he is much less prone to rest upon so unstable a foundation as the world of appearances. Where life and death themselves seem such relative states, both here and hereafter, the death of a fact, like its existence, causes far less disturbance than when it is treated as if endowed with an absolute reality of its own.

That is the strength of the Orient, observable not only in the life of Sages but also in that of quite humble people, subject as they are in other respects to ordinary human weaknesses. For habitual open-mindedness the danger of error will come, not as a result of a rigidity which it precludes, but rather through a too great readiness to accommodate itself, to the point of finding agreement where none really exists and of underrating the importance of forms in a time of crisis; the oft decried use of "dogmatic" definitions in the service of a religious orthodoxy can in such times amount to a solid protection, at least for the generality, though at the same time it will always remain something of a two-edged weapon. In the Eastern religions so long as the traditional structure remained substantially intact this danger of making too free with the formal element was hardly likely to arise; but in very modern times, with the sudden impact of Western profanity upon Eastern minds at a moment when many of the native traditions were already suffering from the degeneration which time must bring to every form itself born temporally, a serious breakdown at the surface level rapidly took place, evinced in many cases by a clamorous depreciation of all formal, that is to say doctrinal, ritual and artistic elements such as had supplied people through the ages with their day-to-day nourishment for the soul—all this in the name of a neo-spiritual "idealism" which, in most cases, amounted to nothing more than ethical sentimentalism and specious universalism, after the Western modernist model. Both in India and elsewhere much weakening has occurred as a result of these tendencies, which that very open-mindedness we have been discussing has, in present circumstances, helped to foster.

Before quitting our subject, allusion must be made to an oft-expressed opinion that with a view to better understanding between the religions of East and West *love* single-handed might forge the necessary link, and this suggestion is one which, more perhaps by its sound than its content, exerts a deceptive attraction upon many minds, both by reason of its obviously sentimental appeal when employed in such a context and also because its vagueness really commits one to nothing, leaving all the problems created by traditional differences where they were. Professions of peace and goodwill are cheaper today than in any previous age, and doubtless the fact that this has corresponded with a time when persecutions and wars, declared and undeclared, have reached a scale and extension without parallel in recorded history is no accident, so that both sets of phenomena can reasonably be traced to the same fundamental causes.

That goodwill, kindly feeling, is one of the conditions of success in every form of co-operation between humans is a truism, but this is by no means enough to ensure any but the most superficial success if only from the fact that a sentiment, however excellent in itself, remains by its nature a relatively unstable thing, which a very small shifting of the focus of attention may easily swing as far as its own opposite, in virtue of the law of polarity which governs the whole manifested universe, and this effect is often seen in wartime. Hence the repeated failures of the various peace movements which have been such a disappointing feature of our times, these having been due, in the writer's opinion, not so much to the absence of sincere goodwill in their promoters (even in "the politicians"!) as to its excess, itself due to an urge to make up for an intellectual lack felt, but not truly understood. Indeed it is a great and common error to suppose that Charity is something that can function unintelligently, for true Charity is grounded less upon kind feeling than upon the nature of things: fundamentally it demands a spiritual attitude, not simply a moral one. Charity is in fact intensely realistic and "practical"—"operative" in the sense given to that word by the old craft initiations—and is itself opposable to that very sentimentality with which it is so often confused. In an ultimate sense Charity rests upon the disappearance of ego-separativity in the face of God, with its accompanying abolition of all sense of otherness towards one's fellow beings, and this highest synthesis of the soul is only realizable in terms of both knowledge and love which at this point coincide: from which it follows that every attempt to reach understanding in the face of differences requires, as its force both motive and directive, the presence of Intelligence, which is something more than mere mind and which, if man were without it,

72

would preclude all hope of reaching an effective conclusion, were it even in respect of the smallest of the problems consequent on existence, let alone the final problem set by existence itself.

Once it is accepted that an attitude not merely benevolent but also derived from a just appraisal of relevant factors is required by anyone who wishes to establish contact (whether only indirectly in the mind or in a more direct and complete sense) with "foreign spirituality"—and few serious-minded people escape this need under some shape or other today—then it becomes a matter of urgency that the operative principles should be presented in a form assimilable by an average intelligent person (we do not say "an erudite person", still less a "theological technologist"), accompanied by a commentary that will combine fairness and accuracy with insight and interpretative skill. It is for the sake of such inquirers, regardless of their angle of approach, that we will conclude this chapter by drawing attention to a pair of books which, in the writer's opinion, fulfil the required conditions in the highest degree—both works have been translated into English (from the French), under the respective titles of *Transcendent Unity of Religions* (Faber & Faber, 1953; Quest [2nd ed.], 1993) and *Gnosis: Divine Wisdom* (John Murray, 1959; Perennial Books [2nd ed.], 1990), their author being Frithjof Schuon.

There would be little point in filling one's own pages with an analysis of these two closely knit and also highly original works of practical theology—practical, because throwing light on some of the most urgent as well as complex questions affecting the spiritual life of individuals and groups; just enough must be said, however, in connection with the present discussion, to show why the appearance of these particular books has been so timely.

Of *Transcendent Unity* one can say that it marshals all the basic information needed in order that this pressing problem of religions and their relations to one another may be properly stated—wherever this is done one is already halfway to a solution. From the very outset, the author lays himself out to deal with the fundamental problem of letter and spirit, or otherwise expressed, of exoterism and esoterism.[5] Besides putting this great question with telling effect he points the way to an effective answer by showing that here is not a case of choice between two alternatives situated on the same plane but rather of recognizing that they refer to things belonging to different orders (thus implying a hierarchical, not a symmetrical relationship between them); a knowledge which once clearly possessed will allow of applying one and the same principle with unfailing discrimination to each case as it arises, without any confusion between the factors concerned. It is this knowledge in fact which confers mastery over forms and constitutes the primary qualification required of one who would build a bridge, for his own sake and for the sake of others, between religion and religion, even while the stream of formal distinction continues to flow in between. This is perhaps the most important, though by no means the only, message contained in the book, for much ground is covered in the course of it and many accessory aspects are dealt with in a manner not less illuminating, such as "the question of forms in art" and its bearing on the spiritual needs of mankind, and also certain matters touching the Christian tradition which occupy the two final chapters.

In comparison with the earlier of the two works, charged as it is with a wealth of illustrative material from which conclusions disengage themselves at a sure but gradual pace, *Gnosis: Divine Wisdom* makes easier reading, being in fact extremely

---

[5] Incidentally he helps to clear the latter term of the reproach that has become attached to it as a result of its tendencious and fanciful employment by various pseudo-mystical and occultist schools such as always make their appearance in times of widespread bewilderment, these times being no exception. Correctly used, the twin terms "exoteric" and "esoteric" are in their way extremely useful ones, as corresponding to two fundamental aspects of reality, and therefore to necessities, spiritual and practical.

concise in its presentation as well as more "poetical" in tone. As far as our present subject is concerned, some twenty-odd pages[6] suffice to cover most of the ground in a manner that is never less than masterly: one would gladly have reproduced those pages in their entirety by way of a final summing up. The rest of the book is taken up with different aspects of spiritual life, including, as in the previous case, one whole section on the Christian tradition which, by its appeal at once intelligent and moving, is well calculated to put heart into many a flagging aspiration.

It is especially in the opening pages of *Gnosis*[7] that the author touches the most tender point in the continual misunderstanding existing among the religions, which to a visiting outsider might indeed seem very strange given both the actual facts and the apparent intelligence and good faith of many of the people concerned—not that the contrary of these qualities does not enter in at times, for the methods used in religious controversy have often been far from edifying: the point he makes in those first pages is that, in many cases if not in all, misunderstanding has been bound up with a proneness to compare elements not strictly comparable, than which there can be no more fatal cause of confusions.

In the spiritual field the fact is that differences of expression often mask an identity of content, while verbal resemblances may, on the contrary, accompany essential dif-

---

[6] We are referring especially to the first few pages of Chapter I and to the sections on "Revelation" and "Natural Mysticism."

[7] As with the word "esoterism" in the other book, here the author is at pains to rid "gnosis", a word that should be sacrosanct if ever there was one, of the prejudice that has in course of time gathered round its use, chiefly from its association in many minds, and often for mutually exclusive reasons, with "gnosticism" and the early heresies of that name. Here this term is restored to its normal connotation, indicating in spirituality its sapiential essence, unitive Knowledge.

ferences. In our time René Guénon was probably the first to point this out clearly: this truth once seen, one becomes wary alike of superficial assimilations and oppositions. Before proceeding to compare two doctrinal formulations arising from a different background one must first master the true language of each, its essential assumptions as also the things left unsaid, otherwise the conclusion will betray one. For this work of "spiritual translation" a fully awakened power of discernment is an indispensable qualification and this means an intuitive, not a merely rational quality. One cannot do better than quote Frithjof Schuon himself in his opening lines which already contain the key of all that is to follow:

> One of the chief reasons for the mutual incomprehension which rises, like an impermeable partition, between the religions, seems to us to reside in the fact that the sense of the absolute in each case is situated on a different level, so that points of comparison are most often illusory ones. Formally similar elements figure in such differing contexts that they change function from one case to another and consequently also change nature: thus it is, because the infinity of the possible precludes all exact repetition.

A clearer picture of the whole situation could not be given.

Considered together these two books are characterized by the maintenance, at every turn, of a sharp distinction between what in any question belongs to its essence and its more accidental and therefore variable factors. The reader is continually being put in a position of having to face his difficulties in all their complexity and irrespective of what may be his own personal leanings; if the experience causes discomfort, this will have to be endured, for the author never makes any kind of concession to intellectual hedonism. At times our author can indeed be very severe in his judgments, but never uncharitable. As for his use of language, whether the theme under treatment be simple or subtle, expression remains that of everyday speech, but used purely and with accuracy;[8] no reader of his need fear that his task will be rendered heavier by a text loaded with ultra-technical phraseology and "long words" such as shallow minds delight in; close attention he is asked to pay, but nothing besides.

If it be asked now what, in the present writer's view, is the chief distinguishing feature of these books, his answer is that they exemplify, in a pre-eminent degree, a possession of "the gift of tongues", the ability, that is to say, both to speak and understand the various dialects through which the Spirit has chosen to communicate itself to men in their diversity and therefore, in practice, also the ability to communicate clearly with one's fellows across the religious frontiers. In other words it exemplifies the power to penetrate all traditional forms as well as to render them mutually intelligible for the sake of those who, not by evading but rather by faithfully observing the claims of form where they properly belong, will make of this obedience not a shuttered but an open window, one through which light and air are able to penetrate and from which the imprisoned bird can start forth on an unhindered flight.

---

[8] This statement refers primarily to the French text which however also translates well into English: those able to read the books in the original are naturally advised to do so. For their information the titles and publishers are given, namely *De l'Unité Transcendante des Religions* (Gallimard) and *Sentiers de Gnose* (La Colombe).

"This noiseless solitude is guide to lasting contemplation." Mila Repa

4
Some Thoughts on Soliciting and Imparting Spiritual Counsel
(To one who provided
the occasional cause for this essay)

The function of *upaguru* or "occasional instructor", to which René Guénon devoted an article (*Études Traditionnelles* January 1948), is one that cannot be defined in terms of any special qualification: any man, thanks to a particular conjunction of circumstances, may some day be called upon to exercise it, and it may even happen that the office in question will devolve, outside the circle of human relationships, upon an animal, plant or even an "inanimate" object that becomes, at that moment, a substitute for the human instructor in bringing enlightenment to someone in need of it—here the word "enlightenment" is used in a relative sense, this goes without saying; but provided the knowledge thus gained really counts spiritually, being thus related in greater or lesser degree to the gaining of Enlightenment in the full sense, then the use of the self-same word is justified. Naturally the function itself is exercisable, in the case of a human being, in more or less active mode, that is to say with greater or lesser awareness of what is involved; in the most favorable case the agent of instruction will accept the responsibility that has come to him as being part of his own *karma*, a by-product of anterior causes, that is to say in a spirit of submission to the universal law of causality or to that Divine Will which translates it in personal terms; but at the same time he will regard it as a spiritual opportunity, an episode of his own vocation or *dharma*, to be welcomed accordingly.

This experience is one which must have been shared by many of those who, inspired by Guénon's example, have themselves come to publish books or essays treating of the traditional doctrines: speaking from his own experience, the author of these notes has in fact repeatedly found himself in the position of being consulted by people anxiously seeking spiritual advice with a view to giving effect, in the face of the modern world and under its pressure, to that which, thanks to their own reading of Guénon or other works imbued with the traditional spirit, had become for them a matter of pressing necessity.

These inquiries, however, though animated by a common motive, have in fact taken on many different and sometimes most unexpected forms, calling for answers no less variable: it is nevertheless possible, looking back, to recognize some features of common occurrence that may allow of a few profitable generalizations touching the way in which a man should prepare himself to meet an opportunity of this kind. It must however be clearly understood that any suggestions offered here, even if they commend themselves, are intended to be carried out, whenever the occasion presents itself, in a resourceful spirit and with the greatest flexibility, lest by faulty handling on one's own part the person most concerned be driven back prematurely on his defenses, as can so easily happen with temperaments either passionately or else timidly inclined. Ability or willingness to discuss a vital matter in a spirit of detachment, as experience has shown again and again, can but rarely be taken for granted in anyone; a certain failure in this respect at the outset must not cause the other person to be written off as "uninteresting", as a result of a summary estimate of his character and motives; in handling such matters a remembrance of one's own limitations can be of great service as a corrective to impatience or complacency.

At the same time, neither is it necessary to wrap up every statement or avoid every straight issue for fear of causing pain, and if some question productive of an answer from one-self couched in rigorous terms happens to awaken an unex-pectedly strong sentimental reaction in one's interlocutor this too must be accepted patiently and without surprise; the cause of such hitches may well lie in the fact that anyone with a mind seriously divided about spiritual questions will neces-sarily be living under some degree of strain and this state of acute doubt may well give rise in season to symptoms of irrit-ability. On the other hand it also sometimes happens that an inquirer, professedly asking for counsel, has already made up his mind, if unconsciously, and all he is really seeking is a peg on which to hang a decision prejudged on the strength of secret desires; in such a case a straight answer, that brings matters sharply to a head, may be the only way left open to one. Nevertheless, these cases are comparatively rare, and the greater number of consultations of the kind here referred to are more likely to follow a line of gradual and also of fluctuat-ing approach.

For the sake of those who, either from natural diffidence or for any other reason, might feel dismayed at the possibil-ity of having some day to impart spiritual counsel to another, and possibly even to one who, at the mental level, is more highly equipped than themselves, it should be repeated that the function here under discussion, that of *upaguru,* is not one that depends on the possession of any kind of transcen-dent qualification, though within the very wide limits defin-ing the field of its possible exercise all manner of degrees are to be found. If it be argued, rightly as it happens, that the function of instructor, even in its most relative sense, will always carry with it some implication of superiority over the person instructed, the answer in this case will be that the mere fact that the latter has come to one seeking spiritual advice itself constitutes recognition of a certain superiority, however temporary and however limited in scope. To accept this fact in no wise runs counter to true humility; for in fact no human instrument as such is ever adequate to a divinely imparted vocation at any degree, therefore also his own unworthiness can never rule a man out altogether. One can take comfort in the fact that the very disproportion of the two terms involved serves to illustrate the transcendence of the one and the dependence of the other: paradoxically, it is the "good man's" personal luster which might, in the eyes of the world, seem to mask the seemingly distant source of its own illumination, but this can hardly be said of the sinner's!

Incidentally this same principle contains an answer to the classical attack of the man of "protestant" turn of mind on various sacred offices because of the occasional, or even frequent, moral deficiencies of those traditionally entrusted with their exercise. The function itself remains objectively what it was at the origins; neither can the saintliness of one holder validate it further, nor the corruption of another invalidate it, be the facts what they will. If reform be needed, it must rest on this principle, otherwise it is more likely to become a wrecking, the displacement of a relatively normal evil by one wholly out of control.

So much for the call to *upaguruhood*: when it comes to the case of a Spiritual Master, however, *guru* in the full sense, his superiority rests on the twin poles of initiatic status, which is not a personal attribute, and of spiritual realization which likewise confers an objective quality that once gained cannot afterwards be forfeited; in that sense the *guru* can be called infallible, and a mouthpiece of the Self. Should it happen, however, that the disciple becomes equal in knowledge to his master, then, if he wants further guidance he will have to go elsewhere, as indeed sometimes occurs in the initiatic life; there are even cases on record when a master, recognizing the fact that a disciple has surpassed him, has exchanged places with him, descending willingly from the instructor's seat to sit at his feet, an example both of the highest humility and also of the purest realism. With the occasional office of *upaguru* the case is different, as already pointed out: apart from the temporary superiority conferred by the occasion, an adviser may well be, on balance, inferior by comparison with the person who has consulted him, though the reverse can just as well be true; in either case this question is irrelevant.

If, however, the questions as addressed by the inquirer are felt to be beyond one's powers of adequate handling it is always open to one—this hardly needs saying—to send him elsewhere to someone better equipped for the purpose; which is not the same as simply wanting to get rid of him, in a spirit of indifference lacking charity.

Cases may also occur which are of a very doubtful character, calling for an attitude of reserve on one's own part; besides which there are all sorts of inquiries having an obviously superficial bearing, when all that is needed is to refer the other person to suitable books which, if read attentively, might at least serve to awaken some understanding as to what the spiritual life really entails and this in its turn might produce consequences of an incalculable kind. The present comments, however, are only meant to cover the case of the more or less serious seeker, without trying to extend the discussion to borderline cases. Having been compiled under the impulse of a recent experience, they have an almost entirely practical bearing, and in any case there has been no intention of treating the subject exhaustively.

A. *For the guidance of the person consulted:*

(1) Speaking generally, it is usually good policy to start off by dealing with whatever question one's would-be client has chosen for a gambit, and this holds good even when one suspects that there may be other and deeper-seated perplexities still unavowed. Very often one's own first contribution will consist in framing the question itself correctly: half the unanswerable questions in the world remain so because they are already vitiated by the intrusion of special pleading (in other words, of passion) or because they harbor some undetected confusion between different orders of reality

with consequent false comparisons—the history of religious controversy abounds in such examples, which does not mean, however, that it consists of nothing but that, as professed enemies of dogma would like to argue. Given that the case is such, however, once a question has been accurately and fairly re-phrased, it will already be half way to begetting its own right answer, which can then be left to the inquirer himself to elicit far better than if one tries to supply it for him. It often happens, however, that the questions addressed to one are of a very general kind, amounting, that is to say, to an inquiry how to find a spiritual way unaccompanied by any pointer indicating a particular line of approach, and in that case it will be advisable to begin by investigating those spiritual possibilities that appear to be most accessible to the person concerned and least beset by practical obstacles, while being careful to leave the door open to other and seemingly more remote possibilities. At the same time there should be a conscious attempt to prevent the scales from being hastily weighted, by either party, in favor of or against a particular solution (unless the form of the question as put is such as to admit of only one answer, which will not happen very often), because the considerations governing any eventual choice of a path are necessarily complex and include not only practical factors of time and place and personal associations, but also factors of psychic affinity or incompatibility which cannot be assessed at a first glance.

(2) One should deliberately frame one's comments and answers on the basis of the traditional norms, with the minimum intrusion of one's personal opinions or preferences: it must all along be borne in mind that one is not called upon to substitute one's personal will for that of the other party, who must on the contrary be encouraged to take proper responsibility for any decisions taken, whether in a provisional or in a more far-reaching sense. One is there, in a situation not of one's own seeking, as the temporary spokesman of tradition itself, across its every form, and this requires an attitude of

calculated detachment, which must not for a moment be abandoned under whatever provocation from the other party or because of some sentimental attachment of one's own. It is neither by getting involved in a debate nor by any one-sided advocacy of this or that but rather by consistently holding the mirror of pure metaphysical knowledge in the face of the other person's aspirations and difficulties that one will best succeed in dispelling the confusions and contradictions that beset the entrance to the Way: these are likely to be more than usually troublesome if the inquirer happens to be an "intellectual" (in the modern sense), one whose mind, that is to say, is haunted by a throng of abstract concepts, besides laboring under the mass of factual information which a man of retentive brain can hardly escape being burdened with under present circumstances.

(3) Sentimental prejudices, if they happen to reveal themselves, should be shown up for what they are; but in doing so, firmness should be duly tempered with courtesy and sympathy, since the realm of the feelings is one where, by definition, violent reactions are in the order of things and once these have been evoked it is not easy for anyone to return to a state of impartial consideration; he must be given time to regain his balance.

(4) One must abstain from engaging in an attempted psychological analysis of the other person: the less one delves into his or her private life, antecedents, etc., the better, and questions of this kind should only be put where some fact or other appears quite indispensable for the purpose of rendering a spiritual problem more "concrete". Once again, it is well to remind oneself that for someone to be seeking advice of this nature does in itself argue a degree, and often an acute degree, of "spiritual distress" that deserves all one's sympathy. It should be added that in trying to probe the nature of another's spiritual need, small, apparently irrelevant signs will often tell one more than any rationalized explanations, since the latter, even when honestly advanced, are almost bound to

take on an apologetic and forensic character, affecting their usefulness as evidence to a greater or lesser extent.

B. *Concerning the need for a traditional framework:*

In the case of one who is already attached to an authentic traditional form, the positive possibilities of that form must first be taken into account, if only for the reason that the individual concerned will already have been molded psychically according to that form, at least in part, and will understand its language without special effort.

As for one who is "unattached" traditionally, the primary necessity of a traditional basis for a spiritual life must, as Guénon has done repeatedly, be stressed in unequivocal terms; an esoterism *in vacuo* is not to be thought of, if only from the fact that man is not pure Intellect, but is also both mind and body the several faculties of which, because they are relatively external themselves, require correspondingly external means for their ordering. This insistence on the "discipline of form" is a great stumbling-block to the modernist mentality, and not least so when that mentality is imbued with pseudo-esoteric pretensions. Therefore it provides, over and above its own correctness, one of the earliest means for testing the true character of a man's aspiration, even to the point of bringing about an immediate "discrimination of spirits": only here again one must beware of making a system of this test, since it has become such a commonplace, on the part of modern writers on spiritual subjects, to decry the value of forms that a person not already forearmed can be pardoned, at least in some cases, for having developed a similar distaste in the sincere belief that he is merely escaping from the servitude of the letter in the direction of "pure spirit"; whereas all he is doing is to substitute mental abstractions for concrete symbols, and human opinions for the traditional wisdom and the laws that express it outwardly. Nevertheless, in the long run, a persistent unwillingness to accept any traditional formation for oneself, on the common plea that there is no form but has exhibited imperfections in greater or lesser degree in the course of its history, must be reckoned as evidence of spiritual disqualification. Form necessarily implies limitation and this in its turn implies the possibility of corruption; it would be futile to wish things otherwise. This fact however does not invalidate the efficacy of a formal disposition for those elements in the individuality that belong themselves to the formal order, of which thought is one. For this reason one must not allow oneself to weaken in regard to the principle of traditional conformity, which does not mean, however, that one should try to ignore incontestable facts concerning various manifestations of human corruptibility that have occurred in the traditional civilizations, especially in more recent times, from some of which, moreover, the modern profanity itself can be traced in lineal descent.

C. *What attachment to a traditional form implies*:

Attachment to a revealed form which, to meet its corresponding necessity, must be an effective and not merely "ideal" attachment, will imply, as an indispensable condition: (a) The taking up of an *active* attitude towards the world, in opposition to the attitude of passive acceptance that has become so general in these latter days, and it also implies a symbolical but still relatively passive participation in the mysteries, firstly through faith and secondly through general conformity to the traditional institutions. This relatively (though not wholly) passive participation is in fact the distinguishing "note" of an attitude properly qualifiable as "exoteric", in contrast to an "esoteric" attitude (b) which, for its part, implies, over and above, an active, truly "intellectual" participation in the mysteries with a view to their effective realization, sooner or later, in the heart of the devotee. In the latter case the more external side of the tradition, with all its component elements, instead of appearing to fill the entire spiritual horizon, will rather be thought of as offering two advantages, namely (i) as imposing the indispensable discipline of form upon the psycho-physical faculties of the being, the rational faculty included, so that they may all serve, and never obstruct, the activity of the central organ or Spiritual Heart and (ii), as providing teacher (when found) and disciple alike with appropriate "supports", symbolic or other, wherewith the more inward activities can be steadied in the course of development, and more particularly in the earlier stages.

These supports if they are to be utilizable in an effective sense, as instruments of a spiritual method, must be formally consistent (hence the objection, voiced by Guénon, against any arbitrary "mingling of forms"); otherwise all kinds of psychological dissonances are likely to arise. The modern mind, with its habit of conceiving progress in terms of an indefinite amassing of things regarded as beyond question beneficial and not so merely under a given set of conditions, finds it especially hard to admit that two elements, each advantageous in its own place, can nevertheless be mutually exclusive and capable, when brought into association, of producing far more harm than good. Behind this reluctance there lies in fact a serious metaphysical fallacy, due to a radical inability to grasp the true nature of forms which, to be such, must each display aspects of inclusion and exclusion, both.

D. *Concerning the nature of tradition:*

For any human being, his "traditional attachment" can be regarded as a minimum condition defining him as human, at least in intention, and this, regardless of the greater or lesser extent of that being's spiritual horizon: in this sense, tradition will appear as the chief compensating factor for Man's fall from Grace, and as a means for regaining a lost state of equilibrium. In a sense, it is untrue to speak of a man's attachment to tradition; it would be more accurate to say that by tradition man is connected with the source of Knowledge and Grace, as by an Ariadne's clue, one that gives him his direction as well as the hope and promise of safety, if he will but use the opportunity it offers him. For every man, his tradition will be evocative of certain spiritual "values", besides providing the ritual and formal supports (as explained before) which are the carriers and catalysts of celestial influences, at all degrees of receptiveness and participation. The tradition will dedicate that man or woman in principle to the Way and it will unlock the door to all the possibilities of realization. Likewise it will serve to "regulate" all the more external aspects of human activity and it will, under normal conditions, suffuse its characteristic "color" or "flavor" over all the elements of daily life.

For an esoterist the same holds good, with the difference that the whole conception of the Way will be raised, as it were, to a higher power, its finality being transposed beyond individual and indeed beyond all formal limits.

E. *Digression on Orthodoxy:*

Faith has been defined as confident acceptance of a revealed truth, orthodoxy marking a parallel conformity of thought and expression to this same revealed truth. It is not our purpose here to attempt a detailed study of this important aspect of traditional participation, the one that imparts to spiritual life its formal consistency. There is however one aspect of the subject which must find a place here because in practice it often plays its part in the difficulties surrounding the early stages of spiritual quest: it is the distinction, not always apparent to everybody, between an expression of traditional orthodoxy in the strict sense and a private opinion which happens to coincide with the orthodox teaching. From the point of view of its objective content, such an opinion can be accepted at its face value since, as St. Ambrose pointed out, truth by whomsoever expressed is always "of the Holy Ghost". Subjectively judged, however, the correctness of an opinion so held, though creditable to its author and in any case welcome, still remains "accidental" and therefore precarious; the traditional guarantees are not in themselves replaceable thanks to any purely human initiative, carried out, that is to say, outside that spiritual current whence the doctrine in question itself emanates.

The same question might also be presented in another way: it might be asked, which is preferable, that a man be regularly attached to an orthodox tradition while holding some erroneous opinions or that he hold correct views while remaining outside any actual traditional framework? To such a question the answer must be, unequivocably, that regular attachment is in itself worth more than any individual opinion for the simple reason that thoughts, whether sound or mistaken, belong "to the side of man" whereas a traditional doctrine, as deriving from a revelation, belongs "to the side of God"—this without mentioning the "means of Grace" which accompany the doctrine with a view to its realization and for which there exists no human counterpart whatsoever. Between the two positions the distance is incommensurable and once this is seen the original question loses all its point. It was necessary to touch on it, however, because the pretension to share in the things of tradition "ideally", that is, without paying the price, is one to which many people are addicted from a somewhat clumsy wish to safeguard a non-existent freedom—non-existent because still waiting to be gained through knowledge.

F.   *Concerning the structure of a tradition:*

Every complete tradition implies three elements, utilizable by all concerned and at all degrees of knowledge though in differing proportions. These elements are: (a) a form of doctrine, expressed in the appropriate "spiritual dialect" (which, to some extent at least, will exclude other dialects), the vehicle of that doctrine being not only the spoken or written word, but also arts, manners and indeed everything great or small forming part of the tradition in question: and (b) certain "means of Grace", whether transmitted from the origins or else revealed at some subsequent time, these being the specific supports of the spiritual influences animating that tradition: and (c) a traditional law regulating the scope of action, positively and negatively, in various ways.

For an exoterist (a), the doctrine will largely be a field for faith in its more ordinary sense, which represents a relatively passive aspect of knowledge, whereas that same doctrine will, for an esoterist, be treated from the point of view of full awareness through "ontological realization", that is to say from the point of view of knowledge in its active mode. The Christian dialect may still continue to apply the word "faith" to the latter case also, but it must then be taken in the sense of "seeing is believing" and mountains are able to be moved in virtue of it. Similarly, in the case of the sacramental element (b), it will be accepted by the exoterist as a mystery which will often amount, for him, to little more than the implanting of a germ, one which, however, watered by faith and warmed by the other virtues, is bound to bring forth fruit in season.

An esoterist, for his part, will share in the rites with the conscious intention of actualizing their fruits in the fullest degree; his attitude is active by definition—if the latter term can be applied to an intention which accepts no limits whatsoever. As for (c), legislative conformity whether ritual or moral, this is required of exoterist and esoterist alike so long as any of the components of a human individuality still remain unordered and uncentered. The final term of this condition of being "under the law" is a converting of one's human status, which since "the Fall", as variously pictured in the different traditions, has been merely virtual, into an irreversible actuality, by a return to the human norm symbolized by the axis passing through the center of all the "worlds" or degrees of existence, that axis being in fact identical with the path by which the Intelligible Light descends from its source in order to illuminate the darkness of ignorance, thus also indicating the direction of escape along the same road.

G. *Concerning "Solitaries"*:

A passing allusion must be made to those rare beings, the *afrad* of Islamic tradition, known also to other traditions, for whom initiation in the Supreme Knowledge comes, so to speak, directly from Heaven, if only to show that the Spirit bloweth where it listeth. These, the spontaneously illuminate, owe nothing to any living master, nor have they any reason to be attached to a visible traditional form, though they might so belong accidentally. The formless Truth is their only country and their language is but the Inexpressible.

Given that their existence does represent a possibility, if a remote one, it is expedient to mention it here: all that need be said on the subject, however, is that any suggestion that such and such a person belongs to this rare category could only begin to be considered on the strength of quite overwhelming evidence; and even then only those who were themselves endowed with the insight born of profound Knowledge would be in a position to hold an opinion on the subject, let alone to claim certitude. As for a person who made such a claim on his own behalf, this would under all ordinary circumstances amount to an evident disproof of the claim, a case of "outer darkness" being mistaken for "solitude" in its higher sense. A genuine state of *fard* (= solitude, whence the derivative *afrad*), like "spiritual silence", "voidness" and other such terms, corresponding, as it does, to a possibility of non-manifestation, would seem to preclude any definable sign of its possession or any organized expression in action.

The true solitaries are in fact but "the exception that proves the rule" and their occasional appearance in the world, necessary in order to affirm the Divine Playfulness, as the Hindus have eloquently called it, does not in any way affect the need for a tradition, as far as the overwhelming majority of human beings is concerned, a need which is moreover attested, if further evidence is needed, by the fact that most if not all Spiritual Masters known to have existed in our time or in former times have spoken in the name of a tradition and have used its appropriate modes of expression when instructing their disciples: whereas it is almost a commonplace for self-appointed teachers to repudiate the traditional norms and to encourage a similar attitude in others, hoping thus to attract the unwary by playing upon their naïve self-esteem as persons who supposedly stand beyond the need of outmoded formal disciplines. This is, moreover, an habitual stumbling-block for the Western "intellectual", as also for his westernized Eastern counterpart, being not the least among his accumulated spiritual disabilities.

H. *Concerning the viability of forms:*

For a tradition to fulfil its purpose in any given case, it must be "viable" in relation to the circumstances of the person concerned, that is to say it must be sufficiently accessible in time and space, as well as assimilable in itself, to render participation "operative". It would, for instance, be useless to try and attach oneself to an extinct form such as the Pythagorean tradition; and even with a still extant form such as Taoism, it would be practically impossible to establish contact with it, save by rare exception, because of the immense physical and psychic obstacles standing in the way of any Occidental who wished to resort to a Taoist Master—always supposing that such is still to be found hidden in some remote corner of the Chinese world, which today is not easy to prove or disprove.

By pursuing this line of argument it will be seen that the range of choice is not actually very wide and that even within that range a distinction has to be made, in the case of a European, between traditions existing in his immediate vicinity, and those which, if assimilation is to become a practical proposition, can only be approached through travel to more distant regions; and even if this be possible, the question of maintaining contact subsequently is not without pertinence, given the small probability, in any average case, that a high degree of contemplative concentration will have been attained soon enough to reduce the formal aspects of the tradition to relative unimportance.

It must not be thought, however, because of the emphasis laid on accessibility, that this condition is to be treated as a completely overriding one or applied systematically to all cases alike. Though it is reasonable to give preliminary consideration to what seems to be the nearest solution, its apparent advantages may, despite all the extra difficulties consequent upon a more remote choice, have to yield before some alternative solution, one governed by considerations of natural affinity, for instance, or by some other factor not perceivable at the outset. It is in fact always good to bear in mind the oft-heard statement that in the end it is the tradition that chooses the man, rather than the reverse. All that human reasoning can do is to prepare the way for the final discrimination prior to which he can only preserve an attitude of "prayerful expectancy".

In the case of an Occidental it is evident, however, that his mental conformation, whether he likes it or not, will have been powerfully affected by Christian ways of thinking and acting and that the very words he uses are charged with inherited implications bearing a Christian tinge: this is as true of those who have cast off (or so they would have it) their traditional yoke as of those who still remain attached to some branch of the Christian Church, at least in name. Such being the case, it would seem most prudent to consider the possibilities offered by the Christian path first of all, provided one does so with a mind unbiased by irrelevancies, whether in a positive or negative direction: this last remark applies equally to both parties in the discussion. As to the question of what criteria may be applied when investigating the spiritual possibilities presently offered by any particular traditional form, this will be reserved for a section to follow.

I.   *A few remarks about existing forms:*

Besides the two Christian traditional forms—their differences need not be stressed in the present instance—which between them cover the European world together with its American and other prolongations, there are also certain Eastern traditions, including the Islamic, which come within the bounds of practicability for Occidentals, at least in exceptional cases; this is especially true of the last-named, which both by reason of a certain kinship with the Christian form and still more by reason of its own structure is particularly fitted to meet the needs of men in the latter days of the cycle, a fact which is not generally recognized in the West, where ignorance on the subject of Islam and consequent prejudice is still rather general. Howbeit, it is in the direction of one or two of the Oriental traditions that those souls who, for any reason, find themselves out of tune with their dechristianized environment usually turn. Whoever does so ought not, however, to underrate the practical difficulties of an Oriental attachment on the part of one who intends to continue living a life which, in all other ways, will conform to the Occidental pattern. Whereas this is a very real drawback, it is not an altogether insurmountable one, though it does mean that rather exceptional qualities are required to overcome it, chief of which is a markedly contemplative turn of mind. Prudence demands that these obstacles should be faced from the start in a spirit of realism, otherwise a revulsion of feeling may wreck the whole enterprise after the first enthusiasm has begun to cool. On the other hand it does not do to be too cautious either, where spiritual matters are concerned; a readiness to plunge boldly for the prize is also a quality of the spirit. The Way is beset with dangers, and to follow it at all is inseparable from certain oft repeated discomforts, which have to be accepted for what they are, as part of the price to be paid by one who would fain walk with the Spirit. It is well to recognize that the very existence, for so many, of an apparent problem of choice is in itself an abnormal happening, due to the chaotic circumstances of the times. The alternative to solving it effectively is a relapse into indifference, a virtual atheism.

J.   *Of attraction and aversion*:

Wherever a person spiritually intent and not already in a tradition evinces a disproportionately violent aversion for a particular form (whatever arguments may be advanced in justification of the dislike) this feeling can be ascribed, roughly speaking, to one of two possible causes: the aversion may be due to the presence, in that person's psychic make-up, of elements which do not harmonize with some of the formal elements of the tradition in question and in that case the feeling of repulsion, though never insurmountable in itself, must be regarded as a negative sign affecting the choice of a form in a manner worth heeding: or else the aversion may be due to an inverted attraction for a form that really, in essentials, agrees with that person's psychic constitution, the apparent hostility then being due either to purely accidental causes such as inherited historical or racial oppositions or else to some deep-seated desire to remain in the profane world which, by covert means, is trying to hinder a positive decision of any kind. The passionate symptoms, in the first case, can be counted as of relatively small importance, froth upon the surface of an otherwise genuine aspiration; but in the second case passion betrays diabolical instigation and means must be found to allay it before judgment on the main issue becomes even possible. Discernment in these matters is never easy for either party to the conversation and the most one can say on the subject, in the early stages at least, is that attraction and aversion are twins, born of one mother, and that the intellect, by referring them both back to their common principle, should be able to effect an eventual discrimination between them. To hate a thing one may actually be very near that thing oneself, though this is not necessarily the case (two causes being possible as mentioned above); that is why one must not be too ready to take expressions of dislike at their face value, where spiritual problems are concerned, but must rather do all one can to restore a state of dispassion, after which difficulties of the kind described are likely to clear up of their own accord.

K. *Concerning criteria:*

Among factors allowing one to distinguish between form and form there will assuredly be some partaking of a subjective character, such as for example the way in which the art belonging to a certain tradition may have been instrumental in giving impulse to one's own spiritual yearnings, while others again will have a more objective bearing, such as the degree of corruption by which one or other form is presently affected, and still more the nature of that corruption, as well as the type of collective psychism prevailing in each of the traditional forms under consideration—a most important element in any attempted judgment. Nevertheless these factors, though they cannot but affect the question, must still count as accessory, if only for the reason that none of them is such as to outweigh all others by its presence or absence alone. The essential criterion still remains to be applied, and till this has happened some degree of doubt will adhere to any choice one may have in mind.

The essential question to be asked is whether the traditional form one is thinking about does or does not, under present circumstances, actually provide the means for taking a man all the way in the spiritual life or not? In other words, are the formal limits such as to leave an open window looking towards the formless Truth, thus allowing room for the possibility of its immediate or ultimate realization? If the answer is in the affirmative then that form, however degenerate it may have become, must still be admitted to be adequate as regards the essential, which is all that, rigorously speaking, matters; if on the other hand that form, however pure it may have remained as regards its more peripheric aspects, does in fact fail to pass the essential test, then there is nothing further to be said in its favor.

When applying this criterion, moreover, important corroborative evidence can be drawn, in support of a positive decision, from the knowledge that some people at least, however few in number, have succeeded at this time, while attached to such and such a form and using the means of grace it provides, in cultivating their spiritual possibilities to the full in the face of whatever local difficulties have been created for them by the traditional environment in question. All the great traditions are necessarily affected at the human and historical level by corruption in larger or lesser measure and even those sanctuaries that hitherto had been most immune, even Tibet, are now feeling the pressure of the modern profanity, over and above all the harm suffered as a result of petrifaction or dilution, which are the two types of natural corruption in a form. In such a changing situation there are many temporary distinctions to be made: sometimes evils which seem most blatant may turn out to have been relatively superficial while others, though less noticeable, may go nearer the essence and it is this last factor that will tell us, ultimately, whether the disease has reached the mortal stage or not.

One thing however is certain in all this, namely that at the level of forms anything like a watertight determination does not exist: for though under the most favorable conditions a given form may be conveniently described as perfect this can only be taken in a relative and therefore transient sense, since the very phrase "perfect form", strictly speaking, is a contradiction in terms. In adhering to the support of a form, therefore, one must never ask to be relieved of every cause of dissatisfaction of body or mind, for that is impossible at the level of the world even under the most favorable circumstances: in those ages which, to us, seem to have come closest to the ideal, the saints of the time were denouncing errors and vices and calling on men to abjure and repent—which does not mean we are wrong in our view of those ages, on the strength of the positive evidence. What it does mean is that every world is by definition a place of contrasts and this will always necessitate an accepting of the rough with the smooth, even when leading the religious life at its best. As a Sufi master once said to the writer: "There is always something unpleasing about any spiritual way".

Actually, the kind of impediment that takes the form of saying "I would so gladly adhere to such and such a religion which attracts me, if only just this one feature in it could be different" is a very common one, especially among persons of apparent goodwill who are second to none in decrying the modern world and its materialism but who, when it comes to their taking any positive step, will invariably find yet another gnat to strain at. Repeated experience has shown that this is one of the most difficult obstacles to surmount from the very fact that the hard core of resistance to the call lies concealed behind such an evident show of theoretical understanding coupled with sympathy for sacred things. To such the answer can only be that revealed religion, like everything else in manifestation, will have its crosses as well as its consolations: to approach the Way with a mind full of inflated expectations of a pleasurable kind, or else with one charged with puritanical gloom, is quite unrealistic. What one needs is to keep a firm hold on essentials, on metaphysical truth, and, for the rest, to view the doings in the world with some sense of proportion though never without discernment, while getting on with the task in hand.

Defects apparent in a form, the inevitable abuses, the relativity of the formal order itself, negative factors though these be from one point of view, have at least one positive compensation inasmuch as by their presence they proclaim the fact that a form, however hallowed, is not God and therefore also the fact of their own ultimate nonentity in the face of His transcendence. It is not the image nor even the mirror that counts, but the Light which reflector and reflection alike veil and reveal.

L. *Further notes on discrimination:*

Both the facts and causes of worldwide corruption not being contestable by anyone who rejects the profane view of things, there is but little profit in dwelling on this subject except for occasional and chiefly practical reasons, otherwise one might soon be reduced to despair. When however a cause does arise for so doing, the need for a nicely balanced discernment will be relatively greater or less according to the nature of one's own natural vocation or, as the Hindus would put it, of one's "caste".

For the man of action, since his focus of attention is external by definition, a more or less dualistic outlook, spelling inherent oppositions, is normal; though an attitude of non-attachment to the fruits of action can also lead him beyond the point where those oppositions have power to bind him. Again, for the *bhakta,* the man of devotional temperament, his whole spiritual field will properly be suffused with an emotional tinge (which does not mean "sentimental" in the sense of inhibiting intellectuality in the way that applies to certain forms of "mysticism" but not to true *bhakti*). In the first of these two human types judgment concerning forms other than one's own may be biased by loyalties, just as in the second case it may be blurred by a loving fervor that has no use for discernment; but in either case an occasional exaggeration on the lines described is of relatively small importance, because the feeling which prompts it, though not exactly desirable, goes with a temperament into the composition of which feeling largely enters as an integrating factor.

Not so, however, with the *jnani*, the man whose vocation is predominantly "intellectual" and for whom, consequently, the intellectual virtues of dispassion and discrimination are essential, and not accessory, constituents of his spirituality. For that man, a just appraisal of "foreign" forms will have positive importance and the reverse also applies inasmuch as criticism that goes beyond its brief, as a result of a passionate intrusion, is liable to have subtle repercussions which, unless neutralized, may seriously affect that person's chances of rendering all forms (including his own) transparent and thus acceding to the formless Knowledge. That is why, if such a thing should occur with an inquirer of markedly *jnanic* type, the person consulted should, even at the risk of incurring a certain suspicion of favoring a particular form, do his best to discourage criticisms which, though partly justified, exceed the limits of accurately balanced discernment, based as this must be on traditional and not on arbitrary criteria. Over this matter of criticism none has been more severe than Guénon, and if he was ready to accept certain forms as being still orthodox, despite admitted corruptions, it would certainly be wrong to attribute this fact to leniency on his part, or to think of outdoing him in Rigor.

Mention has been made occasionally by Coomaraswamy and others of certain Occidentals living in fairly recent times, of whom the poet-painter Blake provides an oft-quoted example, who in their works displayed a power of metaphysical insight that seems, when viewed against the background of their time, to be explainable in terms of a hidden traditional connection or even, as some have maintained, of a quasi-prophetic gift. It would be difficult for a stranger to this field of study to offer an opinion upon the spiritual qualification, or otherwise, of these rather enigmatical figures, of whom a number made their appearance here and there during the centuries following the rupture of the Middle Ages.

However, even where someone has special reason for devoting attention to this problem, it is yet well to remember that for purposes of spiritual precedent there is little to be gained by searching among the anomalies of that twilight period in the West, when the traditional doctrine at its most rigorous and spirituality at its most normal are so much more plainly observable at other times and places. Whatever the intellectual antecedents of these exceptional exponents may be, one has no right to refer to them as "traditional authorities"; the fact that they showed that wisdom was still able to manifest itself sporadically in an age when the forces of materialism and rationalism seemed to be carrying all before them is already much to their credit and one must not try and add to this in the absence of conclusive evidence.

What does however emerge from the foregoing discussion is that there is a distinction to be made between a man of greater or lesser "metaphysical genius" and the normally qualified spokesman of a traditional teaching—though the two things may, of course, coincide in one person, as in the case of Sri Shankaracharya, for instance. The principle of discrimination between the two states just mentioned is this: in the metaphysical genius his human mind will play an essential part, hence the often amazing powers of doctrinal expression displayed; whereas in the traditional teacher, whose mental powers will not necessarily be much above average, the intellect may manifest its presence more or less unsupplemented by special talent—the latter "incarnates" rather than "thinks out" the truths he communicates. It can also be said that the first-named in fact exemplifies the highest possible use of human reason, or in other words the use of reason placed at the service of intellect, while the second primarily exemplifies an effacement of the human individuality (reason included) before the spiritual order and before the tradition that conveys its influence in the world.

Above all, it must be recognized that true metaphysical insight, in any degree, is only possible for one whose mind remains "open" to the things above, otherwise its activities must needs degenerate into philosophizing, whether speciously brilliant or merely dull. It is by applying this criterion that one is able to distinguish without fail between the mind of a Coomaraswamy or a Guénon and that of a ratiocinative or manipulative *virtuoso* of the kind that occurs so commonly today and astonishes by its feats in various departments of the scientific field. The former, thanks to its intellectual non-limitation, is able to reach and therefore to communicate truths of the principial order; whereas the latter can reach no further than the general which, when cut off from the universal, can be a most fruitful source of errors.

It is on the basis of these distinctions that any eventual judgment must rest.

M. *On finding the* Guru:

The question of how a man is to find his spiritual way in the midst of this labyrinth of a modern world is often accompanied by another, closely bound up with the first, which takes the form of asking where, if anywhere, a spiritual master or *guru* is to be found; in any case this second question is always more or less implicit in the first one, unless one is dealing with a person whose horizon does not for the time being extend further than the individual realm and for whom a religious attachment, in its more external sense, will provide all that is needed to regulate his life and quicken his fervor. It should be added that whereas access to tradition is every man's right as well as his duty, the same does not apply to the initiatic path, which is selective by its own nature so that access to a master, even if his whereabouts be known, will always imply some degree of qualification in a would-be disciple before he is accepted. It is moreover evident that spiritual masters are not common anywhere today and that those who do exist are mostly to be found in the East, though obviously this is not a necessary condition. Nor is search for a master made any easier by the existence, in all directions, of bogus masters, usually persons of abnormal psychic development who, unlike the true kind, lose no opportunity of advertising their presence in an endeavor to attract disciples to their side.

In a normal civilization the urge to find a *guru* would arise naturally in a mind already conditioned by a whole tradition and likewise the channel of approach to the *guru* would pass through that same tradition. Passage would, in any typical case, be from peripheric aspects, gradually, towards the center, as represented by that innermost knowledge which it is the object of an initiatic teaching to awaken. But under the extremely anomalous conditions of our time the need for the most inward things will often strike on the consciousness of a person situated outside any tradition, as a result of reading or from some other accidental cause. In that case an aspiration already pointing, at least in principle, towards the center has, as it were, to be "underpinned" by means of a traditional attachment of appropriate form, and the acceptance of things pertaining to the more peripheric orders would, in that case, have to be aroused *a posteriori* for the sake of the higher prize and not just as a matter of course or simply as forming part of the spiritual nationality into which one has been born and the language of which one both speaks and listens to continually. To follow an unusual process is perfectly reasonable in the circumstances.

From the above it follows that once having found his master, a hitherto unattached aspirant would adhere to that master's traditional form, and not to another, for obvious reasons. This would apply both in the case of someone who found his *guru* close at hand or who was compelled to travel far afield for this purpose, for example to some Asiatic country. It is perhaps well to point out, however, that there have been exceptions to this rule, especially in India where the number of Hindus resorting to Muslim masters or vice versa has been quite considerable. Where an ability to contemplate the metaphysical principle underlying all formal variety is common, the latter element largely ceases to oppose a barrier. But even nearer home there have been exceptional cases of this kind so that it would be a mistake to exclude this possibility altogether, even while recognizing that it answers to very special conditions, personal or other, in the absence of which the argument of normality and convenience holds good.

There is one case, however, that still remains to be considered, namely the case of one who, though already seeking a spiritual teacher, has not been able to find one up to the moment of speaking. Is that person to remain idle hoping that something will turn up or can he be doing something already which will favor the purpose in view? Here the lesson offered by the Parable of the Talents applies: to sit back blaming one's bad luck because others have found their teachers or been born in the right country or the right century while one has been able to get no farther oneself than mere aspiration is an unworthy attitude and the passivity it expresses is in itself a sign of disqualification. The initiatic path is active by definition and therefore an active attitude, in the face of difficulties that might even outlast a lifetime, is the proper prelude to entering that path—herein is to be seen the difference between hope, in the theological sense, and mere desire. The true seeker does not only wait for Grace to descend upon him but he also goes out to meet it, he knocks continually at the door, while at the same time he accepts delays not of his own making in a spirit of submissiveness towards the Divine Will, whether this shows itself in bestowing or withholding.

It is in this situation that a man's traditional connections will count more than ever: for then he can reason to himself thus and say "Though at present the mysterious gate appears closed, I can at least use the resources of the existing exoterism, not in a perfunctory way nor for the sake of a minimum of conformity, but generously, by pushing out as far as its very farthest frontier, to the point where the realm of my hope begins. Let me then take advantage of every rite and every traditional rule, and at the same time let me do all I can to fit myself for the reception of the initiatic grace, if ever it comes, both by study of Scriptures and of the more rigorous commentaries ('browsing' is to be avoided, even among traditional things) and also by the daily practice of the virtues and above all by assiduous attention to the smallest details—and who shall say what is small and what great under such circumstances?" An attitude of this kind (the writer had an actual example in mind) is well calculated, if one may so express it, "to attract the grace of the *guru*" when the moment is ripe for such a thing: besides which, twin terms like "exoteric" and "esoteric", convenient though they may be, are meaningless apart from one another, and likewise the supposed line of demarcation between their respective realms is but a point of reference, so that one who has realized the full possibilities of the one realm will, as it were, already have got one foot across the barrier into the other; also that barrier will grow more tenuous and transparent in proportion as the heart of the aspirant, pursuing this form of self-discipline, unhardens itself until one day (God willing) the barrier will simply cease to be—and on that day the *guru* also surely will appear.

A friend to whom the above notes were shown made this comment:

> . . . after all, persons who approach us supposedly do so because they have understood the doctrine expressed in the books (of Guénon and Schuon); that is to say, essentially, they have understood pure metaphysic, which is supra-dogmatic and universal, and likewise the validity of orthodox traditional forms which, for their part, vehicle that metaphysic while adding to it secondary perspectives and spiritual means of varying importance. Even if one does not feel a particularly marked affinity for such and such a religious form, one must know that it is valid, and

this by reason of its own criteria, intrinsic on the one hand and extrinsic on the other; the intrinsic criteria derive in fact from metaphysic, while the extrinsic criteria are of the phenomenal order: for example, there are all kinds of historical, psychological and other criteria of this kind which prove in their own way that Islam cannot but be an orthodox tradition and the same would apply in all comparable cases.

. . . Prejudices cannot stand in the face of those ideas which are supposed to be at the very basis of the search; at most there may be question of a "climatic" preference, such as is legitimate wherever choice is possible, and on condition that the elements governing choice are sufficiently known . . . if such difficulties were to arise in the mind even of a comparatively informed inquirer, in dealing with him there would be no reason to embarrass oneself with too much psychology; it is enough that the inquirer should be "recalled to order" by referring him to the Doctrine.

The all-compassionate Lord

5

The Place of Compassion in Tibetan Spirituality

If during recent times Tibet and things Tibetan have tended to exert an increasing fascination upon Western minds, this has largely been due to two causes, themselves not unrelated, namely to the fact that Tibet was a "closed country", all but impenetrable to foreign exploration, and also to the extreme contrast which, according to every available evidence however garbled, existed between the Tibetan outlook on life and that of our modern secularist society. This contrast almost justifies the statement that all the things which by us are deemed to be most real and necessary were, for the Tibetans, if not quite illusory, at least of secondary importance; while contrariwise, whatever things they, for their part, regarded as primary realities are for the majority of our people including the highly educated—perhaps for them most of all—either all but non-existent or ascribable to a twilight realm of subjective imaginings, one far removed from that region of solid facts, as our minds take them to be, in which we ourselves are wont to dwell and think and act. For most of us, the things pertaining to that other realm, even if we do not go so far as to discount them altogether as being "opium for the people", yet seem so far removed from any possibility of verification as to turn their pursuit into a proposition too doubtful to attract much attention; hence it seems only natural for us to bend our efforts in the direction of a human welfare supposedly attainable at the level of the material world, through exercise of human ingenuity alone, and this attitude is one that is by no means confined to the professedly irreligious, for by far the greater number of those who still claim to hold religious views of some kind nevertheless live and think and act and react as if they have accepted the premises of materialism wholesale; and as for those few who have held back from sharing the general outlook, they tend to be rather suspect in their neighbors' eyes, since their very reluctance to come into line implies casting a doubt upon that solidity of fact which, it is taken for granted by all the others, corresponds to reality.

Yet those mistrusted people, if they were minded to argue the point (as rarely happens) would almost certainly retort in kind by saying that it is they, the materialists and humanitarians, who are truly the unpractical visionaries, the eccentrics, ever content to wander about on the periphery of reality instead of seeking as they might—indeed as they would did they but recognize the true nature of man and his finality—the straight and narrow way leading to the heart of things, and they might even add, unkindly, that the evidences supplied by the world as these other people or the likes of them have been shaping it are not, in themselves, particularly suggestive of a state of human welfare, present or about to be; and in thus calling in question the postulates upon which our whole "progressive" civilization rests these critics would certainly enjoy the support of all true Tibetans. Although in Tibet as elsewhere, men, impelled by their shifting desires, may largely occupy themselves with worldly interests, few of them are prepared actually to defend such an attitude, one which they attribute rather to their own ignorance and consequent feebleness of purpose than to practical good sense; and as for those others, fewer in number, who have taken another line, withdrawing attention from the surface phenomena of existence, it is they who, even in the eyes of worldlings by their own admission, appear as the practical men, the realists. That is also why, even with a seemingly worldly Tibetan, one can never be quite sure that he will not suddenly experience an irresistible call in the opposite direction, and when this happens the casting off of old associations is usually unhesitating, since the power of these things to attach the mind, despite whatever may appear on the surface, remains comparatively slight, as judged from the standpoint of a European in like circumstances—for the latter the resistance both of the social environment and of his accumulated mental habits is likely to be much more persistent, involving more strain before it is overcome.

In Tibet, the transcendent nature of the Contemplative function, and therefore also its overriding necessity for the sake of human welfare, represents an undeniable fact, and all other forms of activity, private or public, are valued in proportion as they contribute more or less directly to the promotion of spiritual interests. What, for the Tibetan mind, is an unthinkable proposition is the possibility that any kind of human existence can remain really healthy while in a state of insubordination, overt or concealed, to the Spiritual Order; to speak of "raising the standard of living" or "establishing permanent peace" under such circumstances would sound like a cruel joke, and so would the phrase "the Welfare State". The secularist conception of man and his interests, according to which contemplative activity, even when tolerated, ceases to be a necessity and becomes reduced to the level of a private hobby, coupled with the conviction that to live "by bread alone" is, for man, actually feasible—this is something so alien to normal Tibetan thinking that it would be almost hopeless to try to put over such a point of view even to many of those who profess an interest in the ways and beliefs of the outside world—I have more than once made the attempt and my Tibetan friends, who are extremely polite, have listened patiently, but it was easy to gauge from the look on their faces how little they had taken in of my laborious explanations.

An attitude of such indifference towards things of a spiritual Order would appear to these people, and indeed to all who still live and think in a traditional manner, to be not so much impious as suicidal. For are not the sages and saints, so they will say, the only efficient protectors of mankind, failing whose presence and applied skill, itself based on awareness and prompted by compassion, everything else would infallibly go to pieces for lack of principle? Furthermore they will go on to point out that the saints in question owe their beneficent power precisely to their own detachment from the world and from all social exigencies, whether these take the form of duties or of rights: having won through to the point where it is possible to contemplate the naked Vision, they have become like a mirror in which those whose eyes are as yet too feeble to bear its radiance otherwise than as viewed "in a glass darkly" may nevertheless discern something of its reflected glory, in a form tempered to their own lack of strength. Truth revealed and veiled, the immediate vision and the vision by reflection, knowledge and faith, realization direct and intuitive or, failing that, a participating at one or more removes, herein is to be found the essential structure of a traditional civilization like that of Tibet, all the values of which are assessable in terms of one or other of these two main categories.

Passing to the human microcosm, the same quality of transcendence, as pertaining to the contemplative function, is recognizable: here the central or "axial" position is occupied by the organ of contemplation, the Intellect or, as some traditions have it, the "Eye of the Heart". The human norm is itself describable by reference to its supreme possibility which is to be an Awakened One, a Buddha, one, that is to say, who has become aware of what he is not and of what things are not (note the negative form which is characteristic) and consequently of what he is and of what things are; as one of the Zen Masters has put it, at first the disciple, his mind still entangled in the cosmic mirage, beholds around him objects such as mountains and trees and houses; then, with the gaining of partial knowledge, mountains and trees and houses fade from sight; but lastly having arrived at complete understanding, the man, no longer a disciple, again beholds mountains and trees and houses, but this time without the superimpositions of illusion.

It is characteristic of the Buddhist tradition, its Tibetan branch included, that it prefers to express truth in terms of an "apophatic theology" (to use a Christian expression), one that lays itself out to unmask and destroy the various limiting concepts that veil the face of the Sun of Knowledge, which, for its part, once the fog of attribution has been cleared away, can be trusted to shine forth by its own light. Roughly speaking, the whole Buddhist technique derives from this conscious avoidance of conceptual affirmations and that is why, in the case of the Buddhist, his immediate attention will be directed, not upon a principle to be realized, upon God, but rather upon the obstacles to be dispelled, the limits to be transcended, upon the Round of Existence, the World.

Such an attitude is already to be found implied in the first of the "Four Truths", starting point of the Buddhist Way as revealed by the Founder, whereby existence is equated with "Suffering", a word which here must be taken to include not only all that commonly falls under that heading, but also that which by contrast and in virtue of deriving from the same duality, passes for pleasurable. What, after all, is the nature of this happiness which all so assiduously pursue? Is it something constant which, once overtaken, can be firmly anchored and confidently enjoyed, or does it not rather show itself as an unsubstantial, elusive thing, one which already, even in the act of trying to perpetuate its savor in the mind, is beginning to dissolve away under one's perception of it, leaving behind only the aftertaste of regret? Youth turns, first imperceptibly and then at an accelerated pace, to age, and good health, however carefully conserved, must yet, before very long, yield, for the sober liver as well as for the rake, before the onset of decrepitude, disease and death: this fact alone makes nonsense of the boastful claims to have extended human life thanks to medical research; for were the span of life to be prolonged by a hundred, two hundred, even a thousand years, would this make death, when it came, any more welcome? Or would it cause a person to use his life with greater mindfulness? The Tibetans have a saying that "the long-lived gods are stupid", for, as compared with existence in the human state, with its more varied blend of the pleasurable and the painful, their mode of existence leans excessively towards the pleasant pole, and this want of tension translates itself into a carefree unawareness which will all the more surely give place to painful experience, when, at long last, the hour of dissolution suddenly shall have struck. In this respect at least we humans are more fortunate, hence the importance of making a full use of the opportunity provided by a human birth "so hard to obtain" as the Indian and Tibetan books are continually reminding us; for now is our chance to break the bonds of ignorance and of its attendant egocentricity, cost what it may, and this it is the privilege of man, in virtue of his "central" position, to accomplish, for just as it is in the nature of fire to burn, so it is in the nature of man—would he but remember it—to become Awake, to be Buddha. Furthermore if it be said, as it sometimes has been, that such an attitude is "fatalistic" or even "pessimistic", the answer will be that such notions as optimism, pessimism and the like belong to the sentimentalist and do not enter into the point of view of spirituality which is always, in intention at least, impartial and resigned.

A genuinely carefree attitude, a serene outlook, these are not to be won by refusing to face facts, and it is rather those who, despite all warnings, insist on laying up their treasure where moth and rust will corrupt it who, as the inescapable hour of disappointment draws near, will yield to despair. Clutching hard at things which in the very course of nature are bound to disappear, they try to put off the hour of awareness, using every possible narcotic device that human ingenuity can invent, the true "opium of the people"; but despite their efforts they are overtaken by fate and certainly their end will be a lamentable one. In many the desire to be deceived is carried so far that even in the hour of death itself people conspire to trick the dying into unconsciousness, an impious proceeding which those who are still traditionally minded, like the Tibetans, will hardly credit. Is it then really surprising that persons brought up in such an atmosphere of escapism—here this much abused word applies with full force—should develop every kind of morbid symptom such as all the palliatives offered by physician and psychologist alike are impotent to remove? In contrast to this mentality, the Buddhist peoples generally and especially the Tibetans are characterized by a conspicuous cheerfulness, one as uncontaminated by optimism as it is free from its more obviously depressing partner, and this buoyant outlook goes hand in hand with an ability to contemplate the mortality of things.

The doctrine of Death and Impermanence, to give it its full name, together with its uttermost prolongation into the doctrine of the emptiness, or lack of self-nature or, in other words, of the negative character attaching to every form of existence whatsoever, remains, throughout his course, the staff on which the Buddhist pilgrim leans, and all possible means are called into play with a view to keeping an aspirant perpetually reminded of it. To mention one example, when the disciple in meditation finds himself thronged by distracting thoughts, often very trivial ones—many of us must have had this experience—a recognized remedy is to go back to the very beginning, letting the mind dwell once again upon the universally shared certainty of Impermanence and Suffering (which is always the first theme proposed at the start of the meditative process) and, as an eminent *Geshe* (Doctor) told me, if this is done persistently the distractions will be stayed. It should perhaps also be explained that in case of the contrary happening, by the disciple's mind sinking into torpor, it is likewise a contrary remedy that may be applied by dwelling on the positive aspect of the world and on the opportunity provided by a human birth, with a view to rousing the drooping spirits.

But to return to the subject of Impermanence; continued meditation upon this theme will, almost inevitably, bring another kind of awareness, pertaining to the fact that there is a shared fatality enveloping all existences regardless of their nature, from long-lived inhabitants of the god and titan worlds, through mankind down to the lowliest animal, plant and mineral forms and again below these to the tormented existences that constitute the hells. In proportion as this welter of common suffering makes itself evident to one's consciousness so will one be moved thereby to Compassion which will go on growing until, having been possessed by it entirely, one will no longer be able to hold back from the next step, which is to become a fully dedicated being by taking the "Bodhisattva's vow", as it is called, in an unshakeable resolve to win Enlightenment, not merely for one's own sake, but for the emancipation of every suffering creature; from that moment onward whatever meritorious deeds one is able to accomplish, instead of being accumulated on one's own account, will be freely shared with all the beings in the universe, regardless of everything but their compelling need.

The traditional form of the Bodhisattva's vow will be of interest; it runs with some omissions as follows: "I, so and so, in the presence of my Master so and so, in the presence of the Buddhas, do call forth the idea of Enlightenment . . . I adopt all creatures as mother, father, brothers, sons, sisters and relatives. Henceforth . . . for the benefit of creatures I shall practice charity, discipline, patience, energy, meditation, wisdom and the means of application . . . let my Master accept me as a future Buddha." Furthermore, these words are uttered as it were in anticipation of a similar vow ascribed to the Bodhisattva himself, the fully enlightened being, already entitled to Buddhahood in twofold virtue of Knowledge of the Voidness of Existence and of Universal Compassion, a vow which is symbolically conveyed—for clearly one has gone beyond the ordinary resources of language—under the paradoxical form of a "refusal to enter *Nirvana* so long as one single blade of grass remains unenlightened".

116

Bodhisattvahood, this is the heart of the matter, as far as Tibetan spirituality is concerned. In a subsequent chapter this theme will be treated in greater detail; but for the time being it is enough to have allowed the reader to gain an inkling of that which, more than anything else, has given the Tibetan world and tradition their characteristic quality; and it is this same flavor, perfume of the Bodhisattva's presence, which is immediately sensed, by anyone who has even a partially awakened perception of such things, on crossing the barrier of the Great Himalaya and setting foot upon the Tibetan plateau proper.

Tibet, largely because of its closed character, has gained the reputation of being a land of mysterious happenings, a "lost horizon", and many things true or fantastic have been published on the subject; but in one respect at least it is possible to substantiate such a description out of one's own experience, for during one's stay there one did become very frequently conscious as of a mysterious presence, using that epithet, however, without any sensational connotation, but rather according to its primitive meaning of something not to be uttered, something that can only remain an object of the unbroken silence of the soul.

All one can do is to repeat that one became conscious more than once of a peculiar quality of transparency affecting the whole atmosphere of the place; it was as if the obstacles to the passage of certain influences had here been thinned down to something quite light and tenuous, obstacles which in the outer world remained dense and opaque. The Himalayan ranges through which one approaches, mounting through their deep-cut gorges, tend to awaken in the mind an ever changing series of vividly separate sense-impressions which in their way are deeply stirring; it would be an insensitive person indeed who did not yield to the magical beauty of slopes all covered with small metallic purple, dark crimson, or white rhododendron from the midst of which blue or yellow Meconopsis poppies raise aloft their crown of flowers; while in damper spots the associated loveliness of dark blue iris and yellow primula seems to offer a foretaste of the delights of *Sukhavati,* the Western Paradise of Amitabha, the Buddha of Light. But once out on the plateau all this is quickly forgotten, for there one finds oneself in a landscape of such ineffable contemplative serenity that all separate impressions coalesce into a single feeling of—how can one best describe it?—yes, of impartiality. It is this quality of the Tibetan landscape which made one call it "transparent", for before all else it preaches the essential emptiness of things and the compassion which is born of an awareness of their vacuity.

If some readers are inclined to dismiss this impression of Tibet as rather fanciful and in any case explainable as an effect, upon an imaginative nature, of a high mountain climate—the valleys are all over 12,000 feet and the air is indescribably exhilarating to both body and mind—this writer can only make answer that though much can reasonably be attributed to such a cause, this is nevertheless insufficient to account in full for the conviction, formed at the time and remaining undimmed after twelve years of absence, that Tibet is a focus of spiritual influence in a particular and objective sense and apart from any power of one's own to respond or otherwise, as the case may be. Essentially, this is a question that pertains to what may properly be called the Science of Sacred Geography, and Tibet is by no means the only example of the kind, though it is one of the most remarkable and extensive.

Were a Tibetan to be asked to account for this special character attaching to his homeland he would doubtless evince no surprise, since for him the explanation would be as plain as the fact itself, and expressible in the following terms: Tibet is in a very special sense the seat, or if one so prefers, the focus of manifestation of that Divine Function or Aspect known as Chenrezig, the All-Compassionate Lord and Good Shepherd, of whom it is said "that he will not enter the sheepfold before all the sheep, down to the last, have been safely gathered within, after which he will follow and close the gate". This symbolical statement is, of course, readily recognizable as a variant upon the one already mentioned, the Bodhisattva's vow "to tarry until the last blade of grass shall have attained Enlightenment".

A seal is set upon the sacred character of the land by the presence at its center of the Dalai Lama, or, to give him his Tibetan title, the Precious Protector, a visible embodiment of the Bodhisattva of Compassion and reminder of his vow, as also a living pledge of its ultimate fulfillment.

It would be possible to give many examples of how strong a hold the idea of Compassion has secured over the minds of the people and there is little doubt that, given a choice, the average Tibetan would name Compassion born of Knowledge as the pre-eminent characteristic denoting the Saint, and any unusual example of the exercise of this virtue, when known, will invariably call forth the fervent admiration of great and small alike. I remember the case of a member of the Tibetan nobility, for instance, who was paying a call on the officers of the Indian contingent stationed at that time under an old treaty at Gyantse on the trade route leading from Kalimpong to Lhasa—since the Chinese occupation these troops have been withdrawn. In the middle of the conversation his eyes rested on a photograph hanging on the wall opposite and he asked: "Is that perchance a picture of Mahatma Gandhi?" and on being told that it was he rose from his chair, removed his hat and with clasped hands bowed reverently before it, in silent worship of the Compassionate Power which had once again chosen to manifest itself among men through the person and example of the saintly Indian leader. His exploits as a great nationalist figure did not count, as far as the Tibetans were concerned: it was the Saint, individual manifestation as they might perhaps suggest, of Chenrezig which, in Gandhi as in any similar case, would draw forth their devotion and their praise: a small incident perhaps, but in its own way typical.

There is no point in multiplying examples; but some allusion ought perhaps to be made to the treatment of animals in Tibet, for in this respect the Tibetans can justly claim to be worthy followers of Chenrezig, since there is no other part of the world where people's attitude towards their animal neighbors shows up more admirably. It must be admitted that most Tibetans are meat eaters since, apart from barley which is the staple food of the country (it is parched and ground and eaten as a kind of stiff porridge), dried mutton is almost the only important foodstuff commonly available, for the plateau produces little else in any quantity and the winters are long. But even so, the Tibetans do not delude themselves concerning the nature of the action involved in meat-eating, in contravention of the first of the "Five Precepts" which by the Buddhist layman are regarded somewhat like the Ten Commandments, nor are they in two minds concerning the probable repercussions of such action, in this or future existences. Because the action is difficult to avoid in the circumstances they do not for that reason try to explain it away by means of moral subterfuges, as others have been prone to do in similar cases: moreover any person who despite difficulties finds the way to abstain from meat, whether he be Tibetan or a foreigner, will invariably be admired as one who has taken, in this respect, the better way.

Meat-eating apart, the treatment of animals both domestic and wild is unusually considerate and the laws that deal with this subject are free from the niggling exceptions with which one has become familiar in much modern legislation aimed at various cruel practices. In the case of horses it is rare indeed to come across a case of beating through ill-temper, and even verbal abuse is uncommon. On arrival at the day's stage after a tiring march across mountain tracks the Tibetan mule-driver will immediately unsaddle, water and feed his animals and only afterwards will he settle down to prepare his own tea, and on the passes, when snow falls, the men will not spare themselves in battling to help their charges over the bad ground. Dogs are very popular all over Tibet, cats though rare are well cared for, horses are especially valued, as one might expect in a country of wide spaces. But it is especially in their attitude towards wild creatures that the Tibetans have much to teach us, for in this matter both the law and public opinion are united in preventing that continual harrying of wild animals and birds, whether for sport or profit or for other reasons, which in so many parts of the world has emptied the countryside of furred and feathered life.

By the "ordinance of mountain and countryside" as it is called, a complete prohibition of hunting is operative in some years, with certain exceptions to the ban in others, but I am not sure of the details. Hunting for any purpose whatsoever is in any case looked on with disfavor by the population, though in frontier regions a certain amount of poaching by collectors of musk for export does take place, as the profits to be had from this trade are considerable. There is also hunting for food and furs by nomads in the far north. These exceptions need to be mentioned lest the picture seem overdrawn. There are very large areas where hunting is under no circumstances allowed; these areas include the proximity of monasteries and also districts regarded as peculiarly sacred such as the wooded circuit of the mountain of Tsari some distance east of Lhasa, which is the scene of a great pilgrimage every twelve years. Given such unstinting protection it will hardly surprise anyone to be told that the wild animals are practically without fear of man, as attested by many travelers, not all of whom however have appreciated this object-lesson. There is tremendous spiritual advantage in the society of animals living in their natural state, an experience that enables man to hark back to his own primordial state as when Adam was dwelling in Eden; but it does not take many shots to tell the animals that man has become their enemy, and once this has happened the spell will have been broken, perhaps for ever. Naturally these descriptions apply to Tibet as it still was at the time of the author's visit: now that the country has fallen under foreign occupation it is impossible to say how much will survive there, either in the way of ideas or of those practices and abstentions which translate them in the field of behavior.

As we have spoken at some length about certain virtues commonly found among Tibetans, it is but fair to add that if Compassion, both as an idea and in its ethical applications, has come to occupy such an important place in their conception of spirituality, this does not mean that the contrary is never to be met with in practice, for that would be an overstatement. For example the family feuds and personal rivalries affecting official life have often taken an extremely vindictive turn. The fact is that Tibetans, though normally good-tempered and generous, are by no means incapable of cruelty and if once they reach the point of wishing to hurt, then their downright nature will not let them stop at half measures, for they are anything but squeamish when it comes to witnessing pain believed to be deserved or unavoidable. Toughness of nerve will always cut both ways. Nor were the methods of the criminal law in Tibet exactly gentle, as evidenced by the following story: he author was talking to a well-to-do peasant of the Chumbi valley, just within the frontier, and he started to give his views on the law and its workings, as he had observed them in India, where the British penal system was in force. "Your methods of law are quite senseless," he said, "no wonder crime is so prevalent among you. For what, after all, do you do to the criminal? You convict a man, say, of housebreaking and then, forsooth, you reward the deed by shutting him up for a few months in a nice, comfortable prison with clothes, good food and everything else found. Perhaps also you will give him some simple work to do, but with plenty of time to himself. What do you expect that man, once let out, to do but resume his lawbreaking habits? In Tibet we don't act in this way, by no means; we give him what for, something to remember! That's the only way to put down crime."

It might be explained perhaps that for an average Tibetan, and even for Orientals in general, solitude is not the hardship that it is, or has become, for the socially over-stimulated mentality of the West, for which a prolonged period in one's own company tends to appear as an ordeal peculiarly terrible. Faced with a spell of enforced solitude, as in prison, the Oriental will easily settle his mind into comparative quiescence, and consequently he will not suffer overmuch; and as for the other discomforts of prison life they may well seem trivial to a Tibetan, accustomed as he is to a way of living that is often extremely hard, though not for that reason lacking in a certain quality which our greater luxury itself excludes. This ability to be alone, in silence, which people there acquire from an early age, undoubtedly is one of the factors that make for meditative concentration; one who becomes fretful the moment he is left to himself is never likely to shine as an exponent of the contemplative art. From this example it can be seen that one's manner of living and one's private habits can have an important bearing upon the question of spiritual competence and it is quite idle to think that one can enjoy the spiritual gifts of the Tibetans (or of some of our own ancestors for that matter) while the whole pattern of one's life and upbringing is based on profane considerations and on evasion of the only thing that really counts. As the Tibetan books tell us, every acquisition entails a corresponding renunciation, one cannot have it both ways, much as the modern world would like to believe the contrary.

We have chosen to illustrate our theme by a number of examples drawn as if at random from among the various currents, profound or comparatively shallow, which together go to compose the complex stream of Tibetan spirituality. One last illustration now awaits discussion, one that is of quite a different order from the relatively contingent questions that have just been occupying the reader's attention, since it will point back again into the heart of things, to that Bodhisattva doctrine which is for the whole Tibetan tradition both its source of inspiration and its reservoir of power. Every doctrine, however, as the Mahayanist books are for ever reminding one, over and above its theoretical enunciation, pertaining to aim and direction, requires a corresponding method to render it effective, otherwise it will remain barren of results. Wisdom and Method, so it is said, are inseparable partners; or else they are respectively compared to the eye which discerns the path leading to the promised land and the legs that will carry one thither. Our example in this case pertains to means, for of doctrine enough has been said for present purposes.

The practice about to be described, if briefly, is one which has been a frequent subject of ridicule by foreigners, associated as it also sometimes is with the use of an auxiliary appliance miscalled a "prayer-wheel", since prayer in its more ordinary sense, does not enter in at all, no idea of petition being implied. The practice in question should properly be described as "invocation" (the Indian "*japa*") and consists, as far as its outward expression is concerned, of the continual repetition of a sacred formula, the aim being to promote concentration by substituting, in place of irrelevant thoughts and other producers of dissipation, something which, being itself a highly concise symbol of the Knowledge to be realized, is able to serve as a catalyst of that same Knowledge within the heart. The Gospels tell us that when one devil has been expelled from a man, if nothing further is done about it, seven worse devils will enter and take possession of the empty place, which they will find "swept and garnished". So it is with distracting thoughts; if a man succeeds in mastering one of them, to the point of arresting it for a moment, others will not fail to crowd in its wake, for the human soul when in a state of ordinary consciousness cannot for a moment remain vacant, and if it be not filled with spirituality then the demons of profanity must enter and occupy it. The object of "invocation" therefore is to substitute the symbol, direct objectivation of the Knowledge aimed at, and keep it turning round, as it were, so that no agent of distraction can even for a moment obtain a footing. This is the nearest one can get to an explanation without going off into technical details, but perhaps it is just enough to afford an inkling of that process of which "invocation" is the operative support.

One of the formulae or "*mantras*" most frequently used in this manner is called the "*Mani Mantra*", consisting as it does of six syllables forming the words OM MANI PADME HUM. If one be asked to give an exact meaning to the words themselves one can only answer that if translated literally they would probably convey little to an average mind, for their meaning, or rather meanings, are not of the kind to be arrived at by an ordinary analytical process, since they depend upon the correspondence existing between different orders of reality. All true symbolism works in this way and that is why it is able to serve as a means for conveying metaphysical Knowledge, such as lies beyond the scope of ordinary language and thought. It is moreover this intentional avoidance of a wording couched in rational form which has frequently caused hostile critics to describe *mantras* as "meaningless", for to those critics they truly are so, but not to everyone. This point needs to be mentioned because people nowadays are apt to regard the spiritually endowed man as being typically a thinker, whereas it is the opposite that is the truth. Thinking has its uses, admittedly, and also—let this not be forgotten—its dangers. Actually, there is no more reason for a spiritual person to be a thinker than a cricketer; occasionally the two things, spirituality and an unusually acute brain, may be found together, of course, as with, say, Saint Thomas Aquinas, but equally often it is the other way: which does not mean, however, that spirituality can ever go hand in hand with shallowness or obtuseness of outlook (as can easily happen in the case of a purely mental agility), if only because spirituality, to be such, implies a power of intuitive vision in greater or lesser degree, and he who is able to embrace a truth as in a single glance has no need to analyze or rationalize an experience which is, for him, beyond all relativity as well as beyond all doubt.

Invocation with a *mantra* can be carried out in several way: most commonly the words are repeated on a rosary, or else they can be rhythmically assisted by the turning of a *mani* wheel as already mentioned, in which case the wheel itself will contain the same formula, inscribed many times over on the paper cylinder which forms its core. The Tibetan word for "invocation" is taken from the purring of a cat, which well describes the murmured repetition; but in cases where the invoking person has attained a higher degree of aptitude, the *mantra* will be repeated silently and without the aid of rosary or other similar instrument. But before going further there is a story to be told.

Some years ago a friend belonging to the Swiss foreign service was visited by a Catholic missionary who had been stationed in the South-West of China, in a district which by race and language is entirely Tibetan. My friend, wishing to obtain an unbiased account of conditions out there, inquired whether the stories he had heard about the Tibetans and their great piety were true or exaggerated, to which the missionary answered without hesitation: "Oh! not in the least exaggerated, the Tibetans are without the slightest doubt the most pious people on the face of the earth." "How do you make that out," said my friend, "can you produce any clear evidence in support of this statement?" "Certainly I can," replied the priest, "for instance, of how many Tibetans can it not be said that their ordinary occupations and the occasional conversations these entail are little more than a passing interruption in what would otherwise be a life of continual prayer?" My friend then asked him why, in that case, was it thought so desirable to change these people's faith. However this is getting away from the point, since all one wishes to do is to emphasize certain facts: as for the phrase "continual prayer", used by the missionary on the basis of Christian terminology, the parallel is inexact and the word "invocation" should have been used, as previously explained. It should perhaps be added that this method of concentrating attention and stilling the mind, frequently employed in India and Tibet and among the Muslim Sufis, is not unknown in the Christian tradition either and any persons who have read the deeply moving *Way of a (Russian) Pilgrim* will have no difficulty in recognizing, in connection with that spiritual current of the Orthodox Church known as "Hesychasm", a method of invocation strictly analogous, as regards its principles and even its details, to what is to be found in the lands further East, a case of spiritual coincidence, not of borrowing in either direction.

Returning to the *Mani* itself, it would not be possible to enter into details concerning the plurality of meanings implicit in this formula or the no less varied manner of its employment as a spiritual support in the course of a more or less protracted initiatic process embracing every degree of competence from the simplest piety to intellection of the most profound mysteries: all that need be pointed out here is the intimate connection of *Mani* with the Bodhisattva doctrine which it symbolizes by means of a closely interlocked verbal synthesis, a connection which is traditionally indicated by the attribution of the *Mani Mantra* to the Bodhisattva Chenrezig himself as its originator.

There are, however, two verses of four lines each, which respectively precede and follow any spell of invocation with *Mani,* and of these a translation will be given, together with a few explanatory comments, as they are particularly striking as illustrations of the point one is trying to make. The introductory verse runs as follows:

Thou who art entirely unstained by sin
Born from the head of the supreme Buddha
By Compassion look upon beings:
To Chenrezig let obeisance be made.

In this context "the supreme Buddha" refers to Amitabha, Limitless Light, who is the heavenly begetter, as also the *Guru* of the Bodhisattva Chenrezig. In traditional symbolism, the world over, Light represents Knowledge, born of which is Compassion, Chenrezig's self. And now for the concluding verse:

> By the merit of this (invocation) soon may I
> Have realized the power of Chenrezig,
> Thereby may beings without a single exception
> Attain to the land of the Norm.

Phrases like "the land of the Norm" or "the Pure Land" are commonly used periphrases for the supreme realization, Enlightenment. It is easy to see from the wording that this verse amounts to no less than an anticipation of the Bodhisattva's vow. Thus every initiate into the *Mani*, even if he be but a novice, is by that very fact already looking forward consciously or unconsciously to a time when that vow can be taken with a more clear and deliberate mind; as for the adept, the *Mani* itself constitutes his call to Bodhisattvahood, while the whole process provides the occasion to obey the call effectively. It is not without reason that the *Mani Mantra* has been described as "the concentrated quintessence of all the thoughts of all the Buddhas".

One day in the Spring of 1951, as the author was about to leave Kalimpong for England, a man brought along a prayer-wheel (by which is meant a *Mani*-wheel) which he wished to dispose of: it was made of silver, most beautifully chased by some artist of the province of Kham far to eastward on the Sino-Tibetan border, for the Khamba smiths excel at every form of metalwork. The man opened the silver container in order to show the roll of writing inside—I expected to find the usual formula, but no one would ever guess what actually came out of the box . . . the Gospel according to St. Mark!

It almost looks as if some local follower of the Christian faith, perhaps even a parishioner of the missionary mentioned before, had placed it there, arguing to himself that by making this small adjustment he would thereby be entitled to continue to use the *Mani*-wheel in the time-honored way, invoking according to his wont—for to the Tibetans one sacred thing is very much like another, and their sense of reverence does not stop short at any confessional boundary.

And after all, who shall say they are mistaken?

Mani wheels

Lachhen Monastery, Northern Sikkim

6

Sikkim Buddhism
Today and Tomorrow

To set out to provide a condensed, but not oversimplified description of a country's traditional life is never easy: whoever undertakes such a task must first ask himself what he considers most essential. Is it the piecing together of a more or less documented account of the people of a given region, their beliefs and institutions, by way of ministering to the insatiable appetite of modern scientific curiosity, after the manner of the countless articles by travelers, ethnologists and others which fill our journals? Or has the task in hand some relation to a purpose which touches one vitally and which, for reasons no less vital, unites one with those who have become temporarily the objects of one's study? It is in the latter spirit that we prefer to approach the study of Sikkim Buddhism as something having its own local character, admittedly, while being a form of that which, knowing no boundaries, touches us all alike. The name Sikkim defines a certain field, to be sure, but the emphasis all along must rest on Buddhism.

I have been acquainted with Sikkim, off and on, for over twenty years, the last visit having taken place in the summer of 1959. I have also enjoyed the society of many Sikkimese friends, both great and small, from whom I have gathered various impressions of their own attitude towards the Buddhism they profess. Lastly I have had access, for an all too brief period and before I was ready to take full advantage of the opportunity, to the presence of one who occupied for many years a pre-eminent place in the spiritual life of the country, the late Abbot of Lachhen. It is on the basis of this fairly wide range of experience that this chapter has been written.

As regards its Buddhist connections, Sikkim belongs entirely to that branch of the tradition that bears the name of Great Vehicle or Great Way, the *Mahayana*, an allegiance it shares with its neighbor Tibet, as well as with China and Japan; and furthermore it is by that section of the monastic congregation that is represented by the Nyingmapa or Order of the Ancients—the rather misleading word "sect" has been purposely avoided—that is to say by lamas of the line instituted by Padma Sambhava or the Precious Teacher, Guru Rinpochhe, as he is commonly called, that Sikkim was both evangelized in the first instance and still is spiritually governed. There is little in Sikkim to remind one of the large and highly organized monastic communities of Tibet itself, for the Sikkimese *gonpa* in its typical form is usually quite small, consisting, more often than not, of an isolated temple with a few outbuildings which are only in full occupation on certain occasions when the monks, many of whom are not celibates, assemble to carry out rituals, either seasonal or else specially commissioned by some local person. The rest of the time they spend in their own homes and take part in the ordinary activities of the peasantry, while the temple itself remains in the charge of a sacristan, who will open it on demand; even in the few *gonpas* of larger size their occupants, except at specified seasons, rarely add up to more than a handful. Thus the Sikkimese monk, on an average, leads a life less distinct from that of the laity than many of his fellows in other lands, an arrangement which, under favorable conditions and in periods of widespread spiritual activity, can have its advantages in that a continual permeation of the lay community by the traditional influence is thus intensified. In times of decay when spiritual initiative is at a discount, however, it brings its own dangers, in that it is often the monk's aspirations that become submerged in the daily round of more worldly preoccupations, instead of the reverse being true.

I have chosen one example of a Sikkimese community (Buddhist goes without saying) in order to let it serve as a type for the whole region: in the present instance the example chosen will be a small settlement in Western Sikkim called Sinen, situated on a spur some three hours' walk above the better known center of Tashiding. Sinen is one of a series of such small pockets of Sikkimese race which extend along the higher ground overlooking the true left side of the Rangit valley, the lower reaches of which have by now become predominantly Nepali and Hindu. In all these places along the edges of the greater mountains the Sikkim way of life is to be found preserved almost untouched, and from what remains it is possible to form an idea of what the whole country was like before the coming of the British opened the floodgates of immigration, with consequent disturbance of the racial balance.

What strikes one most forcibly in any predominantly Sikkimese environment is the successful compromise that has been effected between the interests of the human beings concerned and those of their wild neighbors, animals, birds and plants. How admirably the traditional Sikkimese methods of agriculture agree with the character of the country, where men never seem bent on encroaching beyond reasonable limits nor try by violence to force Nature out of her appointed ways! Apparently the Sikkimese attitude towards natural things has been largely free of that overweening cupidity that has driven so many others, not least in more modern times, to exploit the earth's resources regardless of everything else, whereby so much of the world's surface has already been turned into a semi-desert. In the Sikkimese lands, though a certain amount of clearing naturally took place in order to make room for man's crops, this did not go to the point of wholesale obliteration of the forest and extermination of its animal inhabitants, as in the case of other peoples of a more pushing but really less far-sighted character, and indeed it could well be said that across the Sikkim countryside, so long as its ancient economy remained unaltered (which today is unfortunately no longer the case), was writ large the fifth proposition of the Noble Eightfold Path, Perfect Livelihood, thanks to which man himself was the first to profit since in sparing the trees and the animals he was in fact safeguarding the primitive sources of his own prosperity. Nor was that enlightened self-interest confined to the material spheres only, since Nature in her untamed state has from time immemorial been the nursery of the spirit, as attested by the history of countless Saints and Yogins who have found in the wilderness a favorable field for exercising the Contemplative Life. Afterwards, it may be, led by compassion, they would return to minister to those who were still struggling in the net of worldly distraction, but at first where would they themselves have been without their wilderness?

Standing on any lofty spot and letting one's eye roam over the tangle of ridges and deep-cut valleys which together make up Western Sikkim, one notices that every second spur, of which Sinen is one, is crowned with its temple or small *gonpa,* each a sentinel of the Doctrine looking out across this once blessed region, and it is impossible not to feel a certain contemplative urge oneself at the mere scene displayed before one's gaze, the serenity of which is such as to make one imagine every forest recess or mountain cave as still harboring its hermit Lama, as must have been the case down to quite recent times. Today, however, most of these likely-looking places are deserted and it can be said that, in the higher sense, the Contemplative Life has largely ceased to be followed in these parts, and it is only the more outward things of the tradition which now serve to canalize the spiritual influence, more indirectly therefore and in a less active or conscious way. This is really a cardinal fact concerning Buddhism in Sikkim, one which any honest survey must first of all take into account; for the contemplative or intellectual element (which must not be confused with what is merely mental or rational, due to a loose, modern misuse of the word "intellect"), being the central element in any true tradition, is the one essential factor in the absence of which all the others, necessary as they are in their own relative order, rituals, arts, moral legislation and the Active Life in general, are bound eventually to fall apart through lack of a principle to unify them. Knowledge constitutes the one and only stable guarantee of a normal existence in the Buddhist sense, and by knowledge is meant, not the variegated fruits of individual mental activity, but *That* which comes only by way of direct Intellection, without intermediary, *That* which being ever present shines by its own light so that it is perceptible from the moment that the mentally and physically created obstacles have, through applying the appropriate Method, been rendered fully transparent. It is this end that all spiritual disciplines have in view, and it is for this purpose that one resorts to a Spiritual Master, but it is Contemplation itself which makes of a man a Master, so that here again one is back where one started—Contemplation it is which constitutes the heart of a tradition and if that heart is allowed to grow weak, how then shall the rest of the organism continue in normal health? But let us now resume the description of the *gonpa* of Sinen and its surroundings, since this is to provide us with the pegs on which to hang a number of other comments and reflections each having a bearing on some aspect of the more general question of the present state of Buddhism.

Beyond the end of the spur, towards the main hillside, are to be found dotted about the thatched homesteads of the peasants, as beautiful in their own way as the sacred buildings, beautiful, that is to say, with the pure beauty of functional aptness, of faultless adaptation to landscape and climate and material, and also beautified by the addition of ornamental features, here a boldly decorated window-frame, there a lattice, whereby a touch of lightness is imparted, though never at the expense of structural fidelity. As for the people themselves, they are characterized by an open and cheerful disposition, coupled with natural courtesy and a sense of hospitality unsurpassed anywhere in the world.

On the crest of the spur stands the temple itself which, as is usual in Sikkim, consists of two storeys, one of them being dedicated to Guru Rinpochhe. The walls are formed from masonry of satisfying thickness, crowned with a cane-thatched roof the eaves of which spread out a long distance so as to meet the requirements of a particularly rainy climate; the construction is extremely ingenious as well as beautiful and the fact that it has to be repaired at intervals (of about eight years, so we were told) does not really constitute an argument in favor of altering a type of roofing otherwise so satisfactory; the introduction of corrugated iron in several other places has been a regrettable development, both because of the inescapable shoddiness of the material itself, and also because its use has destroyed the artistic homogeneousness of buildings otherwise beyond reproach, as at Tashiding for instance, not to mention the terrible noisiness of an iron roof during the long rainy season.

Certainly, if one wishes to gain a clear impression of the Sikkimese style in its purest form, one cannot do better than go to Sinen, because of its compactness coupled with the high quality of the work to be seen there: what one perceives is that this local style, though related to the general pattern of Tibetan art, possesses a number of features of its own, one of which is the wealth of bold and original woodwork in the interiors; especially remarkable are the great supporting piers with the spreading, bracketed capitals most splendidly carved and very aptly left uncolored; the great temple at Tashiding provides another magnificent example.

And what manner of men, it may be asked, were the creators of these wonders? The answer is that they were quite simple, normal people not very obviously distinguishable from other descendants of the peasant stock to which they belonged; indeed the only secret of what, to us, appears like "genius" lay in their normality itself, that typically Buddhist virtue (in the sense of conformity to "the Norm", to *dharma*), and doubtless these same men would have felt hard put to it if asked to explain how they went about their creative achievement, and probably their only answer would have been that they had been so taught by their predecessors in the craft, who had shown them how, when one wishes to put up a temple or fashion a pillar, such a way is the "correct" one, as traditionally revealed in the ancient days, and any other way is not. The traditional mind, when artistically engaged or otherwise, is a unanimous mind, and it is its very unanimity and the reduction in the sense of individual selfhood that goes with it which, by thus restricting the agent of restriction, causes that spontaneous and at the same time ordered originality to be released. That is the lesson of all traditional art, and besides its accomplishment how small do the supposed triumphs of artistic individualism seem, when once one has learned to see through the various tricks whereby it is wont to assert itself.

The interior walls of Sinen are covered with ancient paintings, now somewhat faded, but still clear at such times of day as the light is shining in at the right angle. They fall nothing short of the other features already described, and the same applies to the images: certainty, were these things to be found in Europe, Sinen would be a famous place and every precaution would be taken to preserve its treasures by guarding them jealously against the dangers of well-meaning but uninstructed restoration, as well as by an occasional repair rendered necessary as a result of weathering: of the two dangers the first-named is the greater, however. In Europe if paintings like those at Sinen ever had to be retouched, none but experts would be allowed to go near them, who would in any case restrict their own work to the minimum so as to preserve the character of the previous paintings as nearly unchanged as possible. Neglect of these precautions, or rather unconsciousness on the subject, has been responsible for the total destruction, by reckless repainting on the part of inferior artists, of many most precious frescos in Tibet itself, so that it is well to be warned of what is at stake in all similar cases; for the men who could paint like that were men who *knew* something, and by their art they were able to infuse something of their own contemplative experience into the work itself, whereby it in its turn became a source of spiritual edification for the beholder, a "means of grace" in the fullest sense.

If we have given tongue on the subject of Sinen, this was because it provided an example that simply asked one to be eloquent; however, the last thing one would wish to happen is that this pen of ours, by attracting the wrong kind of attention to the place, should help to turn it into a tourist center, for that would be the surest way to destroy it and also the human beings who draw spiritual nourishment from its proximity, by profaning the one and exposing the others to powerful and unknown temptations: of what use is the shell, however beautiful its form, if once the spirit has abandoned it? Sinen deserves to be an occasional center of pilgrimage and otherwise to be left in enjoyment of its own peace; and if anyone, because this is one of the most precious of Sikkim's ancient monuments, makes it his business to watch over its safety, whether officially or otherwise, one can only pray, while sincerely welcoming the intention, that this task will be carried out in the most unobtrusive manner possible, efficiently indeed but with the lightest touch, for then it will be preservation in the truest sense.

Speaking personally, the experience at Sinen was unforgettable, the conviction of a more-than-human influence, a grace, was most powerful. Apart from that, during the brief period when we were camping (my friend and I) under the shadow of its ancient walls that had remained standing, almost alone, when a great earthquake leveled Pemayangtse and so many other temples roundabout, we had a number of opportunities to observe the workings of the tradition in the daily life of the people, both by way of odd conversations and by watching what went on in the vicinity of the temple. During that time, for instance, a service was held for the benefit of a local family, starting off with a procession round the building to the sound of music, the whole performance being conducted in a manner that many a larger place might well have envied for its dignity and spontaneity alike. From watching these operations and also through our talk with the old sacristan whom we found to be well informed about all that related to his temple, we were further confirmed in the impression that, with these people, their conception of spiritual activity is almost exclusively a ritual one coupled with a considerable degree of devotional fervor but lacking doctrinal information of a precise kind. This does not mean, however, that such information is totally wanting (here the professional "scientific" observer obsessed with "facts" is often at sea), since there are ways of conveying knowledge other than by formulations couched in rational and analytical language (the stock-in-trade of the literate mind) and much can be assimilated through symbols, sacred myths and other such instruments and sometimes knowledge gained in this way can reach quite deep. Nevertheless one must admit that a general lack of doctrinal precision, of acquaintance, that is to say, with the elementary teachings of the tradition in their more explicit form, leaves a man in a rather vulnerable state of mind, especially in the face of false doctrines such as are being propagated on all sides in the modern world but which in fully traditional times would never have been encountered at all. The kind of precautions to be taken in times of epidemic must needs differ from those in force under more healthy conditions, when the dangers are relatively sporadic ones.

The rituals themselves, in the minds of these peasants, appear in the guise of an activity necessary for the maintaining of the equilibrium of life, communal or private, as an element on the one hand of order and on the other of protection against dangers both material and subtle, and of course, in a more general way, the rites provide a link with the Heavenly Powers. This attitude, if limited and sometimes marred by superstitious misinterpretation of elements occurring in the rites themselves, is not altogether lacking in realism; for the chief purpose of rites, all the world over, is to keep open channels of communication with something which, if it were once shut off (as happens when the profane point of view has come to prevail, with consequent cessation of ritual activity), would inevitably leave the beings concerned exposed, helplessly, to all kinds of obscure influences of a subtle order, emanating from a level far below the human, and these influences, finding the field clear would tend to extend themselves further and further over the world of men. This is perhaps the greatest danger resulting from materialism, which may be compared to a general encrusting over the human scene whereby the free circulation of the spiritual influence, of which tradition is the vehicle, is hindered more and more, until that crust, which in man is so aptly described as a "hardening of the heart", begins to crack by its own rigidity, whereupon the obscure forces of dissolution already mentioned begin to pour in, reducing everything to a state of disintegration. This, broadly speaking, is the story of the modern world, and the loss of interest in the ritual function (itself part of the process of skepticism in regard to spiritual things, coupled with credulity in regard to a quasi-absolute validity of "facts" and their applications) is not the smallest of the causes bringing about this result.

I have enlarged somewhat on this aspect of the question, not only because it is daily becoming more and more forced on one's attention, but also because, in relation to our immediate purpose, namely an assessing of the chief factors affecting the Buddhist situation in Sikkim, it would be easy to underestimate the value of what exists there because of its being predominantly ritual in form; very many travelers have written down Sikkim Buddhism as being a mere residue, a tissue of superstitions, in which very little of real Buddhism inheres. With this view I disagree because, though doctrinal instruction is admittedly and often dangerously lacking among people of every walk of life (and it is often among the well-to-do that the danger is most apparent, because they are being subjected to much greater pressure from the side of modern profanity than are the simpler folk), yet the sub-structure still carries the original message implicitly, though with a local flavor added as must always be the case: rituals and a hundred traditional practices of lesser degree all help to perpetuate it. All said and done, that which conditions the atmosphere of the place and the attitude of men still, despite all, remains characteristically Buddhist, and no amount of dragging in of historical and ethnological red herrings is able to alter the fact.

There is one last question which, though it is an accessory one, deserves a passing mention, because it has a practical bearing upon the spiritual life as carried on in these parts, and moreover it is a question which has aroused a certain amount of controversy among Buddhists attached to different branches of the tradition: this question refers to the taking of alcoholic liquor in monasteries as well as by the laity which, though disallowed in a great part of the Buddhist world where the primitive injunction against wine still holds good, is permitted by exception to the followers of the Nyingmapa path according to the word of Guru Rinpochhe himself who, for them, represents the supreme embodiment of traditional authority; whence it follows that any fruitful discussion of this question must, if it is to remain "in context", take stock of that fact. Nor need the existence of divergences of this kind within one and the same tradition cause surprise, since at the level of form a certain variability is both normal and indica-tive of vitality, each such variation corresponding to a sepa-rate adaptation in view of the special needs of different kinds of men. Buddhism, no less than other traditions, has given birth to quite a number of different schools, each of which has developed certain ways of its own, and between these ways a certain incompatibility is noticeable in some respects, yet one and all of them still remain essentially Buddhist.

All that need be said in the present instance is that the habitual use of alcohol has its obvious dangers and that while these must not be exaggerated it equally would be a mistake to underrate them; if, for example, the effects are such as to cause an appreciable number of spiritually gifted persons to sink, by dint of hard drinking, into a state of torpor so that their spiritual gift becomes stillborn in consequence, then clearly something must have gone wrong somewhere, since such a result cannot possibly be ascribed to the wishes of the Sage who gave the original permission. Whatever one's personal opinion about the causes at play, the incontestable premise is that Guru Rinpochhe, when he allowed a certain thing did so in awareness of what he was doing, and not from carelessness and still less from a demagogic wish to gain popularity with his followers; in his case a spiritual motive has therefore to be presumed. But actually his attitude need not astonish when we remember that Padma Sambhava was a *Tantrika* and that it is in keeping with the Tantrik methods to utilize various substances in view of their symbolical properties and in disregard, to some extent, of the dangers to which their profane misuse might give rise, one which naturally is excluded from any spiritual point of view by definition. Wine is a case in point, since traditionally it represents esoteric knowledge or, according to another version of its symbolism, the *amrita* or liquor of immortality, itself a symbol of that knowledge which alone is able to bring about release from the limitations of this mortal state; the sacramental use of wine, wherever it occurs, rests on this analogy.

The foregoing very brief reference to the "technical" aspect of the taking of wine will have afforded a slight inkling of what may have lain behind the authorization in question; for reasons of space it is not possible to pursue the matter into further detail. If then the question arises as to how abuse is to be prevented with a view to counteracting the wastage of good human material which undoubtedly is occurring from this cause, the answer would seem to lie in a better understanding of the doctrine covering this particular matter, as well as of the symbolical relationships whence it derives, so that those who are minded to found their practice upon the permission given them by their supreme Lama may do so in accordance with the spirit of his teachings and not, as now often happens, with the letter only.

This brings us to a point where it is possible to pause and take stock of the position, by assessing the principal known factors in terms of positive and negative, following which a few general conclusions may also be drawn. These factors fall roughly under two headings, namely those which consist of elements belonging to the tradition itself and those which, springing from outside causes, affect it indirectly. In the latter category must be placed such factors as the reduction, through changes in the composition of the population during the last few decades, of the area occupied by Buddhism, as well as the shifting of the balance of political power as an additional consequence. Nor should one overlook the increasing social and political disorder to which the entire world has fallen prey and which has spared no country however remote, not even Tibet; anything tending to deprive the Sikkimese of the powerful source of moral support hitherto represented by an undisturbed Tibet must be regarded as a serious loss. Finally into this category must enter one other factor of particular importance, one which ought by rights to belong to the other group but which, because of the spread of modern secularism, is to be found at present among the negative influences—one is referring to school education which, in so far as it affects the outlook of the rising generation, must be regarded as a very potent cause of irreligion.

It would be quite impossible here to embark on anything like a full discussion of this vital subject; but one remark at least should not be omitted, namely that the system of schooling that has been in vogue in all Indian territories since its first introduction by the British reflects in its every method the profane and materialistic outlook of its nineteenth century originators. This affects not only the way in which every subject is envisaged, regardless, that is to say, of any possible connection with principles of a spiritual order, but also, no less, it affects the "imponderables", the background, which will, in the long run, condition the results of the education received even more than what is expressly taught.

It is high time that some people turned their attention to the important problem of what constitutes an acceptable education in the Buddhist sense—the same applies to Hindus and indeed to all who have the spiritual welfare of their children at heart. Such persons should know that it is idle to aim at material benefits apart from the spiritual, for without the latter to give form and direction and meaning there can be no true happiness and no contentment and no prosperity and no culture. One has only to compare impartially the state of mind and the quality of living of the average Sikkimese peasant (despite the comparative fewness of his worldly goods) with the alternation of harassment and boredom and the consequent frantic pursuit of happiness such as passes for life in so much of modern Europe and America, and that in spite of, rather should one have said because of, the quantity and bewildering variety of material possessions which that life demands—one has only to compare them in order to judge which of the two states of mind is the more fortunate. What then, it will be asked, is that essential factor which while belonging to the one mentality is wanting in the other and which has made all the difference? It is awareness of the spiritual order and attention (be it even with a little accompanying superstition) to its claims which in the one case has remained in the forefront and has been allowed to lapse in the other, this it is that has made the difference.

Turning now to the other side of the picture, the field of traditional life as such, a discrimination has to be effected, as already explained, between factors of a positive and negative kind. Of the former, two must be singled out as being of great importance: firstly, there is the maintenance of the continuity of ritual activity, in all its many forms, whereby the channels of spiritual influence are kept open and many adverse influences neutralized, and secondly, there is the immense fund of devotional fervor as displayed by people of every type and kind, whereby they have kept themselves, even when knowledge has been narrowly restricted, in a state of spiritual receptivity, still proof against many a temptation. Who could doubt the truth of this statement who, like the writer, had witnessed the scenes at the building of the *stupa* in memory of their late Abbot by the people of Lachhen, when all from the very old down to children barely out of their mothers' arms bent their backs to the task of carrying the stones with an ardor that no hired laborer could emulate? Or again, could anyone doubt it who, in the same district, had stood close to the gigantic tree-trunks lying ready to be man-handled all the way across a wide tract of mountain country, including a pass of over 17,000 feet, for the purpose of repairing the great temple at Sakya? A modern engineer with all his gadgets would not have found the handling of these great cedars in such country an easy task, but for these peasants it was simply a case of putting a team of sixty or more men and women to each tree who, singing and moving in rhythm, would shift it so many miles each day and then hand over to the next team who, no less light-heartedly, would take it over—and what for?—for merit, that is all, for love of the Divine. None who has come into contact with these things can ever doubt that Sikkim Buddhism still possesses a substratum of spiritual power which would take a lot of undermining, though one knows that the adversary has not spared his efforts and that he has even met with some success.

On the negative side of the balance-sheet it must be said that the strictly intellectual element in the tradition, that of doctrine, both in its more theoretical form and as actualized by method and experience, has largely disappeared and this is a matter for very serious misgiving, since the loss affects the most essential element of all, Knowledge, starting point and final term of all spiritual endeavor. In a more outward sense, this lack expresses itself in a very general absence of doctrinal instruction affecting all classes, even monks, and which often extends to quite elementary information concerning the fundamentals of Buddhism. Further insight into this state of affairs was gained quite recently when some lectures were given at Gangtok upon such themes as the Four Truths and the Noble Eightfold Path, for some members of the audience were led to remark enthusiastically that it was news to them that Buddhism taught all these wonderful things! Such ignorance ought not to be tolerated, for, as was mentioned previously, it leaves a man terribly vulnerable in the face of false doctrines which today are being disseminated on every side both purposely and, still oftener, through unconscious infiltration under the disguise of seemingly innocent things.

If anyone should wonder how such apparent indifference to the need for theoretical instruction should have come about, it can be explained (apart from the more immediate causes which are manifold) by the fact that in former times the traditional structure was so free from fissures that many things were then unnecessary which, under the peculiar circumstances of the last hundred years, have become more and more imperative. At that time one was dealing with what was a practically unanimous society, one in which the authority of the tradition was unquestioned and unquestionable; moreover the level of spirituality itself was undoubtedly higher, thanks to the continual presence in the land of unbroken lines of eminent Lamas and their disciples, and though the imparting of theoretical instruction outside the ranks of the clergy may not have been any more organized then than it is today yet there was, for the reasons given above, a continual outflow of knowledge from the various spiritual centers and a continual contact and exchange between those who knew at first hand and the receptive generality of the people around them, so that the knowledge under its more theoretical form did in fact circulate widely and without let or interruption. This way, which follows the normal mode of traditional inter-communication, is superior to any form of catechism organized according to a set pattern, and while it lasted it provided automatically for ordinary needs; the present generation has inherited the framework, but meanwhile the sources have themselves partly run dry while at the same time adverse forces from outside have increased their pressure. If only this educational problem can be solved successfully, then assuredly the power of underlying devotion among the people is such as to promise incalculable results, because to the warmth of love there will then have been added the precision of knowledge, and both of these together go to make up spiritual health.

Much has been said already, but nevertheless the heart of the matter has yet to be touched, since the theoretical form of knowledge, indispensable though it is at every stage, still remains an experience at second hand which requires faith, the power of confident participation in knowledge, to supplement it; from which it can be seen that this form of knowledge is not in itself complete and self-sufficing, but partial and dependent on something that will quicken its latent possibilities. For theory, doctrine expressed, is after all but a preparation for Knowledge unqualified and the latter is only to be realized intuitively through the Intellect, the true Intelligence, which, for its part is not to be regarded as an intermediary, like another Mind, but as a prolongation of the Knowledge itself, a ray which, though it is not the sun, is not other than the sun.

The highest order of Knowledge—this is the one omission in our balance-sheet which no merely human artifice can rectify; other things can be improvised, more or less, yet without its vivifying presence in the persons of one or two at least who have realized it, the rest of the traditional edifice will remain shaky for lack of intellectual foundation. One must face the truth: today the Great Lights have been dimmed, the twilight has descended. Sikkim has its long tale of saints and teachers second to none; even a few years ago one still heard echoes of great names like Bermiak Rinpochhe and others of like eminence, and the Great Hermit of Lachhen was still there, he could be visited, round him were disciples, but now who is going to fill the vacant places?

Is there then reason for despair? That can never be said, for the Compassion of the Bodhisattva is inexhaustible and so long as one blade of grass remains undelivered he will not quit the Round of Existence nor abandon creatures in their need, only those who want his help must prove that they are in earnest. Therefore, even while not deluding oneself with the idea that the essential Knowledge can either be dispensed with or else replaced by some other thing, one should preserve an attitude of hopeful vigilance and meantime one should continue to work at the preparation of the ground, the field of oneself and others, so that all may be in readiness if and when the Lama reappears. Besides, there is another possibility to be considered in the same connection; if perchance it is known that somewhere in the Buddhist world a Lama is to be found, preferably one of the spiritual family of the Nyingmapa or of one allied to it, who might, in response to pressing entreaty and from compassion, consent to make his home in Sikkim for the purpose of fanning back into flame the still smoldering embers of its ancient spirituality, then assuredly no time should be lost nor any effort spared in securing his help.

Should such a Lama arrive—or arise locally as could still happen—then there is little doubt that his presence would act as a magnet upon all who are endowed with a true qualification, and disciples would hasten towards him from all sides like moths flying into a lamp, and many latent spiritual possibilities would wake up from their present state of torpor at his mere touch, and the holy Nyingma tradition, its intellectual poise restored, might see a day of renewal. This, then, should be one's prayer, that the sun of Knowledge may yet rise over Sikkim and with its warming rays cause to dissolve the mists now veiling the face of Kangchhendzönga.[1]

[1] It might well be asked whether the sudden arrival in Sikkim, in the autumn of 1959, of a number of eminent Lamas fleeing from Communist persecution in their home countries of Tibet and Kham may not have created just that opportunity one had in mind when writing the above words. A reference in *The Listener* (September 17th) to the new Institute of Tibetan Studies in Gangtok, formed with Indian assistance, will have caught the eye of many readers. That important results will follow in the field of Tibetan scholarship is quite likely. This, however, is hardly the kind of thing one is thinking of. The wind of the Spirit, wafting the essential Knowledge, does not willingly imprison itself within the four walls of an institution organized to serve human convenience; it blows as and where it chooses. Mental virtuosity, that the world persistently mistakes for knowledge, is often its deadliest enemy. Scholastic studies can indeed become one of its handmaidens, but as a first condition they must admit their own subordination, otherwise they remain but another form of ignorance. To invite the Spirit, quite other sacrifices are wanted. Therefore we must still end our chapter, as before, on a question mark.

Ultimately, it is a question whether some, if any, are prepared to pay the price—of gaining the "pearl of great price."

The Abbot of Lachhen (1867-1947), a Sage of the Nyingmapa Order

7
Do Clothes Make the Man?
The significance of human attire

"If a man does not honor his own house, it falls down
and crushes him"—*Greek Proverb*

During an exchange of letters that took place between the
late Ananda K. Coomaraswamy and the present writer during
the war years, discussion once happened to turn on the question
of traditional dress and its neglect, a subject which had
frequently occupied my mind in the course of various journeys
through the Himalayan borderlands. We both agreed
that this question was of crucial importance at the present
time, a touchstone by which much else could be judged. Dr.
Coomaraswamy (who henceforth will usually be denoted
simply by his initials A.K.C.) then informed me that his own
earliest publication on any subject other than Geology was
precisely concerned with this question of dress; the paper
referred to bore the title of "Borrowed Plumes" (Kandy, 1905)
and was called forth by its author's indignation at a humiliating
incident he witnessed while staying in a remote district of
Ceylon. He further suggested that I might some day treat the
same theme in greater detail; the opportunity came for complying
with his wishes when I was asked to add my personal
tribute to a world-wide symposium in honor of the seventieth
birthday of that prince of scholars, whose rare insight had
made him the qualified interpreter and champion of the traditional
conception of life not only in India but everywhere.
All that remained, therefore, was for one to apply to the subject
chosen that dialectical method, so typically Indian, with
which A.K.C. himself had made us familiar in his later works:

that is to say, the question at issue had first to be presented under its most intellectual aspect, by connecting it with universal principles; after which it became possible, by a process of deduction, to show the developments to which those principles lent themselves in various contingencies; until finally their application could be extended, as required, to the field of human action, whether by way of doing or undoing. In the present chapter appeal will be made, all along, to the parallel authority of the Hindu and Islamic traditions, as being the ones that between them share the Indian scene; such reference being primarily intended as a guarantee of traditional authenticity, as against a merely human, personal and private expression of opinion on the part of the writer.

Fundamentally, the question of what kind of clothes a person may or may not wear (like any other similar question) is a matter of *svadharma,* an application of that law or norm of behavior which is intrinsic to every being in virtue of its own particular mode of existence (*svabhava*). By conforming to his norm a man *becomes what he is,* thus realizing the full extent of his possibilities; in so far as he fails, he accepts a measure of self-contradiction and disintegrates proportionally.

The late Sir John Woodroffe, in *Bharata Shakti* (Ganesh, 1921)—a work that ought to be in the hands of every Indian and more especially the young—quotes George Tyrrell as having once written: "I begin to think that the only real sin is suicide or *not being oneself.*" That author was probably thinking in individual terms only; nevertheless, his statement contains echoes of a doctrine of universal scope—from which all its relative validity at the individual level is derived—namely, that the ultimate and only sin is *not to be One Self,* ignorance (*avidya*) of *What one is,* belief that one is *other* than the Self—indeed, on that reckoning we, one and all, are engaged in committing self-murder daily and hourly and we shall continue to do so, paying the penalty meanwhile, until such time as we can finally *recollect ourselves,* thus "becoming what we are".[1]

It has been said that there are three degrees of conformity (*islam*) to the truth; firstly, everyone is *muslim* from the very fact of being at all, since, do as he will, he cannot conceivably move one hairs-breadth out of the orbit of the Divine Will that laid down for him the pattern of his existence; secondly, he is *muslim* in so far as he recognizes his state of dependence and behaves accordingly—this level is represented by his conscious attachment to a tradition, whereby he is able to be informed of what he is and of the means to realize it; and thirdly, he is *muslim* through having achieved perfect conformity, so that henceforth he is identical with his true Self, beyond all fear of parting. In Hindu parlance this same doctrine might be expressed as follows: every being is

---

[1] Following Tyrrell, we have used the word "suicide" here in its more usual and unfavorable sense, as denoting an extremity of self-abuse; it can however be taken in a different sense, when it is far from constituting a term of reproach: we are referring to the voluntary self-immolation implied in a phrase like that of Meister Eckhart when he says that "the soul must put itself to death" or in the Buddhist "*atta-m-jaho*" (= "self-noughting" in Mediaeval English) which coincides, on the other hand with *bhavit' atto* (= Self-made become). This whole doctrine, and ultimately our basic thesis in this essay, rests on the principle that "as there are two in him who is both Love and Death, so there are, as all tradition affirms unanimously, two in us; although not two of him or two of us, nor even one of him and one of us, but only one of both. As we stand now, in between the first beginning and the last end, we are divided against ourselves, essence from nature, and therefore see him likewise divided against himself and from us." This quotation is taken from A.K.C.'s two-pronged essay *Hinduism and Buddhism* (New York, 1943); the section dealing with Theology and Autology is strongly recommended to all who wish to understand the meaning of the universal axiom "*duo sunt in homine.*" We say "Be yourself" to someone who is misbehaving: it is in fact, only the carnal self (*nafs*) or soul that can misbehave, the Self is infallible. Hence for the former an ultimate suicide is essential. As between the outer and inner man, only the latter is the Man (the image of God), the outer man being the "shadow" or "vehicle" or "house" or "garment" of the inner, just as the world is the Lord's "garment" (Cp. *Isha Upanishad* 1, and Philo, *Moses* II, 135).

yogi in that any kind of existence apart from the Self is a sheer impossibility, even in the sense of an illusion; that being is *a yogi*—called thus by courtesy, as it were—in so far as he, she or it strives, by the use of suitable disciplines (*sadhana*), to realize Self-union; the selfsame being is *the Yogi* in virtue of having made that union effective. No element in life can therefore be said to lie outside the scope of *yoga.*

What individual man is, he owes, positively, to his inherent possibilities and, negatively, to his limitations; the two together, by their mutual interplay, constitute his *svabhava* and are the factors which make him uniquely qualified (*adhikari*) for the filling of a certain part in the Cosmic "Play" (*lila*), for which part he has been "cast" by the Divine Producer. Neither possibilities nor limiting conditions are of his own choice—not his either to accept, select or evade. The relative freedom of will which he enjoys within the limits assigned to him is but a translation, into the individual mode, of that limitless and unconditional freedom which the Principle enjoys universally.

Individual responsibility, therefore, applies solely to the manner of playing the allotted part; this, however, presupposes some opportunity of comparing the individual performance throughout with its pattern as subsisting in the intellect of the dramatist; but for some means of access to this standard of comparison, all judgment must be exercised at random. The authentic source of such information can only be the dramatist himself, so that its communication implies the receiving of a favor or "grace" at his hands, by a handing-over of the required knowledge, either directly or through some indirect channel—in other words, an act of "revelation" is implied. As for the carrying out of the task in practice, by faithful imitation of the pattern as traditionally revealed, that is a question of using the tools one has been given, never of forging new ones. Furthermore, in so far as one has been led, from any reasons of contingent utility, to extend the range of one's natural tools by artificial adjuncts, these too must, in some sort, be treated as supplementary attributes (*upadhi*) of the individuality: whatever equipment or "ornament" (the primary meaning of both these words is the same) may be required, it must be of such a character and quality as to harmonize with the general purpose in view, which is the realization, first at an individual and then at every possible level, of what one is.

Of the many things a man puts to use in the pursuit of his earthly vocation there are none, perhaps, which are so intimately bound up with his whole personality as the clothes he wears. The more obviously utilitarian considerations influencing the forms of dress, such as climate, sex, occupation and social status can be taken for granted; here we are especially concerned with the complementary aspect of any utility, that of its significance, whence is derived its power to become an integrating or else a disintegrating factor in men's lives. As for the actual elements which go to define a particular form of apparel, the principal ones are shape or "cut", material, color and ornamental features, if any, including fastenings and also trimmings of every sort.

The first point to be noted is that any kind of clothing greatly modifies the appearance of a person, the apparent change extending even to his facial expression; this can easily be proved by observing the same individual wearing two quite distinct styles of dress. Though one knows that the man underneath is the same, the impression he makes on the bystanders is markedly different. It is evident, therefore, that we have here the reproduction of a cosmic process, by the clothing of a self-same entity in a variety of appearances; on that showing, the term "dress" can fittingly be attached to any and every appearance superimposed upon the stark nakedness of the Real, extending to all the various orders of manifestation which, separately or collectively, are included in the "seventy thousand veils obscuring the Face of *Allah*". In view of this far-reaching analogy, it is hardly surprising if, at the individual level also, dress is endowed with such a power to veil (or reveal) as it has.[2]

For the human being, his choice of dress, within the limits of whatever resources are actually available to him, is especially indicative of three things: firstly, it shows what that man regards as compatible with a normal human state, with human dignity; secondly, it indicates how he likes to picture himself and what kind of attributes he would prefer to manifest; thirdly, his choice will be affected by the opinion he would wish his neighbors to have of him, this social consideration and the previous factor of self-respect being so closely bound up together as to interact continually.

According to his idea of the part he is called upon to play in the world, so does a man clothe himself; a correct or erroneous conception of the nature of his part is therefore fundamental to the whole question—the common phrase "to dress the part" is admirably expressive. No better illustration can be given of the way dress can work on the mind than one taken from that little world of make-believe called the theater: it is a commonplace of theatrical production that from the moment an actor has "put on his motley" and applied the appropriate "make-up", he tends to feel like another person, so that his voice and movements almost spontaneously begin to exhale the flavor (*rasa*) of the new character he represents. The same individual, wearing the kingly robes and crown, paces majestically across the stage; exchanging them for a beggar's rags, he whines and cringes; a hoary wig is sufficient to impart to his voice a soft and quavering sound; he buckles

---

[2] The concepts of change of clothes and becoming (*bhava*) are inseparable: Being (*bhuti*) only can be naked, in that, as constituting the principle of manifestation, it remains itself in the Unmanifest. Ultimately, the whole task of "shaking off one's bodies" (or garments) is involved—these including all that contributes to the texture of the outer self "that is not my Self."

on a sword and the same voice starts issuing peremptory commands. Indeed, if the "impersonation" be at all complete, the actor almost becomes that *other* man whose clothes he has borrowed, thus "forgetting who he is"; it is only afterwards, when he is restored "to his right mind" that he discovers the truth of the saying that, after all, "clothes do not make the man".

Shri Ramakrishna Paramahamsa has paid a tribute to this power of dress to mold a personality in the following rather humorous saying: "The nature of man changes with each *upadhi*. When a man wears black-bordered muslin, the love-songs of Nidhu Babu come naturally to his lips and he begins to play cards and flourishes a stick as he goes out for a walk. Even though a man be thin, if he wears English boots he immediately begins to whistle: and if he has to mount a flight of stairs, he leaps up from one step to another like a *sahib*."

This testimony of the Sage can be matched by evidence drawn from a very different quarter. When one studies the history of various political tyrannies which, during recent centuries, have deliberately set out to undermine the traditional order with a view to its replacement by the "humanism" of the modern West, one is struck by a truly remarkable unanimity among them in respect of the policy both of discouraging the national costume and at the same time of eliminating the Spiritual Authority as constituted in their particular traditions. These dictators were no fools, at least in a worldly sense, and if they have agreed in associating these two things in their minds and in making them the first target for their attack, even to the neglect of other seemingly more urgent matters, that is because in both cases they instinctively sensed the presence of something utterly incompatible with the anti-traditional movement they wished to launch. As they rightly divined, the costume implied a symbolical participation (*bhakti*) in that "other-worldly" influence which the Spiritual Authority was called upon to represent more explicitly in the field of doctrine.

The Tsar Peter I of Russia seems to have been about the first to perceive how much hung upon the question of dress, and when he decided that his country should "face West", politically and culturally, he made it his business to compel the members of the governing classes to give up their Muscovite costume in favor of the coat and breeches of Western Europe, while at the same time he seriously interfered in the constitution of the Orthodox Church, with a view to bringing it under State control on the model of the Protestant churches of Prussia and England. Likewise in Japan, after 1864, one of the earliest "reforms" introduced by the modernizing party was the replacement of the traditional court dress by the ugly frock-coat then in vogue at Berlin, by which the Japanese officials were made to look positively grotesque; moreover, this move was accompanied by a certain attitude of disfavor towards the Buddhist institutions in the country, though government action concerning them did not take on an extreme form. In many other countries of Europe and Asia reliance was placed rather upon the force of example from above; the official classes adopted Western clothes and customs, leaving the population at large to follow in its own time, further encouraged by the teaching it received in westernized schools and universities.

The classical example, however, is that afforded by the Kemalist revolution in Turkey, a distinction it owes both to its far-reaching character and to the speed with which the designed changes were effected as well as to the numbers of its imitators in neighboring countries: in that case we have a military dictator, borne to power on the crest of a wave of popular enthusiasm, as the leader in a *jihad* in which his genius earned him (falsely, as it proved) the title of *Ghazi* or "paladin of the Faith", who no sooner had overcome his foreign enemies in the field than he turned his power against the Islamic tradition itself, sweeping the *Khalifat* out of the way like so much old rubbish and plundering the endowments bequeathed to sacred use by ancient piety; while under the new legislation *dervishes* vowed to the Contemplative life were classed with common vagabonds. It was another of Kemal's earliest acts to prohibit the Turkish national costume, not merely in official circles but throughout the nation, and to impose in its place the shoddy reach-me-downs of the European factories. Some thousands of *mullahs*, who dared to oppose him, earned the crown of martyrdom at the hands of the hangmen commissioned by an arak-drinking and godless "Ghazi". Meanwhile, in the rest of the Moslem world, hardly a protest was raised; in India, where the movement to defend the *Khalifat* had been of great political service to Kemal in his early days, only the red Ottoman *fez*, adopted by many sympathizers with the Turkish cause, still survives (though proscribed in its own country) as a rather pathetic reminder of the inconsistencies to which human loyalties sometimes will lead.

It may now well be asked what, in principle, determines the suitability or otherwise of any given form of clothing, and indeed what has prompted Man, in the first place, to adopt the habit of wearing clothes at all? It is evident that a change so startling as this must have corresponded to some profound modification in the whole way of life of mankind. To discover the principle at issue, one must first remember that every possibility of manifestation—that of clothing for instance—has its root in a corresponding possibility of the Unmanifest, wherein it subsists as in its eternal cause, of which it is itself but an explicit affirmation. Metaphysically, Being is Non-Being affirmed, the Word is but the uttering of Silence; similarly, once Nakedness is affirmed, clothing is "invented". The principle of Clothing resides, therefore, in Nakedness. In seeking to throw light on this fundamental aspect of the doctrine, one cannot do better than refer to the Cosmological Myth common to the three branches issued from the traditional stem of Abraham, of *Seyidna Ibrahim*. According to the Biblical story, Adam and Eve, that is to say, primordial mankind in the Golden Age (*Satya yuga*), were dwelling in the Garden of Eden at the center of which grew the Tree of Life or World Axis (*Meru danda*). The Axis, which "macrocosmically" is assimilated to a ray of the Supernal Sun (*Aditya*) and "microcosmically" to the Intellect (*Buddhi*), occupies the *center* of human existence, all other faculties of knowledge or action being grouped hierarchically round the Intellect as its ministers and tools, none encroaching, each keeping to its allotted work in conformity with its own norm (*dharma*); this state of inward harmony being, moreover, externally reflected in the peaceful relations existing between Man and all his fellow-creatures around him, animals, plants and others. It is also recorded that Adam conversed daily and familiarly with God, that is to say, the individual self was always immediately receptive of the influence emanating from the Universal Self, "one-pointed" (*ekagrya*) concentration being for it a spontaneous act requiring the use of no auxiliary means. Such is the picture given of the state of normal humanity, or the Primordial State as the Taoist doctrine calls it, which corresponds to that state known as "childlikeness" (*balya*) in the Hindu or "poverty" (*faqr*) in the Islamic doctrine, the latter term betokening the fact that the being's Self-absorption is free from all competing interests, here represented by "riches"; for this state "nakedness" would not have been an inappropriate name either.

The Bible story goes on to describe the loss of that condition of human normality by telling how Eve, corrupted by the Serpent (an embodiment of the *tamasic* or obscurantist tendency), persuaded her husband to taste of the forbidden fruit of the Tree of Knowledge of Good and Evil, with fatal results; that is to say, the original unity of vision gives way to *dualism,* a schism takes place between self and Self, in which essentially consists the "original sin" of Christian theology, containing as it does the seed of every kind of opposition, of which "myself" versus "other" provides the type. And now comes a detail which is of particular interest for our thesis: the very first effect of Adam and Eve's eating of the dualistic fruit was a feeling of "shame" at their own nakedness, a self-consciousness by which they were driven to cover their bodies with fig-leaves, thus fashioning the earliest example of human clothing.[3]

The rest of the symbolism is not hard to unravel. For one still in the state of *balya* the thought never could arise "I must be clothed", because *balya*, by definition, implies the clear recognition that the individuality, including all its sheaths (*kosha*) variously diaphanous or opaque, is itself but a cloak for the true Self; to clothe it would be tantamount to piling dress upon dress. From this it follows that, for one who has realized that primordial state, the most natural proceeding would be to discard all clothes; one is on sure ground in saying that the unclothed ascetic or *nanga sannyasin* adequately represents the position of one who is intent on rejoining the Self.

Once there has been a departure from the indistinction of this primitive nakedness, the various traditional ways part company thus producing a wide diversity of types in each of which certain aspects of the symbolism of clothing are predominant, to the partial overshadowing of others; this, indeed, is the general principle of distinction as between any one traditional form and another, by which each is made to display a "genius" for certain aspects of the truth, leaving to

---

[3] In connection with Adam's "shame" a Jewish traditional commentary, (Philo, IA 11.55 f.) offers a strikingly concordant testimony, as follows: "The mind that is clothed neither in vice nor in virtue (i.e. does not partake of the fruit of the Tree of Knowledge of Good and Evil), but is absolutely stripped of either, is naked, just as the soul of an infant (= *balya*)." It should likewise be noted that in Judaism the High Priest entered *naked* into the Holy of Holies—"the noblest form, if stripping and becoming naked," noblest, that is to say, as distinguished from e.g. Noah's nakedness, when he was drunk. In the same connection Shri Krishna's theft of the *gopis*' clothes (*vastraharana*) has an obvious bearing.

its neighbors the task of emphasizing the complementary aspects.

Space does not allow of a detailed study even of the main types into which clothing can be classified; there are, however, one or two which must be mentioned: the first of these, as a letter received from A.K.C. himself once explained, represents the most characteristic constituent of Hindu clothing both ancient and modern, and consists of a length of material woven all of a piece, without joins—the "tailored" styles, as worn by Indian Muslims for instance, come into another category. In this type of single-piece wrap as commonly worn by Hindus, therefore, we are dealing with a "seamless garment", like that of Christ.

It will be remembered that at His Crucifixion the soldiers who stripped Jesus of His raiment were unwilling to tear the seamless robe, so they cast lots for it. As for the Savior Himself, He was raised naked on the Cross, as was only fitting at the moment when the Son of Man was discarding the last remaining appearance of duality, assumed for "exemplary" reasons, and resuming the principial nakedness of the Self. Christian theologians have often pointed out that the symbolical garment of Christ is the Tradition itself, single and "without parts", like the Supreme *Guru* who reveals it; to "rend the seamless garment" is equivalent to a rupture with tradition (which must, of course, not be confused with an adaptation of its form, in a strictly orthodox sense, to meet changing conditions).

Tradition is a coherent whole, though never "systematic" (for a "system" denotes a water-tight limitation of form); once torn, the seamless garment cannot be "patched" simply by means of a "heretical" (literally "arbitrary") sewing on of elements borrowed at random—those who think of saving their tradition by compromising with a secularist outlook might well take note of the words of Christ: "No man putteth a piece of new cloth into an old garment, for that which is put in to fill it up taketh from the garment, and the rent is made worse" (St. Matthew, ix, 16).

Some mention must also be made of what might be called the "monastic habit", founded on a general type consisting of some plain material shaped to a rather austere design or even deliberately put together from rags, as frequently occurs in Buddhism. These forms of apparel are always meant to evoke the idea of poverty and may be taken to symbolize an aspiration towards the state of *balya*. To the foregoing category might be attached, but in a rather loose sense, the self-colored cotton homespun (*khaddar*) which, in Gandhi's India, had become the emblem of a certain movement. In this case, too, the idea of poverty had been uppermost; but it must be said, in fairness, that some of its supporters, possibly affected by an unconscious bias towards westernization, often were at pains to disclaim any other purpose for their hand-spinning than a purely economic one, that of helping to reclothe the many poor people who had been deprived of their vocational life and reduced to dire want under pressure of modern industrialism. This was tantamount to admitting that *khaddar* had a utilitarian purpose but no spiritual significance and that the movement to promote its use was essentially "in front of (= outside) the temple", which is the literal meaning of the word "profane". It is hard to believe, however, that such could have been the whole intention of the saintly founder of the movement, since he had never ceased to preach and exemplify the doctrine that no kind of activity, even political, can for a moment be divorced from faith in God and self-dedication in His service, a view which, more than all else, earned for him the hatred of the "progressives" of every hue, who were not slow in applying to him the (to them) opprobrious epithets of "mediaeval", "traditional", and "reactionary".

Apart from the two special examples just given, we must confine ourselves to a few quite general remarks on the subject of traditional dress, for all the great variety of types it has displayed throughout the ages and in every part of the world.

By calling a thing "traditional" one thereby relates it immediately to an idea which always, and necessarily, implies the recognition of a supra-human influence: to quote a phrase from A.K.C.'s writings: "All traditional art can be 'reduced' to theology, or is, in other words, dispositive to a reception of truth." Thus, the costume which a man wears as a member of any traditional society is the sign, partly conscious and partly unconscious, that he accepts a certain view of the human self and its vocation, both being envisaged in relation to one Principle in which their causal origin (*alpha*) and their final goal (*omega*) coincide. It is inevitable that such a costume should be governed by a *Canon,* representing the continuity of the tradition, the stable element, Being; within that canon there will, however, be ample room for individual adaptation, corresponding to the variable element in existence, impermanence, Becoming.

In tribal civilizations, which are most logical in these matters, the art of dress and self-adornment is carried to a point where the details of human apparel are almost exact symbolical equivalents of the draperies, head-dress and jewels that indicate its *upadhis* in a sacred image (*pratima*); moreover, such costume is usually covered with metaphysical emblems, though its wearers are by no means always aware of their precise significance; nevertheless, they reverence them greatly and undoubtedly derive a form of spiritual nourishment and power (*shakti*) from their presence. Furthermore, it is at least rather suggestive that tribal costume often entails a considerable degree of nudity, and is, in appearance, extremely reminiscent of the dresses of gods and goddesses, as portrayed in the ancient paintings and sculptures; so much so, that a friend recently suggested that the forms of tribal life in general constitute survivals from a period anterior to our present Dark Age (*Kali-yuga*). It is not surprising that both "Christian" missionaries and the apostles of modern materialism (the two seemingly contradictory motives being, indeed, not infrequently found in the same person) should be glad whenever they succeed in inducing some simple-minded peasant or tribesman to forego the natural safeguards provided for him by his native dress and customs; for after that he is only too easily demoralized and will fall a ready victim to their properly subversive persuasions.

One last type of clothing now remains to be considered, that specific to modern Europe and America, which is also the type that is threatening to swamp all others, to the eventual abolition of every distinction, whether traditional, racial or even, in more extreme cases, individual. This "modern dress", through its development parallel with that of a certain conception of Man and his needs, has by now become the recognized uniform to be assumed by all would-be converts to the creed of "individualism", of mankind regarded as sufficing unto itself; it is somewhat paradoxical that partisans of a violent nationalism (which in itself is but an offshoot of individualism) have often been sworn opponents of their own national costume, just because of its silent affirmation of traditional values; some examples illustrating this point have already been given in the course of this chapter, and readers can easily find other similar cases if they but care to look around in the contemporary world.

In this context some mention should be made of a variant on human clothing of recent occurrence, that of "party uniform" as introduced in the totalitarian states of the last decades. One has but to remember the "Blackshirts" of Mussolini's Italy or the "Brownshirts" of Hitler's Germany, for instance, whose respective uniforms were so designed as to suggest ruthlessness and brutality together with a kind of boisterous "camaraderie", indicative of party loyalties. In totalitarianism of another hue, it is a wish to affirm the "proletarian ideal" that has been uppermost. A striking example of party uniform having this idea in view is provided by that in vogue among members of the Chinese Communist party which in its calculated drabness expresses its purpose in a way that verges on genius: nothing could better indicate the total subordination of the human individual to the party machine than that shapeless tunic-like jacket, buttoned up to the chin, sometimes with a most hideous cap to match such as lends a peculiarly inhuman character to any face which it happens to surmount. The most interesting point about this type of costume is that it amounts, in effect, to the parody of a monastic habit; that is to say, where the austerity of monastic dress, in all its various forms, is imposed for the purpose of affirming a voluntary effacement of the individual in the face of the Spiritual Norm, the party uniform in question likewise is meant to suggest an effacement of individuality, but one that operates in an inverse sense, in the face of the deified collective principle known as "the Masses", supposed source of authority as well as admitted object of all human worship and service. It is the ideal of a humanity minus Man, because none can be truly human who tries to ignore his own symbolism as reflecting the divine image in which he has been fashioned and to which his whole existence on earth should tend by rights. Moreover, it is no accident that all these types of uniform have been derived from Western, never from a native form of clothing.

The above admittedly represent extreme perversions, not less instructive for that. When one turns again to western dress, however, under its more ordinary forms, it is at least fair to recognize that it has lent itself, more than other forms of clothing, to the expression of profane values: this has been true of it, in an increasing degree, ever since the latter half of the Middle Ages, when the first signs of things to come began to show themselves, in the midst of a world still attached to tradition—or so it seemed. It took a considerable time, however, before changes that at first were largely confined to "high society", and to the wealthier strata generally, were able seriously to affect the people as a whole. Over a great part of

Western Europe the peasant costume remained traditional, and even with all the extravagances that had begun to affect the fashions of the well-to-do a certain "aristocratic" feeling remained there that it took time to undermine completely.

Now if it be asked which are the features in modern dress which correspond most closely with the profane conception of man and his estate, the answer, which in any case can but be a rather tentative one, will include the following, namely: the combining of pronounced sophistication, on the one hand, with "free and easiness", on the other, coupled with the frequent and gratuitous alterations introduced in the name of "fashion", of change for the sake of change—this, in marked contrast with the formal stability of traditional things—without forgetting either the manifold effects of machine production in vast quantities by processes which so often denature materials both in appearance and in their intimate texture—unavoidable or not, all these are factors that tell their own tale. Also chemical dyes, which have now swept across the world, are playing their part in the process of degradation and even where traditional costume still largely prevails, as in India, they and the excessive use of bleaching agents have together done much to offset such quality as still is to be found in the forms themselves; in most of the East the same would apply. Nor must such factors as the enclosing of feet formerly bare inside tight shoes or the disturbance to the natural poise of the body resulting from the introduction of raised heels be underrated. These and many other more subtle causes have operated in turning Western dress into a vehicle of great psychological potency in a negative sense. Besides, there is the fact that wherever ornamental features occur in modern clothing, these never by any chance exhibit any symbolical character; in other words, ornament, at its best as at its worst, has become arbitrary and therefore profane.

An objection might, however, be raised here which is as follows: the Western dress of today is, after all, but a lineal development of what formerly had been, if not a specifically

Christian form of costume, at least one that was habitual in Christian Europe, one that could therefore claim to be in a certain degree traditionally equivalent to whatever existed elsewhere; it may be asked, how comes it then that its present prolongation is opposable to all other known types, so that it alone is compelled to bear the stigma of providing a vehicle for anti-traditional tendencies? Historically the fact just mentioned is incontrovertible, no need to deny it; but far from invalidating the foregoing argument it but serves to render it more intelligible: for it must be remembered that error never exists in a "pure" state, nor can it, in strict logic, be opposed to truth, since truth has no opposite; an error can but represent an impoverishment, a distortion, a travesty of some particular aspect of the truth which, to one gifted with insight, will still be discernible even through all the deformations it has suffered. Every error is *muslim,* as it were in spite of itself, according to the first of the three degrees of conformity as defined in a preceding section, and it cannot be referred back to any separate principle of its own, on pain of accepting a radical dualism in the Universe, a ditheism, a pair of alternative, mutually limiting realities. Anything can be called "profane" in so far as it is viewed apart from its principle, but things in themselves will always remain essentially sacred.

In the case of dress, this it is that explains the fact that many Westerners, though now wearing a costume associated with the affirmation of secularist values, are less adversely affected thereby (which does not mean unaffected) than Asiatics, Africans or even Eastern Europeans who have adopted that same costume; with the former, alongside anti-traditional degeneration there has been some measure of adaptation bringing with it a kind of immunity—the disease is endemic, whereas in the second case it has all the virulence of an epidemic. Furthermore, since, as we have seen, some positive elements, however reduced, must needs persist through every corruption, those to whom this form of dress properly belongs are enabled, if they will, to utilize whatever qualitative factors are still to be found there; though the reverse is equally possible as evidenced both in the case of the affectedly fashionable person and of his shoddier counterpart, the affectedly unkempt. The position of the Eastern imitator, however, is quite different—for such as he the change over to modern dress may easily involve so complete a contradiction of all his mental and physical habits as to result in a sudden violent rending of his personality, to the utter confusion of his sense of discrimination as well as the loss of all taste in its more ordinary sense. Indeed such cases are all too common.

Some people affect to believe that a movement to submerge specific differences reveals a unifying tendency in mankind, but they are suffering under a great delusion in that they mistake for true unity what is only its parody, uniformity. For any individual, the realizing in full of the possibilities inherent in his *svabhava* marks the limit of achievement, after which there is nothing further to be desired. As between two such beings, who are wholly themselves, no bone of contention can exist, since neither can offer to the other anything over and above what he already possesses; while on the supra-individual level their common preoccupation with the principial Truth, the central focus where all ways converge, is the guarantee of a unity which nothing will disturb; one can therefore say that the *maximum of differentiation is the condition most favorable to unity, to human harmony*; an immensely far-reaching conclusion which René Guénon was the first to voice in modern times, one which many may find difficult of acceptance just because of that habit of confusing unity with uniformity that we have just referred to. Against this peace in differentiation, whenever two beings are together subjected to the steamroller of uniformity, not only will both of them be frustrated in respect of some of the elements normally includable in their own personal realization, but they will, besides, be placed in the position of having to compete in the same artificially restricted field; and this can only result in a heightening of oppositions—the greater the degree of uniformity imposed, the more inescapable are the resulting conflicts, a truth which can be seen to apply in every field of human activity, not excepting the political field.

Enough has now been said to enable the reader to appreciate the general principle we have set out to illustrate: if the subject of dress was chosen, that is because it lent itself most easily to such an exposition; but it would have been equally possible to pick on some different factor pertaining to the Active Life, to the *karma-marga,* such as the furnishing of people's homes, or music and musical instruments or else the art of manners; since each of these is governed by the self same law of *svadharma* and it is only a question of effecting an appropriate transposition of the argument to fit each particular case. Behind the widespread defection from traditional dress and customs there undoubtedly lurks a deep-seated loss of spirituality, showing itself on the surface in a corresponding diminution of personal dignity and of that sense of discrimination that everywhere is recognizable as the mark of a character at once strong and noble. In the East, as we have seen, the tendency in question has gone hand in hand with what Henry James described as "a superstitious valuation of European civilization" and this tendency, despite the much lip-service paid to the new-fangled idea of "national culture", is far from having exhausted itself. This is further evidenced by the fact that imitation rarely stops short at those things that appear indispensable to survival in the modern world, but readily extends itself to things that by no stretch could be regarded as imposed under direct compulsion of contingent necessity. The operative cause therefore is to be sought in an overpowering psychological urge, the urge to experience certain possibilities of the being which tradition hitherto had inhibited, possibilities which can only ripen in forgetfulness of God and things divine: traditional dress being a reminder of those things has to be discarded; the modern civilization being the field for realizing those possibilities has to be espoused. Naturally, when one comes to individual cases, all manner of inconsistencies and oscillations will be apparent; the inherited past is not something that can be expunged for the mere wishing. All one can do, in discussing the matter, is to treat it on broad lines, leaving any given case to explain itself.

By way of striking a more cheerful note in an otherwise depressing story, the fact should be mentioned that Indian women, with but few exceptions, continue to wear the *sari*, that most gracious form of feminine dress, both at home and abroad. Their gentle example has actually spread to unexpected quarters; many African women visitors to this country have appeared clothed in an Indian *sari*, the colors and designs of which were however drawn from the African tradition itself. This adopting of a foreign traditional model instead of the ubiquitous Western one, by adherents of an emergent nationalism, is hitherto quite unprecedented; in its way it is a small and heartening sign, one of which all former subjects of colonialism might well take note. Indeed, sometimes one is tempted to believe that West Africans, in these matters, have tended to show more conscious discrimination than many of their fellows belonging to other continents and this impression has been strengthened by the frequent sight of Nigerian Muslim visitors of commanding stature and of both sexes walking our streets properly clad in their splendid national costume. May this example offered by Africa find many imitators!

To finish, one can but repeat the principle governing all similar cases: one's native attire—or indeed any other formal "support" of that order—is an accessory factor in the spiritual conditioning of a man or woman and this is due both to any associations it may happen to carry and, at a higher level, to its symbolism as expressed in various ways. The assumption of modern Western dress has often been the earliest step in the flight from Tradition: it would be but poetic justice for its divestment to mark the first step on an eventual path of return—too much to hope perhaps, yet the possibility is worth mentioning. In itself such action might seem little enough, for dress is not the man himself, admittedly. Nevertheless, if it be true to say that "clothes do not make the man" yet can it as truly be declared that they do represent a most effective influence in his making—or his unmaking.

Chenrezig Bodhisattva of Mercy

8
The Dalai Lama
His function, his associates, his rebirth

Ever since Tibet and its institutions began to exercise the attention of people in the West, that is to say since the beginning of this century, the Dalai Lama and the, to us, very strange manner of his selection has been an object of widespread curiosity; in a larger way this curiosity has attached to the existence, here and there throughout the Tibetan world, of those revered figures labeled by travelers, though most improperly, with the title of "Living Buddhas",[1] of whom the Dalai Lama, as also the Panchhen Lama (often miscalled "Tashi Lama"), are but two examples among others. However, the fact that the Dalai Lama is also the temporal ruler of Tibet—or was until the time of the Chinese Communist invasion—has focused interest on his person in a very special way,[2] since nowhere else in the world is the supreme governor of a country chosen by the method of "reincarnation"—we use this term here advisedly, though as will be shown further on, it is a loose term and does not correspond very exactly

[1] One must protest still more strongly against the blasphemously suggestive term "God-King," as applied to the Dalai Lama in the popular press and also by some who should know better.

[2] Quite recently this interest has been quickened as a result of the publication of H. Harrer's now famous book *Seven Years in Tibet*. The portrait painted there of the youthful Dalai Lama, whom the author got to know intimately and to whose character he pays high tribute, as well as the tragic circumstances that surround the latter part of the story, will not have failed to evoke much genuine sympathy. The keynote of this account is the personality of the man himself, and comparatively little light is thrown upon the nature of his sacred office which, for the author, is not a primary concern.

with the facts of the case. First of all, however, let us try to define the position of the Dalai Lama as he appears in the eyes of his own subjects.

It is important to understand from the outset that that function of his which chiefly attracts the interest of Europeans, namely his political rulership, important though it is in its own way, must yet be counted as a sideline; one might almost say that a similar, though less categorical reservation applies to his ecclesiastical status, as an eminent member of the Buddhist clergy, since in this sense the Dalai Lama can count a number of colleagues of more or less comparable rank both in Tibet itself and in other Buddhist countries. If the Dalai Lama has sometimes been likened to the Pope and his great residence on the Potala Hill overlooking the city of Lhasa to the Vatican, this comparison contains a fallacy, since his functions are not specifically related to the defining of doctrine, as in the case of the Roman Pontiff. It may well happen that spiritual knowledge and therefore a qualification to pronounce on doctrinal matters with sureness is also to be found in a Dalai Lama, but when this happens it must be ascribed, not to any specific capacity inherent in his office, as some might be led to suppose, but to a metaphysical realization, the fruits of personal endeavor in the spiritual field.

In fact, the Dalai Lama's essential function is neither the exercise of the Temporal Power nor yet the Spiritual Authority (though both of these belong to him in eminent degree), but it is a function bound up with the fact that he is the representative on earth of a celestial principle, of which Compassion or Mercy is the chief characteristic: this principle, under its personal aspect, is known as the Bodhisattva Chenrezig,[3] "he of the penetrating vision", more familiar in the West under his Sanskrit name of Avalokitêshvara, of

---

[3] Generally speaking, the word "Bodhisattva," formed as it is of two roots meaning respectively "Enlightenment" and "being" stands for the penulti- mate degree in the spiritual hierarchy, the one just previous to the attainment of Supreme Knowledge, of Buddhahood; but in *Mahayana*

which the name Chenrezig is a rather free translation: the Chinese *Kwan-yin* (in Japanese *Kwannon*) denotes a corresponding aspect in the Far Eastern tradition. It should moreover be noted, in this context, that Chenrezig, as Bodhisattva, is, on the heavenly level, regarded as having issued from the brow of Opagmed (Sanskrit *Amitabha,* Japanese *Amida*) whose disciple he also is (Amitabha is the Buddha presiding over the Western Quarter and symbolizing the divine aspect of "Limitless Light"). This Buddha, as tradition declares, projects his influence upon mankind through the person of the Panchhen Lama already referred to; whence some people have been led to argue that since a teacher always ranks as senior to his disciples, therefore the Panchhen Lama, as the Buddha Opagmed's representative, should logically occupy a rank above that of the Dalai Lama as representing Chenrezig. However, this argument is an oversimplified one and does not correspond sufficiently with the facts of the Tibetan scene, where Chenrezig actually represents the active power of Opagmed as exercisable in the World; therefore, in relation to human beings and human needs, he is their point of contact with the Luminous Source which, for us, manifests itself here below in the form of the Divine Mercy. Furthermore, it is Chenrezig who is the appointed protector of Tibet and of the Buddhist tradition there, and in this respect his office has been revealed in a more "specific" form than that of the Buddha of Light, though in a principial sense the latter does constitute the primordial source of Chenrezig's merciful power. In fact the functions of the two great Lamas are bound up with one another, even as are those of their heavenly prototypes, that of the Panchhen Lama being relatively "static", while that of the Dalai Lama is more "dynamic", wherein are

Buddhism, which is the traditional form prevailing in Tibet, as well as China and Japan, this word is a keyword to the understanding of the whole tradition and indicates the goal of the spiritual life, as will be explained more fully in the following chapter.

also reflected the distinctive characteristics of Buddhahood and Bodhisattvahood respectively.

Reference has just been made to the fact that Chenrezig is the Protector of the Tibetan tradition and the lands where it holds sway, and this likewise defines the primary and essential function of the Dalai Lama: his presence at the heart of the Tibetan world is a guarantee of heavenly protection, hence the title of "Precious Protector" under which he is generally known. Through his person flows an uninterrupted current of spiritual influence, characteristically compassionate in its "flavor", and it can be said, therefore, that the Dalai Lama's office, in relation to the world generally and Tibet in particular, is neither chiefly one of rulership nor teaching but an "*activity of presence*", one that is operative independently of anything he may, as an individual, choose to do or not to do.

If it should seem astonishing to some people that a spiritual influence should thus be transmitted through a succession of human intermediaries, all one need answer is that this is no more impossible, or unlikely, than that such transmission should become focused on a place or an object, such as the grotto at Lourdes, for instance, or a wonder-working relic: for it is evident, if one thinks about it, that a power deriving from a higher order of reality, as in this case, would not encounter any obstacle in penetrating the substance of something belonging to an order limited by conditions from which the higher order in question is free—which is all that is meant when using terms like "lower" and "higher" in such a context. Incidentally, an understanding of the metaphysical principle here illustrated will help to remove a common stumbling-block in the way of those who nowadays find miracles and supernatural happenings generally hard of acceptance; since it follows from the same principle that an event which at one level of reality, such as that of our world, not only seems but also is miraculous, yet remains perfectly normal at another level of existence, one that is free from some or all of our limitations, so that the event in question can properly be regarded at one and the same time as a miracle and as a natural happening, without any kind of contradiction being implied thereby. Thus to the sufferer whose disease is lifted from him at Lourdes the miraculous nature of his cure is no figure of speech but actual fact, and we as his fellow-humans will likewise share in his attitude; but to the power that works the cure (in this case the Blessed Virgin) the effect produced is but a normal function of her own spiritual eminence, or, as the Tibetans would say, it is the "skillful means" which must inevitably accompany knowledge such as that spiritual degree itself implies.

After this brief excursion into a wider field, some further illustration of the Dalai Lama's function can be provided by comparing it once again, but this time in a positive sense, with that of the Pope. The succession of Roman Bishops and Dalai Lamas are alike in that each vehicles a specific spiritual influence, instructive and protective respectively, and in both cases the exercise of the function in question is unaffected by the individual character of the holder of the office for the time being,[4] whose competence can only be open to question if for some reason or other it be supposed that the traditional conditions governing the appointment have somehow been

---

[4] Between a sacred function and its human or other "support" there can be no common measure, but only a symbolical relationship, since they belong to different orders of reality. In the face of the sacred whatever is merely human will be inadequate by definition, this being as true of a saint as of a sinner, a fact which retailers of misplaced moral criteria often overlook: it was failure to grasp a metaphysical principle that explains the unsoundness of the arguments leveled by the early reformers, for instance, against the papal authority on the grounds that individual popes had repeatedly shown themselves morally unworthy of their calling. In Tibet this manner of confusing things of different orders could hardly occur, as evidenced by the case of the Sixth Dalai Lama whose looseness of living provoked much scandal, without however leading anyone into the error of projecting his personal defects upon the influence of which he was the occasional vehicle.

disregarded in a vital way;[5] the same criterion would apply in a priestly ordination or any other comparable case. At the same time it may be pointed out that an influence that has been vouchsafed in given circumstances of time and space can, and eventually must, be withdrawn into the source whence it emanated and this will occur at such a moment as the cycle of its "providential" manifestation has been completed. The Tibetans, for their part, are not unaware of this possibility, since it is generally expected that the dynasty of Dalai Lamas will some day come to an end, and that time may not be far away, judging by recent happenings. The thirteenth Dalai Lama, in his famous "Testament", had in fact foreshadowed this possibility, but time alone can show whether this particular spiritual cycle is about to close or not.

Similar considerations apply in the case of all other *Lama Tulkus*[6] (to give them their proper name); each of them corresponds to a link in a chain of spiritual influence attached to a specific center, such as a certain monastic foundation where

[5] A case in point is that of the present occupant of the Panchhen Lama's throne at Shigatse, whose status has been widely called in question because of his failure to comply, when still a candidate, with the proper canonical tests, as requested by Lhasa at the time; besides which, the fact that the Chinese from the outset tried to exploit his claims for political ends (if indeed they did not engineer them in the first instance) only serves to make the position still more shaky. If he now reigns at Shigatse, he does so thanks to Chinese bayonets; and meanwhile, the real identity of the Panchhen Lama remains an open question, with the promise of fresh complications if ever the matter of the succession is able to be raised again.

[6] The word "*tulku*" (spelt *sprul-sku*) can perhaps best be translated by "emanation body"; but this rendering does not do full justice to the many subtle implications with which the root *sprul* is charged. In some contexts it could mean "a miraculous manifestation," while in others our word "phantom" might even be used. It is moreover well to remember that, to the Buddhist mind, everything presenting any kind of appearance, whether sublime or of a lowly order, will always have a certain character of illusion attaching to it and must in any final analysis be transcended. It is in the nature of things, according to the Tibetan view, that Heavenly Figures and also saints and Lamas who have attained a certain degree of Knowledge should be able to

succeeding occupants of the abbatial seat will provide in turn the traditionally acknowledged "support" through which a given angelic or saintly power continues to manifest itself outwardly. In every case the methods of selection are similar, though differing in detail, that is to say, when one holder of the office dies, search is made for the child on whom, as proved by certain signs and confirmed by certain tests, the influence in question has devolved,[7] or to use a looser phrase, in whom the spirit of his predecessor in the line has been reborn: but the latter term, even when employed cautiously, is so apt to give rise to misconceptions that some further discussion of both its legitimate and abusive connotations will not be untimely.

In popular parlance, all the world over, the word "rebirth" suggests the idea of an individual constant passing after death into a different body, like someone who discards one dress in order to put on another. Hence the common question "What was I in a former life?" or "What shall I become with my next rebirth?" and so on. Whether such a question is a reasonable

project their influence, if their beneficent mission should require it, in the form of one or several *tulpas*, of gentle or else terrible appearance, even at a distance in both space and time. The present writer was once actually told by a Lama from the easterly province of Kham that he believed him to be a *tulpa* of the slayer of the apostate king Lang Darma, who lived in the ninth century, this opinion having been formed on the strength of something the writer had published which seemed to agree with indications given by that Lama's own teacher concerning a foreigner who would defend the faith in time of danger: this by way of example of how far the *tulpa* idea can extend.

[7] H. Harrer's book cited in an earlier footnote quotes an eye-witness account of the discovery of the present Dalai Lama which is both extremely circumstantial and deeply moving. To give another instance, the present writer was friendly with the Enche Kazi, a Sikkimese gentleman whose son was actually the first in succession of a new line of *Tulkus*, the founder of which was a saint who went under the name of Precious Doctor (Lamas' names always indicate a function, they are never individual) and who died in a valley close to the Indian frontier in 1937. This friend related the story of how his child was picked out and it certainly contained some remarkable details. Later the writer visited the youthful Precious Doctor in his own monastery.

one or an expression of human folly depends largely on what construction is to be put upon the word "I"; we all of us are continually taking this "I" of ours for granted, yet few pause to think of the fact that in the question "Who or what am I?" is contained the very key to wisdom and that, failing a correct answer, the person concerned must continue to be the plaything of ignorance.

The great Traditions, each in its own spiritual dialect, have given form to the answer and have indicated ways and means to verify it: it is doubtful, however, whether any has gone so far as Buddhism in attacking the error that arises from a confusing of true selfhood with the accidents of becoming, so that the doctrine of *anatma*, "non-selfhood", has come to be regarded as one of the distinctive features of Buddhist teaching, being for it quite fundamental.

Buddhism in fact refuses to recognize the nature of self in any of those factors whereby beings are rendered conscious of their own separate existence and its whole "spiritual technique" is expressly designed for the purpose of undermining reliance upon that kind of evidence. From the Buddhist point of view any tendency to identify oneself with a soul supposed to pass over unaltered from existence to existence is as deceptive, in its way, as the similar tendency to identify oneself (and the self of others) with the body—which in practice is what most people do most of the time, and this in spite of the fact that the body is foredoomed to old age and death and eventual decay, as all men know; but over this matter the I-consciousness is apt to brush aside all inconvenient evidence. Buddhism follows the same line of argument in respect of all the constitutive factors which together go to build up the empirical personality, for in its eyes all these things alike are but part of the "cosmic dream" from which there must be a complete awakening[8] before talk about true selfhood can

---

[8] The root meaning of "Buddha" is "the Wake."

even begin. This personal composite, as Buddhism sees it, is something which, having arisen by interplay of anterior causes, must necessarily, in the fullness of succession, be decomposed when once the particular group of possibilities it represented have "ripened" to the point of completing their cycle in the sphere of relative existence. The sense of a fixed "I" opposable to "other", which is the factor on which the existential illusion chiefly feeds, is but an item in a process of becoming, one of a series of effects fated in their turn to provide causes for further modifications in the ceaseless Round of Existence, *Samsara*, the "World's Flow".

Enough has been said to show that popular views on "rebirth" are the result of viewing the authentic doctrine of transmigration through the dualistic eye of human wishfulness, instead of through the single eye of the Intellect (not to be confused with the ordinary organ of thought, which today usually usurps its title):[9] the above criticism especially applies to that kind of "reincarnationism", as it might well be styled, which expects a continuous series of rebirths to take place in human form, ignoring the obvious fact that the universe offers other-than-human possibilities in a multitude compared to which the chances of human birth are rare in the extreme; the Buddha Himself stressed in vivid language the exceptional nature of the opportunity afforded by birth into the world of men, hence also the folly of wasting it in profane pursuits. Assuredly, failing Enlightenment, there is rebirth; but whether this occurs in human or other form, there still is no question of an individual identity bridging the gap between birth and birth, the relationship being more comparable to the kindling of one fire from another: the new

---

[9] The third or frontal eye portrayed on Hindu and Buddhist images represents this organ of transcendent knowledge, which may be compared to the "single eye" of the Gospel. It has no connection whatsoever with any acquiring of extraordinary powers whether physical or psychic.

fire is not the old fire, neither is it wholly other than that fire, the truth lying, here as elsewhere, in a mean between two apparently contradictory propositions, at a point not assignable to the positive category or the negative either. This is the doctrine of the Middle Way, characteristic of Buddhism, as applying to the case in point.

If the doctrine of non-selfhood embraces all modes of existence, it spells no exception in the case of those peculiarly favored persons whose vocation it is to offer their being as a channel for the spiritual influence as described in connection with the Dalai Lama and other *Lama Tulkus*. As individuals the members of a line of *Tulkus* must be regarded as quite distinct and as such they plainly are subject to the ordinary vicissitudes of human existence: it is the influence that has seized on their persons which can be said to take successive birth in the line concerned, while they themselves, in their personal capacity, have been reborn of the matured seed normally contained in the fruit of anterior causes.

Once such rebirth as a *Tulku* has taken place, however, it is quite in order for that Lama, on occasion, to speak in the name of the influence he represents, in the first person, while taking up an attitude of effacement as regards the individuality which for the time being has provided its vehicle; even when referring to events that took place in a distant past such an attitude on his part is perfectly consistent.[10] This also fits

---

[10] Thus the late Panchhen Lama (to mention one such example) when meeting a British representative welcomed him with the remark that he was especially glad to see him inasmuch as he had similarly welcomed his predecessor Captain Bogle: the meeting referred to actually took place in 1774! A somewhat comparable though obviously very different illustration is afforded by the "recognition," on the part of a child candidate, of ritual objects that had belonged to the defunct Lama, such as his rosary, bell, etc. These are placed among a number of other exactly similar ones from which the child has to make his choice. This is not the least extraordinary side of these elections to Tulkuhood, of which the one described in H. Harrer's book (the passage about the finding of the present Dalai Lama)

in with the general mentality of the Tibetans who, unlike the more individualistic Europeans, will always tend to stress a person's functional rather than his private aspect, and it is remarkable how readily the simplest people, instinctive metaphysicians that they are, will improvise functional titles to fit all manner of cases, thus avoiding use of personal epithets. In these matters the judgment of ordinary folk sometimes is unexpectedly acute and even so-called popular superstitions[11] are not always as foolish as they seem to sophisticated minds: one must however beware of going to the other extreme by trying to erect a new doctrine on the basis of popular interpretations, as in the case of certain current reincarnationist beliefs, not to mention the virtual deification of popular opinion which is a common feature of both the "democratic" and the totalitarian systems of our time.

Up to this point we have concentrated our attention upon the essential aspects of the subject: one or two more contingent aspects, however, also deserve mention; but first of all, a word of explanation must be given concerning the

---

provides one most striking example. On all these occasions the child's individuality is entirely dominated by the spiritual influence, not only in a symbolical but in an actual sense.

[11] A superstition (derived from Latin *superstitio* = something left over, a residue) can be the result either of survival in people's minds of one or more accessory features of a true doctrine, coupled with forgetfulness of the essential, or else of an over-simplification of that same doctrine. Such distortions are inevitable in any traditional civilization, but so long as the integral doctrine is understood at least by some this evil will not amount to anything serious and it can always be combatted by pointing out where the features in question properly fit into the whole. This is the way of true reform, in the sense of re-form; mere scoffing, itself born of ignorance of the true facts of the case, always goes with a subversive intention. The almost total absence of superstitions in the above sense in the civilisation self-styled as "progressive" is nothing to be proud of, spiritually speaking: moreover these comparatively harmless forms of the evil have been replaced there, inevitably, by other superstitions of a far more dangerous kind, those characterized by "scientific" pretensions, with consequences, all over the modern world, that speak for themselves.

use of the term "Lama" itself—for though it is so familiar it is often in practice employed in an ambiguous sense, calling for correction. The root *bla*, which gives the true spelling, in its basic meaning implies the idea of *superiority*, nothing else. In Tibetan the title "*Lama*" is not, as in our languages, applied indiscriminately to all members of the monastic congregation, but to three cases only, namely when referring to a *Lama Tulku* as already explained, or to a notable saint and especially the head of an initiatic line, or else to one's own spiritual Master, one's "*guru*", who, for oneself, is "my Lama", I being his disciple. All other uses of this term can be regarded as more or less improper.

Reference has several times been made to the tests to which children believed to be *Tulkus* are subjected in order to substantiate or invalidate their claim. The question may well arise as to whether these tests are always honestly carried out or whether sometimes undue influence is not exerted by interested parties. Though it is impossible to answer this question outright in view of the number of cases concerned as well as the large period covered, one has the impression that until fairly recently a "simoniacal" election to the position of *Lama Tulku* was, to say the least of it, highly unlikely, because the whole weight of tradition was there to impose observance of the proper conditions and, still more important, because people, almost without exception, were in a frame of mind when the consequences, both temporal and posthumous, of attempted sacrilege would have seemed too appalling for anyone to risk incurring them.

Of late years, however, it must be admitted that some suspicious occurrences have taken place in this sphere and that the spiritual authorities whose duty it is to watch over all matters of traditional regularity have sometimes seemed to take up a more passive attitude in the face of possible abuse than would have been the case some time ago: all such relaxation of vigilance must be reckoned a danger-sign, especially at a time when the pressure of profane influences is bringing ever increasing "scandal" all over the world. It is said, for instance, that there has been a noticeable increase in the number of *Tulkus* professedly discovered in well-to-do families, which formerly happened but rarely; the reason for this may well be a wish, unconscious or half avowed, in the minds of some of the members of the lamaseries concerned, to draw the wealth of a big family towards their own community by electing its child as abbot. These cases are still probably few, but they do nevertheless provide a cause for anxiety. Finally one can also ask oneself whether the credentials of all of the many *Tulkus* popularly admitted as such are equally reliable, for in some cases at least it is doubtful whether every precaution has been taken to verify the authenticity of the claim to this position of spiritual eminence. Here again, the traditional authority alone is competent to make inquisition into such matters, for obviously they cannot be decided off-hand, on mere suspicion or under pressure from unqualified opinion.

One last question now lies before us, as being likely to spring up in the minds of some readers: why, they might ask, has the phenomenon of the *Lama Tulkus* been confined to the Tibetan world and might not something of the same kind have been expected to occur in other places also? To this question a number of answers may be given, some of them partly conjectural, none of them watertight: rather is it a case of "situating" the whole question accurately and leaving intelligence to draw the right conclusions than of trying to find a nicely rounded off solution; for a slick answer, even if it succeeds in satisfying the mind for a time, is ultimately always open to suspicion.

First of all, it is good to remind oneself of the truth that the Spirit bloweth where it listeth, "playfully" as the Hindus put it, and also that each spiritual manifestation is in its way unique and if it takes form, this will necessarily imply a certain degree of "localization", as for example in the already mentioned case of Lourdes. One might as well ask why the Blessed Virgin chose that place and not Perpignan in order to manifest her healing power; but this question is really pointless, for after all what was to prevent her? Moreover every manifestation in the world reflects symbolically the uniqueness of the Creative Act which caused it to be, hence the impossibility of duplicating even the most insignificant being or event. In a final analysis not only those phenomena that move us to wonder but every phenomenon whatsoever is transparently sacred (for him that has eyes to see) because it reveals its prototype, just as, to the profane mind, it will seem grossly opaque to match the hardness of his own heart, in the sight of which Heaven itself cannot but assume the guise of Hell; in fact it is a selfsame reality that underlies both states, which of them will make its appearance depending upon the attitude of the beholding subject, a truth which Buddhism has thrown into particular relief.

These more general considerations apart, two reasons can be advanced in order to explain the incidence of Tulkuhood in Tibet and associated countries and not elsewhere, one being connected with the extreme vigor of the traditional spirit in that region, which acts as a catalyst for special graces: this is a first reason, the second is complementary to it, namely that it may also be a case of this phenomenon sometimes occurring in other places but, in the absence of traditional criteria whereby it can be recognized, remaining unnoticed. To these two reasons a third can be added: in the case of other traditional civilizations still substantially intact (we do not speak of the profane modern world) the occurrence there of different but equivalent phenomena may well, on pain of redundancy, exclude this particular form of spirituality. Probably the truth lies somewhere between all three explanations.

It is also worth noting one or two cases, as recorded in history, which, if not identical with the case of the Tibetan *Tulkus*, are at least comparable to it in a highly suggestive manner. One is the succession of sacred cats in ancient Egypt which acted as supports for the influence personified as the goddess Pasht: these consecrated animals were also recognized by the presence of special signs and when one died its successor was searched for in much the same way as in Tibet.

Still more extraordinary is the case of the identification, by the Islamic order of Begtashi dervishes, of one of their own saints with the Christian St. Spiridon who lived many centuries earlier—he was one of the Fathers of the Council of Nicaea where he won fame by silencing the heresiarch Arius. The body of this saint now lies in a chapel in the island of Corfu and this shrine has been greatly enriched by gifts received from Muslim as well as Christian donors, thanks to the traditional identification mentioned above. If such a fact surprises us, this would hardly be the case with a Tibetan who would easily explain the matter in terms of two *tulkus* of the selfsame influence.

In the course of this survey of a complex subject we have repeatedly alluded to the fact that the essential function in the case of both Dalai Lama and other *Lama Tulkus* is one of presence. Personal presence therefore is most important, so that to move too long or too far afield is the worst thing that could happen, as far as the Lama's principal function is concerned.

When the crisis brought about by the Chinese ultimatum was at its height I happened to be staying in Kalimpong, a small market town on the Indian side of the frontier. Great was the excitement when it became known that the Dalai Lama and his government were on their way down from Lhasa with the intention, as everyone then believed, of flee-ing into India. There was even talk in some circles of their eventually being taken overseas to some spot whence the yoke of national resistance could make itself heard. At Kalimpong itself a house was already prepared for the sacred sovereign's reception and when at last he reached the Chumbi valley just short of the border, the final step across was thought to be a matter of hours. But then he—or his advisers, for he was still very young—hesitated and for several weeks they stayed where they were, while the Chinese for their part halted their advance. With hope of outside help fading, negotiations began and eventually ended, as everyone knows, in a capitulation which left Tibet with a faint semblance of local autonomy but incorporated her to all intents and purposes, as a "colonial" enclave, in the new Chinese state. Foreign friends of Tibet who in all sincerity had advocated the Dalai Lama's escape into exile were disappointed, yet I believe that that decision to stay, hard though it must have been in some ways, was a right one at that time and having regard to the peculiar nature of his spiritual ministry; to have interrupted that ministry in time of great need for purely political reasons however strong would have undermined the traditional loyalties as nothing else could have done under the circumstances: certainly this was the view expressed by all Tibetans with whom I discussed the matter—and I made a point of doing so on every possible occasion; whether they were monks or laymen, officials or commoners, rich or poor, all were agreed that if the Dalai Lama's presence were removed from Tibet it would be a calamity that would have incalculable repercussions in every sphere. Never, I believe, has there been greater unanimity of opinion among any people nor a clearer understanding of the reasons governing the choice between two courses. For once one could fairly apply the dictum *"vox populi, vox dei"*, since it was unquestionably the spiritual interest which, as against other more worldly considerations, prevailed.

The traditional doctrine itself helped to encourage this decision: one of the names under which the Bodhisattva Chenrezig goes is the All-Merciful Shepherd-like Lord, concerning whom it is said that the shepherd declines to enter the sheepfold before the last of his flock are safely inside; only then does he enter and close the door: the sheep are all the suffering beings of the Universe "down to the last blade of grass" and the gate is the gate of Enlightenment that leads into the sheepfold of *Nirvana*. This redemptive symbolism, reminiscent as it is of the Good Shepherd of the Gospel, expresses the very spirit of the *Mahayana:* if then the Dalai Lama, at his own level, chose to model his conduct upon that of his prototype, can one criticize him? The good shepherd does not abandon his flock, especially when wolves are about.

The story however has a sequel. Sometime in the summer of 1954 reports appeared in the papers according to which the Dalai Lama, now grown up, was being pressed by the Chinese to go to Peking for a stay of unspecified duration: this to the great distress of his own people, who were vociferous in their protests and pleadings. At the very time, almost at the hour when he was setting out on his enforced journey a fearful flood, caused by the collapse of the barriers of a lake which then discharged itself into a river, swept over the southern part of Tibet, carrying death and devastation to all the places along the river bank; a conjunction of events sufficiently extraordinary to cause some to ask themselves whether this was not perhaps a heaven-sent warning, called forth by a long series of profanations of which this was but the most recent example. Nor can such an explanation, in any similar case, be ruled out; for the two things, natural happening and supernatural interference, do not exclude one another in the complex pattern that the causality of the Universe is continually weaving around us. Even a quite ordinary event, in fact, displays two faces, the one apparent to the senses and the other intelligible through its symbolism, and it needs the art of discernment in order to read beyond and between the apparent "facts" to the point of being able to interpret the "signs of the times", and discernment itself is pre-eminently a spiritual gift.

The Dalai Lama's absence at Peking proved shorter than had been expected: in heeding popular outcry and letting him return the Chinese acted in a politic way which, had they followed it more wholeheartedly, might have taken them far towards winning over the Tibetans, whose chief wish was to be left undisturbed; an older China might have profited by this chance, but with the Communists their ideological fury came in the way. For a time, indeed, Lhasa breathed again, hoping against hope—it was the lull preceding a new and still more violent tempest which, starting from the easterly provinces of Kham and Amdo where Chinese interference was being most strongly felt and resented, gradually spread across the country till suddenly, in 1959, armed resistance broke out at Lhasa itself, provoked by the belief that the Dalai Lama's personal liberty was threatened: the story of his reluctant but by then unavoidable escape to India, under cover of spontaneous demonstrations by the citizens who thought only of his safety, has often been told and need not be repeated here.

When all is said and done, interest in the tragic events that have overwhelmed Tibet, indignation at the savaging of a people, and sympathy for the man himself must not cause one to lose sight of the essential fact about the Dalai Lama, namely that his is an *activity of presence,* nothing else; all the rest about him remains accessory and contingent. It is, however, inevitable that at the popular level the reverence and loyalty of which he is the focus should result in a certain blurring of the outlines, by a confusing of function and person, as invariably happens in such cases. It is as when, in a Catholic country, the papal infallibility, as traditionally determined, becomes confused in the popular mind with the more or less profound opinions of the person temporarily called upon to fill the sacred office. Such confusions, inescapable as they are, do not present a serious danger, provided they do not go too far; but in a time like this, when so many ill-wishers are out to discredit religion itself by seizing on every possible failure on the part of its followers, it is highly important that the true doctrine should be restated in generally intelligible terms and with the severest accuracy.

One can but repeat it: inasmuch as he is a human being and thus subject to individual limitations and their consequences, the Dalai Lama, though he can become a saint through spiritual effort or display such and such shortcomings or remain in the human sense undistinguished (all these cases have occurred historically), can neither add to nor subtract from the influence that, for the time being, has chosen to radiate through his person. It is but natural that when a Dalai Lama acts in an obviously merciful way (as when the thirteenth of the line abolished various cruel punishments used of old) people should say "it is Chenrezig that has spoken"—this statement is not wholly false as far as it goes, since compassion, when genuine, is always referable to its source; and conversely, if a Dalai Lama fails in some respect or other, it is no less natural that this failure should be glossed over as something in no wise attributable to the Bodhisattva as such. But nevertheless an element of error is there and it is well to point it out when treating of this theme: indeed to do so amounts to a voicing of that compassion which can never remain truly itself if discrimination be denied its rights.

The Round of Existence

9
The Tibetan Tradition
Its presiding idea

Some years ago, when writing my book *Peaks and Lamas,* I set myself the task of describing, stage by stage, those wanderings along the Himalayan borderland which had led me to the discovery of that form of spirituality that has its home on the snowy tableland of Tibet. It goes without saying, however, that the picture presented at that time remained incomplete in many ways; anything like a detailed analysis of the various strands that together go to weave the web of Tibetan life could only be undertaken by one who had first gained access to Tibet proper, where the civilization in question could be studied under its most typical as well as its most vigorous form; but it was not until 1947 that the necessary authorization to enter the country was granted. Nevertheless, enough had been learned up to date to allow of a number of generalizations affecting the whole Tibetan world, since it is plainly evident that through its far-flung territories a certain type of human existence is recognizable, owing both its essential unity and its outward form to the influence of the selfsame tradition, having done so, moreover, for many centuries. One has but to compare the account contained in the biography of the poet-saint Mila Repa[1] with what is to be seen today to become convinced of the extraordinary unity, as well as vitality, of Tibetan institutions. Apart from such changes as

---

[1] Mila Repa lived in the eleventh century A.D. His "legend", in autobiographical form, is one of the most moving spiritual documents of the world. It exists in several European translations of varying quality, including a most perfect rendering into French by Professor Charles Bacot.

must come, almost imperceptibly, with the mere passage of time, the ways in which people think, act, and speak and the standards by which they judge men and things do not appear to have altered in any very fundamental way since those early days, and the life of Mila Repa still provides the best-drawn picture of Tibetan life that exists, besides offering a most vivid commentary on that doctrine which, above all else, has given to that life both shape and direction.

The last remark calls for some additional comment, since it contains an allusion to a question of very wide import, one that is of general applicability to all traditional civilizations and not merely to Tibet—namely, the question of what is the principle of discrimination between one form of the Perennial Wisdom and another, causing them to be externally distinct as well as consistent internally; for without the operation of some such principle there would be no excuse for a formal discontinuity as between the several traditions, serving as they all do as ways of approach to the imperishable Knowledge, from which every thought of distinction is manifestly to be excluded, whether of form or otherwise.

The fact is that every civilization that can be called authentic is endowed with a principle of unity peculiar to itself, which is reflected, in varying degrees, in all the institutions of the civilization in question. By a principle of unity is meant a predominant idea, corresponding to a given aspect of the truth, which has been recipient of particular emphasis and for the expressing of which, if one may so put it, that civilization shows a peculiar "genius". Emphasis on an aspect must, however, have its price: that is to say, the highlight of attention cannot be focused on one aspect of reality without producing its compensating shadows, affecting other aspects. Each separate formal embodiment of the traditional wisdom, therefore, corresponds, as it were, to a difference of intellectual perspective; and the key to the understanding of whatever is explicit or implicit in any given form resides in a thorough assimilation of the dominant idea running through that form—in other words, of its principle of unity.

In seeking to determine which is the principle of unity animating the Tibetan civilization one must beware of being satisfied with an easy answer, such as saying that this principle is no other than the Buddhist doctrine itself; for though this statement is correct as far as it goes, it lacks precision, failing as it does to indicate which one, out of a whole body of ideas comprised within the one doctrinal plan, has been recipient of that greater emphasis required for the molding of an entire traditional structure according to a particular form, and, as it were, in its image. Though one knows that Buddhism, by imposing certain fundamental ideas, has become the rule of life over very wide areas extending from Ceylon to Japan and that this has produced a certain community of outlook among all the peoples that have come within the Buddhist orbit, one cannot fail to recognize that in this general whole certain clearly distinguishable forms of civilization are to be found, the intellectual frontiers of which are not primarily determined by the Buddhist influence. The common presence of Buddhism does not, for instance, warrant one's placing the Chinese and Tibetan civilizations under one heading, even though they are next-door neighbors; and if Buddhism is admittedly a factor affecting both, this fact has been insufficient to produce any very marked likeness in their respective points of view, let alone identity.

The chief difference between them lies in the fact that whereas in Tibet the Buddhist tradition is everything, having completely replaced its Bön-po predecessor, in China Buddhism was something in the nature of a graft, admittedly a most timely and successful one, upon a civilization of which the pattern, in all essentials, had already been set before the importation of the foreign influence. Since nothing in the existing Chinese form was found to be actually incompatible with the Buddhist point of view, the latest arrival from India found no difficulty in taking its place in the traditional life of the Far East on equal terms with its two other great constituents, namely Taoism, representative of an intellectuality so refined as to be adapted for the use of an exceptionally qualified *élite* only, and Confucianism. This latter is not, as is commonly supposed, a separate creation, still less a "religion", but corresponds to that side of the Chinese tradition in which all without exception are able to participate, concerning itself as it does with social institutions and human relationships in general—the latter being given expression especially through its characteristic concepts of the race, the family and the family ancestors. It might also be mentioned, in passing, that in the course of time Buddhism and Taoism engaged in many intellectual exchanges, some of which gave rise to that school, so rich in spiritual initiative, that is commonly known in the West under its Japanese name of Zen.

Similar considerations apply equally well in India during the centuries when Hinduism and Buddhism co-existed there as separate currents of tradition: both continued to belong to the same civilization, the characteristic forms of which had been laid down at a time long anterior to the specific formulation of the Buddhist teachings. In any case, both in virtue of its origin and by the nature of its thought, Buddhism remains an Indian doctrine, having derived most of its basic conceptions, if not all, from the common root-stock of the Indian metaphysic. It is not on that score that Buddhism can be called original; nor, indeed, does it put forward any such claim, since the Buddha Himself was always at pains to repudiate, as a monstrous heresy, any suggestion that he had come to teach something new in the matter of doctrine; it is only modern Western writers, themselves imbued with humanistic prejudices, who have been determined at all costs to discover in Buddhism a radical innovation amounting to a revolt against the traditional spirit, and in the Buddha an early revolutionary working on Protestant lines.

Where Buddhism was highly original, however, was in respect of its methods, affecting both the way of expounding the ever-abiding principles and the forms of spiritual discipline that went with their knowledge. Indeed, but for a large measure of originality in the manner of restating the eternal truths the Buddhist apostles would have been unable to carry out their appointed task of adapting the Indian metaphysic so as to render it eventually assimilable by non-Indian peoples, especially by the Yellow races, whose mentality was so very different from that of the Indians.

The Tibetan branch was one of the latest offshoots from the main stem of Buddhism, having only come into being during the seventh and eighth centuries after Christ, chiefly through the work of Indian monks from Bengal and Kashmir. While accepting all the basic ideas taught by the Buddha, which it continued to share with all the other peoples of similar spiritual allegiance, Tibet early developed certain clearly marked features of its own, to the point of giving rise to a distinct form of civilization, comparable, on every count, with the other principal traditional forms of the world. This is possibly due in part to the incorporation of such features of the previous Bön-po tradition as could usefully be readapted; it seems unlikely, however, that any element specific to a form actually in process of replacement by another form would retain sufficient intrinsic vitality to provide a whole civilization with its principle of unity, in the sense given to that term at the beginning of this chapter—that is to say, with an idea both distinct and powerful enough to create and nourish its own forms, conferring on them the means for perpetuating their own character through long ages and of impressing it firmly and unmistakably upon the face of things and upon the thoughts of men.

In fact, the idea that enjoys pride of place in the Tibetan tradition is one that figures in the Buddhist doctrine as originally introduced from India. This presiding idea, coloring the outlook of sage and simple peasant alike (as we were repeatedly enabled to observe during our journeys), is the conception of Bodhisattvahood, the state of the fully

197

awakened being who, though under no further constraint by that Law of Causality which he has transcended, yet freely continues to espouse the vicissitudes of the Round of Existence in virtue of his Self-identification with all the creatures still involved in egocentric delusion and consequent suffering. Such an attitude must not, however, be confused with a kind of sentimental "altruism" in the social sense; indeed a moment's reflection will show that one who has finally been set free from the false notion of a permanent "I", personally experiencable, is at the same time automatically rid of its correlative notion of "other". The Bodhisattva behaves as he does precisely because, for him, any kind of conceptual polarization is inoperative, because, to his singleness of eye, all contrasted pairs such as the Round of Existence and *Nirvana*, Bondage and Deliverance, Body-Mind and Spirit, together with all the subsidiary oppositions born of such contrasts, are alike canceled in the unity—or, as the Tibetans would say, in the "two-lessness"—of That which he himself realizes as the All-Principle (Tibetan *Kun-ji*), eternal Cause and ground of all phenomenal existence.

The Bodhisattva's compassion, or what in human language is described as such, translates into individually intelligible terms the universal "non-altruity" of his point of view; even while in *Nirvana* he experiences the world, according to that measure of reality which belongs to it—and one must not forget that suffering, in the deepest sense of the word, is inseparable from the very fact of becoming, which cannot in any sense be experienced without it. Likewise, even when dwelling in the midst of a changeful world, he does not cease to know the changeless bliss of *Nirvana,* and if to us the two experiences seem distinct and mutually exclusive, they are not so to the possessor of true insight, because such a one never feels tempted to abstract one or other of them from the unity of their common and transcendent principle, so that, from his point of view, they are not even conceivable apart. Thus the Bodhisattva, through a perfect realization of his own essential identity with all beings, thereby suffers with them and for them, as the eternal victim self-immolated upon the altar of their existence; but even in that suffering itself he perceives the joy unspeakable—both the light and its inseparable shadows alike yield up their closest-guarded secret under the scrutiny of his incorruptible impartiality.[2]

The status of a Bodhisattva has been defined (though, strictly speaking, the very word "definition", implying as it does the idea of limitation, is here inapplicable) as that of one who realizes Wisdom as Knowledge of the Void, and Method as Universal Compassion; the first-named representing the purely transcendent aspect of his realization, while the second implies an unblurred recognition of the Face of Divinity even through the veil of separativity as constituted by the worlds—in other words, a not merely theoretical but an effective awareness that the transcendent aspect of Truth is not other than the immanent and vice versa. Thus, if the being is first called upon to seek "deliverance" from form and its restrictions in order to become awake to that reality which dwells "beyond names and forms", yet, in the deepest sense of all, it can be said, following the *Lankavatara Sutra*, that there is really nothing to be acquired, nothing to be delivered from, no Way, no Goal, no Round, no *Nirvana*, nor indeed

---

[2] A parallel, though one very different in its formal expression, can be established by reference to Christian theology, in that it can be said that the ultimate goal of the Christian life consists in giving complete effect to the Doctrine of the Two Natures, central theme of the Christian tradition as such, whereby Jesus, the Man of Sorrows, and the Glorified Christ eternally seated at the right hand of Power are simultaneously realized as one and not two; or, in other words, the Christ who suffered crucifixion temporally upon the tree at Calvary and upon the cross of His own incarnation as a finite being, and indeed cosmically upon the very fact of Creation itself, and that Word of God by whom all things were made, though they respectively suggest notions of suffering and blissfulness that to the eye of ignorance seem mutually exclusive or, at best, successively realizable, are essentially inseparable conceptions neither of which can be fully realized in isolation from the other.

anything needing to be done or undone. However, lest this kind of paradoxical statement, so common in the Mahayanist writings, should be unconsciously twisted into an excuse for taking up a "quietist" position, it is well to remember that the knowledge in question itself implies the most intensely "active" attitude conceivable, a concentration so impenetrable that it is a matter of indifference to its possessor whether he happens to find himself in the most secluded of mountain retreats or engaged on exemplary and redemptive work among the crowded habitations of men, or else in one of the heavens—or the hells. His is not a solitude that depends on any special conditions of place or time, true solitude being indeed but another name for that Voidness which is also the Fullness, a first-fruit of that self-naughting which is also Self-knowing.

Three levels are broadly distinguishable in respect of the comprehension of the Real: first, things may be regarded from the point of view of Ignorance, which is that of the ordinary man, concerned as he is with appearances and with his own reactions to them. It is he, the "common man", held up to flattery in our day as if he were a very pattern of humanity, who is the pathetic dreamer, the incorrigible sentimentalist, the romantic, in contrast to the spiritual man, now at a discount, who is the only true realist, the "practical man" in the widest sense of the word. From an ignorant or "profane" point of view things are considered under the aspect of separativity only, and treated as if they were self-contained entities, that is to say, as if each of them were "carrying within itself its own sufficient cause". Under such circumstances the manifested world appears in the guise of an unresolvable multiplicity, in which the individualization and consequently the opposition of persons or things (through their mutual limitation and inescapable competition) is raised to the highest possible power, thus spelling insecurity and suffering for all concerned: such being, moreover, the inevitable fruit of dualism, of participation in the Tree of Knowledge of Good and Evil.

Secondly, there is the view that comes with an awakening perception of the fallacy underlying the world and its formal appearances. In that case the disillusioned being seeks deliverance in the formlessness of the Unmanifest, where all things subsist unchanged and unchangeable within the bosom of their parent cause, in a state that might be described as one of permanent actuality, whence their coming out to be manifested in one of the worlds can only partake of the nature of an illusion; that is to say, their existence pertains to a lesser order of reality that masks, by the various phenomena it gives rise to, its own lack of true selfhood.[3] This point of view corresponds with the attainment of a *Nirvana* still able to be regarded as one of the twin terms of an opposition, the other term being that state of Ignorance mentioned previously, whereby beings remain imprisoned in the Round and subject to change and suffering. Those who attain such a state of knowledge are usually referred to, in the Mahayanist books, under the name of *Pratyeka Buddhas* (the Tibetan equivalent means Self-Buddhas), with whom are also coupled those whom the Tibetans call "hearers" (in Sanskrit known as *Sravakas*) and who are supposed, though somewhat unfairly, to represent the devotees of the rival Hinayanist school, that to which the southern Buddhists, those of Ceylon and Burma, belong. These two types have provided a favorite

---

[3] One must remind the reader that current loose speaking has practically converted the word "illusion" into a synonym of "unreal"; and this in turn has given rise to frequent misunderstandings on the subject of the Buddhist teachings about the illusory nature of the world and its contents. Nothing can ever be opposable to reality; something that is truly unreal cannot enjoy any kind of existence, not even in imagination; whereas an illusion is something that more or less makes game of the senses of an observer by seeming to possess a character other than its own; typically by appearing more self-sufficient than it really is.

target for criticism on the part of all the Mahayanist writers, whose mention of them has come to constitute a kind of refrain, a matter of "method", probably, rather than one to be taken as referring to actual facts. Thus it is said that the *Sravakas* and *Pratyeka Buddhas* rest content with deliverance as far as they themselves are concerned (hence the name *Self-Buddhas*), but fail to include in their point of view all their fellow beings still condemned to struggle in the whirlpool of the Round; in other words, they succeed in breaking loose from the world and its illusion, but they are unable to reintegrate it positively, stopping short, as they do, at negation. For such as they, therefore, *Nirvana*, Deliverance, though undoubtedly attained in one sense, yet remains essentially as the Non-Round; just as the Round itself continues to be similarly regarded as Non-*Nirvana*, without any means being found of reducing the contrasted experiences to unity. Thus the withdrawal of attention from the world as such, which marks a legitimate and indeed a necessary stage in the process of enlightenment, if it should ever be taken for a final term, can land one in an intellectual blind alley, bringing about a kind of lofty self-imprisonment, a withdrawal into a blissful supra-consciousness which yet implies privation of the one essential thing, since it stops short of the supreme non-duality.

Thirdly and lastly, there is the point of view (if one can still describe as such what is really a total synthesis embracing all possible points of view) of Bodhisattvahood, whereby the essential non-duality of the Round, represented by Form, and of *Nirvana*, represented by Voidness, is clearly perceived as Knowledge compared to which, as a typical Mahayanist writer would probably have added, "all the virtues and achievements of countless millions of *Pratyeka Buddhas* and *Sravakas* during successive aeons are nothing worth." This supreme realization, goal of the spiritual life, goes under the name of the *Prajna Paramita* or Wisdom Transcendent (the Tibetans actually give it as "the transcending of Wisdom"); and a

Bodhisattva is one who has succeeded in realizing this doctrine effectively, so that it can be said that possession of the *Prajna Paramita* constitutes the characteristic *note* by which the Bodhisattva is to be known.[4]

Once having realized it, and from the very fact of having done so, the Bodhisattva, though no longer involved in Existence under any law of necessity, freely decides—so the saying goes—"to remain in the Round as long as a single blade of grass shall remain undelivered from suffering," so that one and all may pass together through *Nirvana*'s gates as the single, recollected Non-Duality they already are in essence. Needless to say, however, the sentimentalism of the masses, even in Tibet, does not spare this doctrine altogether, for even there people will persist in reading into its symbolism some kind of moral lesson, according to which the Bodhisattva, in contrast to the selfish *Pratyeka Buddhas*, "refuses *Nirvana*", out of compassion for the beings (ourselves!) undergoing the painful experiences of the Round of Existence. Rightly interpreted, even such a colored picture is not entirely devoid of sense; its underlying implications are fairly clear, but naturally the tendency of simple minds is to take each detail separately and literally, thus sacrificing the unity of the idea in favor of some version more in accord with their own individualistic bias.

There is, however, one difficulty of interpretation which does actually arise from the fact that, according to the usual

---

[4] There is a famous formula that expresses this doctrine as concisely as possible; it is taken from the *sutra* bearing the same title of *Prajna Paramita* and runs as follows: —

> Form (it is) void:
> The Void Itself (is) form.

By these words the Supreme Identity is given expression, hence this sentence may be regarded as an epitome of all Knowledge. In Tibetan, the fact that a separate word "is" does not enter into the composition of this formula, greatly adds to its doctrinal power.

convention, Bodhisattvahood denotes a state penultimate to the attainment of Buddhahood and not the supreme realization itself. Thus it is said that the Bodhisattva "takes possession" of the final revelation that makes of him a Buddha, and similarly the Buddha is spoken of as having been "still a Bodhisattva" at such and such a time. In face of what has been said above it may well be asked how a Bodhisattva can be regarded as inferior in status to a Buddha, seeing that Bodhisattvahood, as we have already seen, corresponds by definition to the state of one who not only has realized the Void, in a transcendent sense, but also has realized it in the World itself, in an immanent sense, this double realization (as we are still forced to describe it) being for him not two-fold but one and only. It is evident that the attainment of this, the supreme unitive Knowledge, is in fact that which constitutes *Nirvana* or Buddhahood, so that it is difficult to see how Bodhisattvahood can be referred to as a penultimate state at all—yet the very existence of the two separate terms must be intended to correspond to some reality in spite of an apparent redundancy affecting their use in certain contexts.

The explanation appears to lie in a variable use of the name Bodhisattva itself. In the first place it can be used more loosely, in order to denote the all-but-perfected saint, on the threshold of Buddhahood, or even any unusually saintly person—I was once told, for instance, that "we will find you 'a Bodhisattva' to be your teacher." In the second place it can be used in reference to one who is identical with Buddha by right of Knowledge, but who, in the exercise of his work of salvation for the benefit of creatures, *recapitulates* the stages of the Way for *exemplary reasons*, as a "shower of the Way".[5] In that sense he redescends into the Round rather than remains in it, though the latter impression may be produced on the

---

[5] This title is one that is habitually bestowed on the Buddha Himself.

minds of beings, prone to deception by passing appearances. One then has to do with an *Avatara* (to use the well-known Sanskrit term); that is to say, with a specific descent of the Principle into Manifestation, a descent—to quote the words of Ananda Coomaraswamy—of the Light of Lights, as *a* light but not as another Light. As we have just pointed out, such a descent implies the assumption of a limit—in other words, of an individual form, or of something analogous if the descent were to take place into a world other than our own, defined, as it would then be, by another set of conditions; but such a self-limiting need not shock us, since the realization of the *Prajna Paramita,* of the essential non-duality of the Void and Form, obviously carries with it the power of assuming any and every form at will, as well as no form. Thus it is written of him who is established in this Knowledge that "there will be no end of my Avataras, who will appear in inconceivable millions of numbers and shapes, and who will adopt various methods suitable for the control of every kind of being."

At this point it may be advisable to guard against a possible misunderstanding as being one likely to arise in consequence of certain prevailing tendencies of present-day thought. That such might well be the case is evidenced by the following question that was recently put to me by a friend who asked whether, according to the precedent of the Bodhisattva's non-withdrawal from the Round of Existence, one was not justified in regarding as fundamentally sound the attitude of the man who says that he is prepared to make the best of the world as he finds it, enjoying life as far as he can, without troubling his head overmuch with thoughts of the beyond and the hereafter; was this not an indication of a more realistic outlook, it was asked, than the "other-worldliness" of the typically religious view of life?

At a first examination it might indeed appear that those who argue thus are not entirely at fault. Nevertheless, there is a fallacy lurking behind the question so put, even without taking into account the mixture of motives behind it, motives that are bound up with a hankering, on the part of the modern world, after a belief that the fruits of spirituality can be enjoyed without renouncing certain cherished habits and prejudices of an egocentric nature; while there also enters in sometimes a not entirely ununderstandable feeling of sympathy for the good-natured tolerance of the man who is prepared to live and let live, as contrasted with the narrow exclusiveness that so frequently mars the purity of an otherwise sincere religious outlook.

The real defect in the argument, however, is of quite a different order from these superficial matters of feeling, residing as it does in a false assimilation made on the strength of a purely specious likeness between the attitude of the amiable, easy-going and commonsense person already mentioned and that of the Bodhisattva, with his realization of universal nonduality. The two cases differ fundamentally for the simple reason that in the first instance the world is accepted *passively*—that is to say, is taken at its face value, under the aspect of separativity extending to everything within it, without any serious attempt being made to reduce things to unity through the knowledge of a principle superior to their multiplicity and distinction. The phenomenal reality of the world is thus treated as if it were valid in its own right; in other words, it is considered from the point of view of Ignorance, and this is as true in the case of a man who tries to make the best of things as of a confirmed pessimist. At most one has to do with a more amiable brand of profanity, as compared with what is obviously a more disagreeable one.

Such a view of things does in fact start off by ignoring what is a prime condition for any aspirant towards Bodhisattvahood; namely, an understanding of the essentially impermanent character of the world and its contents, not merely in a theoretical sense, as when one studies a doctrine through books, nor in an "ideal" sense, through developing a kind of vague sympathy for that same doctrine, but effectively, so that the knowledge in question may take root in one's very being, causing the self-sufficiency of separate objects to lose all its fascination for the mind; for only when attention has been thus withdrawn from whatever is fragmentary and perishable will it be possible to become poised in "one-pointed" contemplation of That which alone possesses the true nature of Selfhood, "being unto Itself its own sufficient Cause."

One of the author's early teachers, the monk-painter Gyalthsan of Phiyang in Ladak, repeatedly said that without an effective grasp of the Doctrine of Impermanence all further progress in the Way was an impossibility; in this negating of all that is in itself negative (because regarded in abstraction from its principle) is to be found the clue to the mystery. It can thus be readily understood that if the Bodhisattva is free to remain in the world for the sake of the creatures still subject to the delusion of separativity, he does so with his eyes open. Where they see "other" things all around them, things that seem to them only too solid and substantial, he only perceives their voidness, or in other words their lack of genuine Self-nature. Multiple forms that, to the creature, appear opaque and self-contained have become for him of such perfect transparency as to reveal, or to veil no longer, the supreme Suchness, devoid as it is of all particularization, restriction, relativity, distinction, and the like. Nay, more, to his singleness of eye, the negative Voidness of worldly objects and the positive Voidness that translates a freedom from form and all other limiting conditions are but one Voidness unqualified, coinciding, as they do, in that ultimate Reality concerning which all one dares to say is "Not this, not this."

Whereas the profane man, the "ordinary person", is in the Round by compulsion of mediate causes, "under the law" as St. Paul would have said, the Bodhisattva is there but "in sport", that is to say freely, in virtue of his identification with that which being alone absolutely unlimited is also alone absolutely free. Where the former submits to the world and its ways, with or without a semblance of willingness, but in any case in passive mode, the latter may be said to reintegrate the world in active mode; while somewhere midway between these two positions can be placed the *Pratyeka Buddha* (with whom the common run of religious-minded persons might be associated, since their picture of a personal salvation is in many ways comparable with his, though on a more restricted plane), of whom it can be said that he has effectively rejected the bonds of worldly existence (by realizing its impermanence), but has stopped short of reintegrating it. In his case it is rather *Nirvana* that is accepted in passive mode, as against the Bodhisattva's realization, which is active through and through to the point of melting away every factor of opposition in the ultimate crucible of non-dual knowledge. Thus, for him, the realization of the impermanence of the world and the eventual reintegration of that world hang together: the first, leading to Knowledge of the universal voidness, corresponds to Wisdom, and the second, symbolized by the Bodhisattva's Compassion, corresponds to Method, this two-fold realization being, as already mentioned, the "note" by which true Bodhisattvahood can be recognized. This disposes of any claims made on behalf of the man who attempts to integrate either himself or the world without at the same time fathoming their impermanence in more than just the superficial sense of a theoretical admission that everything must some day have an end. It was important to clear up this point before returning to the consideration of the Bodhisattva as he appears from the standpoint of humanity—that is to say, under the inevitable fragmentation into aspects that goes with any view short of his own all-embracing comprehension. From the point of view of individual beings, that aspect of his realization which strikes them most vividly is his Compassion, the fundamental character of which has, I hope, been made somewhat clearer as a result of the foregoing rather long-drawn out theoretical explanations.

It must be repeated that this "Cosmic Charity" (to borrow an expressive term belonging to the Islamic doctrine) is something essentially different from the ordinary human feelings of pity, hopelessly tangled, as they usually are, with self-pity; though it would also be true to say that whatever is genuine in human pity is a reflection, at the individual level, of the limitless compassion flowing out of the Bodhisattva's heart, for which reason even that feeling is able to be taken for an adequate symbol of its universal prototype. It is also good to remember that perfect charity is not a quality opposable to justice, to order or harmony in the widest sense, since its realization is an impossibility in default of an equally perfect impartiality or "non-attachment". Towards the suffering beings in the Round, continually drugged with the three poisons of Ignorance, Anger and Desire-Attachment, the Bodhisattva, like the good physician that he is, will exercise his merciful office not with a view to a mere assuaging of symptoms that will leave the more deep-seated causes of the disease untouched; but in the manner most conducive to his patient's real recovery he will be prepared to employ every kind of "skillful means", which may at times partake of the severest character, and he will show himself under every appropriate aspect, from the gentlest to the most appalling, nor will he stop short at any ministration however pleasant or however rigorous until, as the saying goes, "the last blade of grass shall have attained Deliverance."

This lesson is clearly brought out in the iconographical representations of the various Bodhisattvas such as are displayed on the walls of every temple, for they are made to appear not merely under their benign or attractive forms but also in a guise grim and fearsome to behold. Even the All-Merciful Chenrezig himself, the supreme protector of Tibet and explicit type of a Buddha's mercy, displays awe-inspiring forms for the sake of sinners and their conversion. Similarly, the Bodhisattva of Wisdom, *Jampal*, can also appear as *Dorje-Jigched*, the Ever-subsisting Maker of Fear, chosen to be the chief tutelary of the Yellow-Hatted Order, this aspect being depicted as a most terrible apparition, many-headed and provided with countless limbs, clasped in the arms of his equally bloodthirsty Consort-Energy and dancing ecstatically upon the prostrate bodies of men and animals, whose ignorance makes them his victims. Those who are able to penetrate into the symbolism of this redoubtable double of the All-Wise One will also know that his dance is no other than the Round of Existence itself and his kingdom the very process of Becoming. If the presence of an individual form, with the restrictions that this implies, spells a proportionate measure of suffering for the being concerned, that suffering (which must of course be interpreted in the widest possible sense of the word) can itself be considered under either of the two complementary aspects of justice and mercy: under the first, because privation, such as is implied by the existence of a limit of any kind, produces suffering of its own accord, because, fundamentally, the suffering *is* the privation and not something added to it by way of retributive sanction or otherwise—though at a certain level of realization the latter symbolism is both theoretically legitimate as well as useful practically when considered from the point of view of the being's own spiritual development; under the second, because suffering, in so far as it leads men into self-questioning, is able to become a pointer towards the spiritual path, being thus indeed counted as the first of the Four Truths that together constitute the Buddha's call to a radical change of heart, to that *metanoesis* which is so inadequately rendered by the word "repentance" with its implicitly sentimental notion of regret. Viewed under such an aspect, therefore, suffering must be regarded first and foremost as part of the mechanism of a merciful providence, but for which there would be small hope of deliverance for anyone. It is not a question of trying to explain away the facts of suffering "optimistically" by resorting to the use of a euphemistic phraseology, but of showing the place that it occupies in relation to the aspect of divine Clemency, as well as its more obvious connexion with the complementary aspect of Rigor.

The above considerations also have some bearing on a point that has often worried European students of Eastern doctrines, who fail to understand how Desire, whether admitted to play the leading part in the Round of Existence ascribed to it by Buddhism or not, can ever come to be extinguished in a being; since it is evident that it cannot be restrained by sheer will-power such as can only stop short at dealing with the action prompted by this or that desire, either by way of impulsion or repression, whereas the desire itself will have arisen, in the first place, out of the substratum of the being's unconsciousness where the will is inoperative; this, quite apart from the fact that the nature of Will itself is too closely related to that of Desire pure and simple to provide an entirely adequate instrument for its control. For the average Western mind, with its habit of concentrating all its attention on problems of moral casuistry—that is to say, on questions concerning the right or wrong use of will-power in respect of actions—the Buddha's teaching on the subject of desire and its cessation is apt to prove extremely puzzling.

Yet this side of the doctrine is not so abstruse as to defy at least a theoretical grasp of the principles underlying it. What is usually missed in the argument is the fact that, just as in the case of suffering, unsatisfied desire, though in one sense an evil in that it interposes a distraction between the being and its realization of unity, is also just (therefore a good) in so far as it genuinely registers a lack of something—the pertinent question is a lack of what? In fact all our separate desires are proportioned exactly to the measure of our privation of the One Essential, and if we treat different things as successively desirable or the reverse, this habit arises from a failure to understand that nothing whatsoever can be called desirable excepting only *The Desirable,* whence it is easy to see that the extinction of all desire and its fulfillment hang together, in exactly the same sense as death to self (the "self-denial" of the Gospels) and birth to Self spell one and the same thing. Our alternate loves and hates, from the most trivial to the most noble or ignoble are, one and all, an unconscious tribute laid by Ignorance at the feet of Knowledge, so that, in that sense, they once again are as much an expression of the Divine Mercy (because their attendant suffering is the factor that continually impels a being to seek a way of liberation) as they are an expression of the Divine Rigor through the privation registered by their very presence, which constitutes its own automatically operative sanction.

Let us return, however, to the consideration of the symbolism behind the great variety of forms described in the Tantric books or otherwise occurring in works of art of Tantric inspiration, a symbolism that, moreover, provides a most important *technical* resource for the practice of the various spiritual disciplines attached to the Tantric doctrines, both Hindu and Buddhist. Thus one is led to see that the kindlier aspects can, when necessary, be made to function as their own apparent opposites, by which means both the complementarism and the interpenetration of the aspects of mercy and severity are vividly brought out, only to be succeeded by the coincidence of those same two aspects in a "two-less" identity that dissolves all the force of their opposition. Again and again the symbolical relationships are reversed in an unending play of antithesis and identification, as beatific forms give way to fierce ones, the most repellent features of which are, however, in their turn found to symbolize characteristic attributes of the benign aspect and so on; until in the end, by dint of alternate manifestation, interchange and dissolution of forms, Form itself loses its restrictive power over the mind of the devotee, leaving him henceforth free to contemplate through the eye of true Intelligence the non-duality of That which is to be known by those who find the way to carry their solitude ever with them, even in the world. So is one brought back once again to the Bodhisattva's knowledge, whereby the immanent is seen to be ultimately indistinguishable from the transcendent, the phenomenal from the real, the world of forms from the Void Itself. In all this there is never a question of any "monistic" or "pantheistic" confusion—one is bound to mention this point in view of repeated attempts to foist these purely Western notions, not very old at that, upon Oriental thought, from a variety of motives—but of the realization of a unity which is called "two-less" from the very fact that in it all things are essentially "fused but not confused", to quote a phrase of Meister Eckhart.

This two-less Knowledge, possession of which constitutes the Sage, is as the warp to the entire weft of Tibetan tradition. One encounters it at every turn, now more explicit, now at once veiled and revealed by symbols, now faintly echoed in the thoughts and words of quite simple people, like a theme that unfolds itself in continual self-pursuit through an endless series of episodes and modulations, a fugue that will not modulate into its final close "so long as one insect or one blade of grass remains undelivered from the Round." The Bodhisattva provides the specific type of the spiritual life in Tibet, and it is in such terms that the idea of "sanctity" is always interpreted in all the lands where the lamaic tradition holds sway.

Space does not allow of anything like a comprehensive survey of the manifold applications to which the conception of Bodhisattvahood has given rise in all orders; nor would such an attempt work out profitably for the reader, since it could only result in leaving the essential idea snowed under a mass of indigestible, if separately interesting, detail; the important thing to grasp, however, is that it is this doctrine that gives its form to the idea of spirituality as conceived in all the Tibetan world, especially under its two principal aspects of Compassion and Skillful Means. Sufficient has been said concerning what the former is or is not for little room to be left for misunderstanding as to the nature of this characteristic trait of the Bodhisattva; while in regard to the latter one can only point out the fact that the saint, in Tibet, is regarded first and foremost as one endowed with "skill", as it were an "artist in spirituality", and only secondarily under the aspect of individual goodness. Here one sees a certain difference of point of view, as between the Buddhist and the ordinary Christian picture of sainthood, bound up with the degrees of emphasis respectively given to ethical and intellectual values. Not that one wishes to suggest the existence of a fundamental incompatibility between the two conceptions; all that need be pointed out is that in the Buddhist tradition the practice of those portions of "the Eightfold Path" that relate to action and moral behavior in general, though considered indispensable just as in the case of the sister tradition, are on the whole taken for granted when speaking of the saints, the chief attention in their case being drawn to the purely intellectual virtue of Perfect Contemplation, which forms the climax of the eightfold catalogue; whereas in the case of Christianity, though its teaching on the supremacy of Contemplation over Action does not differ in principle from that of the Oriental traditions, there has been a certain tendency, much increased in modern times through the intrusion of "humanism" (itself an anti-Christian movement), to overstress individual and especially social considerations. Moreover, abuses apart, such a tendency always goes to a certain extent with the "religious" as compared with the purely metaphysical point of view, influencing not only popular conceptions but also many perfectly orthodox formulations of the doctrine itself.

Two examples will have to suffice as illustrations of the workings of the Bodhisattva idea in the spiritual life of the Tibetans. The one applies to the people at large, though admittedly at many different degrees of comprehension; the other to those who have proceeded a considerable way in the direction of realization, or at least whose aspirations and efforts are definitely set in that direction. The first example is taken from the widespread practice of invocation, usually on a rosary, of the Mani formula already mentioned in an earlier chapter, which itself embodies a traditional communication the origin of which goes back to the Bodhisattva Chenrezig, the Patron of Tibet, for whose influence the person of the Dalai Lama himself serves as a focus.

When a person is about to begin saying his rosary he often preludes his reciting of the actual formula by a short dedicatory verse in honor of Chenrezig, its originator, addressed to him under his alternative name of the All-Compassionate. After this follows the repetition of the Mani, for a longer or shorter time, with more or less concentration as the case may be. When these devotions are finished, the invoking person (who incidentally will have been the recipient of an initiation authorizing him to use this particular ritual support) concludes with another short verse, already quoted once, the gist of which is as follows: "By the merit of this (invocation) to (my) self having accrued (i.e. by my having realized) the power of Chenrezig, may beings without a single exception be established in the land of the Norm (that is to say, may they attain the supreme realization)." However attentively or carelessly these thoughts may be uttered, they contain an explicit as well as implicit reference to the "Bodhisattva's vow" not to enter *Nirvana* before all beings have been delivered from the Round and its suffering; the important thing to note in the present instance is that this formula postulates a point of view that does not stop short at a personal deliverance, like that for which the *Pratyeka Buddhas* are constantly being reproached, since is goes as far as actually to envisage a redescent into the world with a view to its eventual reintegration in the divine Non-duality. That it should be possible for a conception of this order to be attached to a spiritual practice as popular as the Mani has become in Tibet is extremely significant.

Naturally too much must not be read into the above statement; the fact is that Tibetans, like other people, do often dream of spending more or less prolonged periods of care-free enjoyment in other and happier worlds, such as the Western Paradise presided over by Chenrezig and his teacher the Buddha Amitabha. The simple-minded likewise indulge in visions of a happy rebirth in a literal sense here on earth, forgetful as they are of the oft-quoted phrase declaring "the individual(ity) to be perishable, and devoid of true

215

self(hood)"; yet the fact remains that even in the case of a method so generally practiced the expressed intention goes far beyond the individual order, and indeed to the point of embracing the totality of beings and worlds in a single universal synthesis in which individual distinctions find no place; so that it can justly be claimed that the *metaphysical horizon* against which the invocation is to be carried out is literally limitless by its own showing and that no concession of principle has actually been made by way of encouraging self-interest of a limiting kind.

All that now remains is to speak of those who occupy the other end of the intellectual scale from the many simple people who, in comparative unconsciousness, give utterance to the Bodhisattva's awe-inspiring vow as they finish telling the beads of their rosaries: we are thinking of those persons (and they are by no means rare in Tibet) who have felt the call to self-dedication in the spiritual life so imperatively as to be unable to divide their energies any further, as between the pursuit of the supreme knowledge and ordinary private interests of whatever order. These people commonly go under the name of *naldjorpas* meaning "obtainers of tranquillity", because they have cut themselves free of the multi-directional pulls of a life lived more or less profanely, leaving themselves in a state of "one-pointed" contemplation that no distraction coming from outside is henceforward able to disturb. This uncompromising expression of the urge towards spiritual wholeness will provide us with our second example, which can, however, only be described in the most general terms, since one who has not himself realized, in a high degree, the descent of the Bodhisattva into his own heart is unfitted to offer any really profound comment on the subject; and the same applies to his hearers, who unless they are able, by resorting to the appropriate means, to approach a similar realization, will be equally incapable of understanding the deeper significance of the doctrine offered to them. All that one can be concerned with here is not so much the nature of

the *naldjorpa's* experience in itself—about which one is not in
a position to pronounce—as the part which that experience,
whatever may be its nature, plays in the Tibetan tradition as
a whole and what kind of influence it represents in regard to
giving its specific form to the idea of sainthood lived according to the Bodhisattva pattern.

One reservation must be made, however; not everyone
loosely described as a *naldjorpa* is so effectively, and due allowance must be made for some who, though possibly qualified
to embrace the life of spiritual abandonment, have for one
reason or another strayed from the strait and narrow path,
whether by yielding to the lure of unusual psychic and physical powers (such as often develop incidentally as a result of
following certain disciplines) or from any other cause equally
irrelevant.[6] These people, though they may continue to style
themselves *naldjorpas* and be accepted as such, have really
arrived at an intellectual dead end, or even worse in some
cases. Nevertheless the real thing not only exists, but it is that
element which, above all, lends color to the whole spiritual
life in Tibet, constituting, as it were, the *axis* in relation to
which all else must be situated and ultimately judged.

The genuine *naldjorpa*, in principle as in practice, stands
outside the pale of society, so much so that if he has been a
monk he usually casts off the monastic habit (and the rule
it represents) as a sign that he has cut adrift from all that
goes with organized existence, letting "the wind that bloweth

[6] Professed spiritual seekers of European origin seem especially prone to
develop an unhealthy interest in extraordinary phenomena of all kinds,
and that despite the calculated warnings of so many of the great teachers of
both East and West. An innate curiosity as well as an experimentalism that
is constantly being stimulated by modern "scientific" training and propa-
ganda is largely responsible for this tendency, which is only too apt to turn
into an insatiable craving, as a result of which the person concerned, when
he does not suffer serious psychological perversion, at least becomes fatally
imprisoned in the world of appearances and in an egocentric enjoyment
of marvels, real or supposed.

where it listeth" carry him in whatever direction it will. Often he is to be met with among the hermits dwelling on the edge of the great glaciers, or else wandering along one of the many tracks that lead hither and thither across the plateau, and even sometimes, as in the case of the late Abbot of Lachhen for instance, staying quietly not far from human dwellings, in fairly close touch with social life though no longer involved in it. Or again, if he be so minded, there is nothing to prevent him from seemingly participating in outward activities—activities which other men may interpret as they please, but which, for him, will ever remain an expression of his own untroubled solitude of spirit.

Most, if not all, of these contemplatives are initiates of some particular spiritual line of which a number exist, each having certain methods peculiar to itself such as will entail the presence of special qualifications in those who aspire to practice them. Through an unbroken traditional succession from Master to pupil, each such line may be said to constitute a separate current of spiritual influence, a channel that after issuing from the same parent stream will by and by go to lose itself, with all the others, in the uncharted ocean, large as the Bodhisattva's compassion, which is called Knowledge of the Voidness.

One misconception must be avoided, however, since it is likely to arise with certain habits of mind and since it also makes a peculiarly subtle appeal: the Bodhisattva's vow must never be taken to imply that the saving of mankind, or even of all creation, should become *an end in itself* for the apprentice in spirituality. Nothing short of the naked Truth, shorn of all contingencies and restrictions, merits to be called Desirable, its pursuit alone can be called Activity unqualified; only one who has been stripped of his attachments to everything except the Truth without a rival or associate can hope to attain that Truth. Having attained it, he does, in fact, become qualified to save the world, but should he at any stage yield to the supremely diabolical temptation (the one offered by Satan to Christ upon the high mountain) of making the world's salvation into his overriding aim, then he must pay the price of his altruistic idolatry and remain irremediably chained to the world and its otherness. A hair separates the two positions, and one can only recall in this connection the remark quoted earlier to the effect that saving the world is the Bodhisattva's sport. The danger of which we have been speaking represents the ultimate temptation of the saint, being both the hardest to detect and the most fatal if yielded to. This warning is, moreover, operative not only at the highest level but even at inferior levels too; to causes of this order must be ascribed the non-success that in so large a measure attends the well-meaning and often strenuous efforts of humanitarian-minded people the world over, for it is their very obsession with the cause of "others" that spells eventual defeat, in spite of their own obvious sincerity.

Tibetans, on the other hand, even the comparatively ignorant among them, seem to have retained some grasp of the principle at work; they look upon the *naldjorpas* as being first and foremost protectors of humanity, without whose "actionless" activity the ship of mankind would irremediably founder. Unentangled, as they are, in either duties or rights, whether of the family or the state or of a professional kind, it is their very impartiality towards worldly affairs that constitutes their power, one in which other men who are still, to a greater or lesser extent, "involved" in various ties of an individual and social kind can also participate, if indirectly. For this reason, it would appear not so much wicked as *suicidal* if society were, on any plea, to try to place restrictions in the way of those who wish to join the ranks of this spiritual élite, even while frankly admitting that those ranks will contain a certain proportion of self-deceived persons and even some who might be tempted to make capital out of the reverence in which they are held by the people at large.

Moreover, no one would ever think of impertinently questioning the motives or methods of anyone so engaged. Every

Tibetan understands that sainthood, at any degree of realization, will imply a different set of values from those that govern
the judgment of the ordinary man: what the latter regards as
important and obvious will often, to the spiritually minded,
seem trivial and, in any case, highly contestable. Indeed, the
last statement itself betrays an inaccuracy: for one who *knows*,
by the direct insight born of realization, the kind of questions
that trouble the ignorant do not even arise, nor do they enter
into the realm of choice or discussion. True intelligence flies
straight to the mark; it requires no tortuous marshaling of
pros and cons to bolster up its conclusions. Nothing would
seem more illogical to the Tibetan mind than to expect the
same kind of judgment from a Knower, even from one who
is so to a qualified extent only, and an ignoramus, which, in
the deepest sense, is the state of the majority of mankind,
including most of those whom the world looks on as learned
or strong or efficient; for it is they, and those who admire
and follow them, who truly are the unpractical visionaries, as
compared with the *naldjorpa*, who is the unshakable realist
because like Mary in the Gospel he "hath chosen that good
part".

It must not be thought that this recognition of the freedom to be earned through following the spiritual path will
imply any kind of antinomianism, though some may have
been tempted to think so. A realization that places one in
a state of complete harmony with the source of all law can
absolve one from its manifold applications but cannot oppose
one to it in principle; moreover it is knowledge that provides
a valid sanction for all applications on the legal plane (one
is referring to law in the very widest sense of the word), and
not vice versa. At the very highest level, therefore, the realization that "His service is perfect freedom", from being merely
theoretical becomes effective, and one who attains this state
can rightly claim that he is no longer "under the law", but is,
as the Hindus would say, henceforth "beyond caste".

The foregoing observation, however, gives rise to another, no less important in its way, since it affects those people—and they are not a few—who have come to yearn for a life of non-attachment, but who think that they will attain it by a premature and purely external casting-off of the bonds of form, whether religious or other. This state of mind on the part of the would-be "mystic"[7] is frequently evidenced by the habit of ceaselessly tilting at "orthodoxy", professedly in the name of "the spirit" as against "the letter", and by an instinctive fear and suspicion of whatever pertains to the formal order in general. Into this attitude of mind many different elements have entered—individualism, sentimentalism and humanistic influences generally. What these people miss is the fact that there are two ways of being outside form, the one supra-formal, because form has been transcended, the other infra-formal, because its possibilities as a "support" of realization at a certain level have been neglected. The one gives access to the formless Truth, seat of freedom and universality, the other represents the most abysmal kind of ignorance, compared with which the formal attachments affecting even the most narrow-minded person must be looked upon as a state of comparative liberty. Form, to be transcended, must first of all be realized and thus integrated; it is impossible to *skip* the experience of form, and the wish to do so, in the name of personal liberty, merely betrays a futile kind of self-conceit. This temptation is especially strong among Western advocates of a return to spiritual values at the present moment, by reason of the individualistic turn of their minds, fostered in the course of their education. On this whole subject of form a great

---

[7] It should be noted that any thoughtless use of the term "mystic" and its derivatives has here been carefully avoided. Whatever meaning this word may originally have borne, later and, more especially, recent usage has so confused the issue as to make it difficult of application outside the sphere where it belongs historically, namely that of Christian theology coupled with certain modes of realization attached to the same.

confusion of thought has occurred, which has not spared even those who appear, in other respects, to be highly gifted. What so many people refuse to face is the fact that in a time of intellectual confusion, form, "the letter", provides almost the last thread connecting fallen man with the sources of his spirituality, so that it would be almost true to say that today it matters more to observe forms correctly than to be "good"—a hard saying, perhaps, and a paradox, but one worth pondering over.

In a country like Tibet—or indeed anywhere in the wide world where the continuity of tradition has hitherto remained substantially unbroken—an intending *naldjorpa* will necessarily set out on his journey from a point situated somewhere in a traditional whole all the constituent forms of which will themselves already have been molded or *informed* under the influence of the selfsame idea that he is in process of realizing integrally and beyond every limitation of form. For this is in fact what tradition means—it is time people were reminded of it—namely, an effective communication of principles of more-than-human origin, whether indirectly and at several removes, through use of forms that will have arisen by applying those principles to contingent needs, or else immediately, after an "exhausting" of whatever makes for formal restriction of any kind, including the human individuality itself.

Thus the true *naldjorpa* (after whom the aspirant is similarly named only in anticipation and, as it were, by courtesy) is both he who realizes fully and effectively what others at best learn only partially through the various theoretical formulations of the doctrine as well as through their own participation in the traditional institutions generally, and also he who, through a similar realization, himself becomes at one with the eternal fountainhead of tradition; for him his approach to the goal is rather in the nature of a homecoming, a recollection, than a fresh acquisition in the spiritual field; while, on its side, the tradition, as revealed through the line of realized sages and their successors, is but a redescent, spontaneously undertaken, into that same world of men whence the *naldjorpa* had originally started out on his way, in the days of his comparative ignorance. The intimate interconnection between the two functions is not difficult to perceive.

Nor is it difficult to recognize the prototype of which this picture is a tracing: the twofold course of outgoing and return, which true insight knows as "not-two", the laborious ascent towards the highest eminences of awareness and the "compassionate" redescent into the valley, is not all this but another version of the oft-told tale of Bodhisattvahood presently renewed, whereby it is also made plain that Tradition is itself an aspect of that providential redescent into the Round, one of the "skillful means" wherewith the Bodhisattva "playfully" works for creatures? A traditionless existence, whether for a single individual or a whole group, is one in which the presence of the Bodhisattva passes unnoticed, in which the *naldjorpa* is without honor, in which mankind, refusing to listen to any talk of self-abandonment, is abandoned to its own devices, as the very name of "humanism" so plainly confesses. This is the first of the lessons to be learned by a sojourn in the places where tradition still prevails, where it has not yet been entirely forgotten that without the guidance, both direct and indirect, of those who have themselves taken possession of the summit, thus qualifying themselves, if need be, for a retracing of the way for the benefit of all the creatures whom "otherhood" still holds under its spell, the supreme peak will remain for ever unclimbable.

One can but repeat it: a personal reintegration in an authentically traditional form, as well as a "normal" participation in its attendant institutions, is an indispensable prelude to any adventure into the path of non-formal knowledge; by this means the individuality is conditioned, "tamed" as the Tibetans would say, in preparation for the supreme task that lies ahead. To those aspirants after the spiritual life who, in a purely negative sense at least, have come to reject the modern world and its profanity, but who, as far as any positive action is concerned, waver on the threshold perplexed by doubts as to the next step to be taken—to such as these the only advice that can be offered is the traditional one: namely, that they should first put themselves to rights as regards the formal order (wherein they are situated in virtue of the fact of being individuals at all) by regular adherence to a tradition; after which they should make use to the fullest extent of "the means of Grace" provided within the framework of that tradition, all the while testing their own success or otherwise by reference to its theory—that is, to its canonical formulations. Lastly, if and when a call to the beyond becomes irresistible, they should place themselves under the guidance of a spiritual master, the *guru* or "Root Lama" who is destined to introduce them into the path followed through the ages by the blessed company of the "thus-gone" (*Tathagatas*)—call them Buddhas, Yogis, Sufis, or what you will.

But one must beware of unauthorized teachers and bogus initiations; for the modern world has produced a heavy crop of self-appointed guides, mostly men who toy with the equivocal term "mysticism"; here again traditional "orthodoxy" is about the only available touchstone and safeguard, a case of form acting as a protective envelope for the formless, by lending to it its body. But protection always will be purchased at the price of restriction—this rule holds good in all orders, the social order included—hence the danger of "idolatry", which precisely consists in ascribing to any form in itself the unqualified character that belongs alone to the integral and formless Truth. Anywhere short of the goal, the way of realization will imply a certain polar balance between these two conceptions, the provisional and "symbolical" validity of forms and the untrammeled freedom of voidness. The Way has been fittingly called "narrow" and compared to walking along a razor's edge: by describing His tradition as the Middle Way the Buddha was expressing a similar idea. Bodhisattvahood is the virtue of being freed from both horns of the perennial dilemma, Form *versus* Void, by realizing them alike in their common and essential twolessness. Likewise the Bodhisattva's compassionate mission for the sake of dwellers in the land of Becoming is itself the free expression of that same non-dual Knowledge that is, for him, the source of his redemptive power as well as his own intrinsic qualification.

Religious texts

The Lord Buddha

Afterword
The Everlasting Message
(in commemoration of Buddha Jayanti, 1956–7)

The Full Moon of May 1956, ushering in the year of *Buddha Jayanti,* two thousand five hundredth anniversary of the *Parinirvana* of the Buddha, was the occasion of joyful celebrations in all places where memory of the Great Pilgrim is treasured. Throughout the Buddhist world, during the months that followed, devout souls gathered round *stupas* and temples bearing their offerings, while others, as in the present case, added their personal tribute under form of a spoken or written dissertation on one or other aspect of the holy message which, by the mouth of the Lion of the Sakyas, once was uttered for the illumination of a darkened and suffering world.

If then, in His time, mankind was already regarded as in urgent need of light, what is to be said about the present time? For never, in all recorded history, has there been a generation whose prevalent preoccupations were so far removed from the things that the Buddha came to teach, nor ever before—at least so far as our present information extends—have men shown themselves so enamored of the things that must bind them fatally to the wheels of *Samsara,* that ceaseless round of "concordant actions and reactions" in which beings, driven to and fro by their desires, are ignorantly struggling. Therefore any reminder is timely which might serve to recall the attention, be it only of a few, to those principles of which tradition, in its every authentic form, is the implacable witness; since without some such reminders what other inducement would there be for people to come out of their present state of complacent passivity in the face of the modern world and its profane suggestions? For the truth is, things have now come to such a pass that little short of a total act of self-examination is of any avail, because such a reorientation of one's whole outlook must precede any true reform. The Buddha taught just this when He named "Perfect Vision" as the first milestone along the Noble Eightfold Path. In fact, from the moment that what might be termed "a *nirvanic* view of things" has begun to unfold itself, obstacles in the way of the complete vision will already be in process of losing some of their opacity; where, on the other hand, a *samsaric* view of things is still openly or else tacitly accepted, all striving for human betterment is thereby self-condemned to futility, and its fruits, however sincere may seem the intentions behind the effort, will continue to be the fruits of ignorance containing, as they do, seeds of impermanence and further suffering.

A quickened awareness, this is the primary need. The alternative to its awakening is to pay the price of unmindfulness down to the last penny, a price which, when viewed on a world scale, is represented by the twofold possibility of mass destruction, Mara's fiery volley, and the would-be creation of a fool's paradise upon this earth, one in which human "welfare" is conceived as being actually realizable minus any spiritual norm, the old seduction by Mara's daughters presented in up-to-date disguise; nor is it even certain which of these two possibilities offers in the long run the more terrifying prospect.

For those who are compelled by force of circumstances to face a crisis of these proportions, recollection, a return to first principles as also to their own center, becomes a matter of the utmost urgency. Such a process of recollection will moreover, if it is to be of real effect, embrace both *prajna* and *upaya*, wisdom-with-method, that inseparable syzygy; that is to say, it will require both a clear perception of the essential aspects of *dharma* and also their actualization through a life remodeled in conformity with that wisdom. Focusing one's attention upon *dharma*—this in fact is vision ("theory" according to the root-meaning of the word), a vision which is no sooner unfolded than applied through a deploying of the appropriate *upayas* or spiritual means. At the level of forms and in practice, these will include both ritual conformity, in the widest sense, and the cultivation of the virtues as being contributory but indispensable factors in any awakening to Knowledge. For similar reasons, the field of *upaya* will also extend in the direction of artistic and scientific conformity to traditional canons, by a conscious selection and use of spirituality compatible instead of self-contradictory "supports", all of which must, for their proper discernment, be considered from the complementary viewpoints of their utility and their implicit symbolism.

An important thing to bear in mind, as regards the proper framing and balancing of one's life, is that spirituality always calls for concomitant means that are best described as "concrete"; it abhors abstractions, whereas the profane mentality delights in them: this gives the measure of the difference between a traditional doctrine, "non-human" both as regards its source and its finality, and a "philosophy", or in other words a system formed out of the products of human ratiocination and little else. No phrase could in fact be more inappropriate than "Buddhist philosophy" (or "Hindu philosophy" for that matter,[1] though both these expressions are commonly heard today, even from the mouth and pen of

---

[1] By rights the expression "Christian philosophy" should also be taboo, but for the fact that the Church has to some extent admitted its use and inasmuch as a philosophical element derived from classical antiquity entered into the formation of Christian theological language—to its detriment as some would maintain: discordance between this element and those belonging to the primitive Semitic stem of the tradition may well explain a certain tendency to fall apart discernable throughout Christian history. Rationalism itself, whereby Christian faith has been gradually undermined, has its distant roots partly in the too secure conceptualism of the mediaeval scholastics and partly in Greek philosophical thinking as again popularized by the Renaissance.

some who should know better), and its loose employment in any context is but to lend countenance to a modern tendency that would reduce the Buddha's own function and that of other great Revealers to purely human stature by eliminating the transcendent element and by treating the sacred teachings as if they were simply an outcome of more or less well-turned thinking. It cannot be said too often, a Buddha is not "a thinker", in the current sense, or even the best of all thinkers, nor is He a "social reformer", an early revolutionary or an ethical philosopher—all of which labels have been applied to him at different times by exponents of Western modernism and by their Eastern imitators.

That the Buddha was a man and therefore could also exercise reason when necessary, no one has ever called in question, for were this not true how could the perfectibility of human nature have been exemplified in his life? But that is very different from saying that the Buddha is "mere man", for if He were, or if anybody were, then the Deliverance from existential bondage that He preached would be but a chimera, since it is, to say the least of it, contradictory to suggest that what *per se* is conditioned in terms of such and such limits can somehow escape out of the circle of its own limitations by climbing up the ladder of those limitations alone. Such a suggestion contains an evident absurdity, which does not however prevent some people from giving it utterance, probably out of an unconscious urge to make Buddhism fit in with the sentimental cult of "humanity" which is now in fashion. A parallel absurdity is the notion according to which the relativity constituted by the phenomenal world is something absolutely irreducible (thus precluding all possibility of liberation, *moksa*), a belief which for a number of more contingent reasons or else from sheer want of metaphysical insight is to be found in several schools of Christian thought as well as among those professed materialists to whom this doctrine more properly belongs.

His realization while in the human state, in the case of a Buddha, is in fact a demonstration of the latent Buddhahood in man, recognizable to the eye of Intellect even behind the veil of ignorance that masks its presence, and it is by virtue of this conjunction alone that Deliverance is possible. Naturally, the same would apply in respect of any other form under which a Buddha chose to appear in this or other worlds, for in this respect all *Samsara* is one and the human state, though "central" by comparison with other beings situated at the same degree of existence, is not for that reason to be regarded as privileged in an absolute sense, otherwise the many references in the sacred books to the possibility of "deliverance down to the last blade of grass" would have no meaning. Nevertheless, the fact of being situated upon the axis that runs through the center of all the worlds justifies the common dictum about "human existence hard to obtain" and the importance of not wasting that rare opportunity: for Deliverance, from any situation that is, by comparison, peripheric and however extended its intrinsic possibilities may be, must necessarily involve first becoming human (or the equivalent), that is to say becoming centered on the axis itself, which is the *sutra* in a pre-eminent sense, the thread of Buddha-nature running through the heart of every being.

Regarded from man's own angle the *sutra*, inasmuch as it connects him with the center, is that which shows him his direction, spiritual life, the path of initiation; and that likewise is the general sense of *sutra* under its more usual, scriptural connotation as treating primarily of means for regaining a center that had become hidden to human view. Regarded from the complementary angle, that is to say inasmuch as it connects the center with man, the *sutra* marks the channel for the Buddha's influence, tradition, the downflowing of Grace. Either of these aspects may be stressed on occasion, for reasons of opportunity or method, but neither can be denied or ignored altogether, since they are as inconceivable apart as the two images that coincide in ordinary bodily vision.[2] Buddhism comprises its ways of Love or Grace as well as its more typical ways of Knowledge and *yogic* endeavor and any one of these ways may on occasion be called "the way", as constituting an adequate specification thereof in view of a particular set of human circumstances.

Whatever may be its apparent form, no way that can properly be described as Buddhist can fail to be an intellectual way fundamentally, just as no way can exclude the element of Grace if only because of the obvious inadequacy of human resources, any distinction as between way and way being merely a matter of which element happens to occupy the foreground of the picture and which remains relatively masked. Similar considerations apply even to that broader distinction of ways indicated by the terms *Mahayana* and *Theravada.* Such a distinction is valid in its place and within given limits. Only if it be taken to represent an irreducible opposition is there call for protest, because such an opinion itself springs from a certain confusion between formal or methodic and more essential factors.

Without the Buddha's Grace human effort would be like casting stones about in a vacuum; but if that effort be withheld then man himself will be the author of his own failure. The eternal message, *akaliko dhamma,* is no other; for us there remains but to pay heed by applying its lessons in the manner best suited to our nature, here and now.

---

[2] For a more detailed discussion of this subject, which is one of great practical importance, see Appendix I.

Vision of *Jiriki*
Bodhidharma, Patriarch of Zen, crosses the ocean of
transmigration on a reed

Vision of *Tariki*
Amitabha Buddha welcomes his devotee into the Western Paradise

Appendix I
The Twin Sources of Power

The Japanese tradition makes a sharp distinction between those methods respectively called *jiriki* (own power) and *tariki* (other power) as representing two main types of spiritual endeavor; any doctrine or method can then be assessed in terms of predominance (never total absence) of one or other of these two contrasting but interdependent elements. *Zen* Buddhism for example, with its insistence at every turn upon a self-reliance heroic well-nigh to the point of dispensing with all physical or mental supports and consolations, quite evidently represents an extreme case of the *jiriki* approach; on the other hand *Jodo* (Pure Land) Buddhism, with its whole-hearted reliance on the saving grace of *Amida Buddha* supported by the invocation of his Name,[1] provides a classic example of the *tariki* way. If there is not an incompatibility of principle between these two ways, it might well be asked, where then is to be sought, in each of the examples mentioned, the sister element, the one that remains recessive to the other's dominance?

The answer to the first part of the question being in the negative, it would seem, with the Zen exercitant, that he draws the *tariki* element first of all from the traditional background taken as a whole, which fosters in him certain attitudes without his having to give them much conscious thought; this leaves him free to devote all available initiative to the end immediately in view, spurred as his efforts will be thanks to that peculiar use of paradox and "spiritual conundrum" whereby Zen shows its affinity to Taoism. For the

---

[1] Technically known as *Nembutsu* from the words *Namu Amida Butsu* = "Hail to Amitabha Buddha."

fervent devotee of Amida, on the other hand, it is the unflagging and centered attention required by the invocation as such, if it is to be properly exercised, that constitutes the *jiriki* element of his spirituality; if with him this element remains formally unacknowledged, this is because all activity deployed along this way is ascribed, *a priori,* to Amida Himself, and not to the invoking subject. For the latter his intellectuality consists in "recognizing" the Grace in which, in common with all his suffering fellow beings, he is steeped and his one effort is to lay open his own brittleness of heart to its mellowing influence till the love of Amida shall have caused egocentricity to dissolve away without residue, when the Pure Land will automatically open its gates.

It might furthermore be pointed out that acceptance, for spiritual reasons, of any kind of formal discipline carries with it certain *tariki* implications, since whatever is imbibed through the mediacy of an apparently outside authority, either impersonal as in the case of the traditional environment or as personally exercised by one's own Spiritual Master, must logically be entered on the "other" side of the reckoning and not in the "own" column. In fact, followers of all spiritual schools, Zen included, have in common this submission to a *guru;* and as for discipline the most highly developed forms of it are to be met with among the ranks of *jiriki*—none is second to the Zen aspirant in this respect—whereas in the *tariki* schools emphasis is more often laid upon the "light" character of the means offered (Indian *bhakti* is no exception): "my yoke is easy and my burden is light" says the Beloved, for He knows his devotee's weakness in these latter days. Thus by a continual interplay of compensations balance is maintained across the manifold blendings to which, in any traditional scheme, *jiriki* and *tariki* lend themselves: advisedly we chose extreme cases the better to illustrate the point at issue; but obviously many other examples could be found in which the two elements are blended in more equal proportions, though practically always with some bias in one or other direction.

If discussion on this subject has seemed to extend itself somewhat, this was but in order to show how *jiriki* and *tariki* both together reside in the nature of things and do not derive from any arbitrary preference on the part of this or that person or school. Once this truth has been clearly grasped, it will be possible to follow that kind of path that best accords with one's own intellectual and temperamental capacity, free from danger of slipping either into intellectual smugness or else into a desiccating asceticism to which the *jiriki* way, if the companion element be denied its just rights, may so easily lead, or even to a Buddhist version of the Pelagian heresy: not that *jiriki-tariki* complementarism is confined to the one tradition, for it enters into all spiritual life whatever its form, the Christian included, and the problems it raises are seen to be much the same everywhere. An exaggeration of the *tariki* point of view would logically result in complete Quietism on the plea that faith alone justifies, but as that attitude is difficult to maintain in practice, refuge is likely to be sought (and recent history confirms this view) in a studied doctrinal vagueness coupled with moralistic extravagance, a road leading, as it were by default, to the deification of the human community, the results of which we know.

In practice those Europeans who feel the attraction of Eastern doctrines look almost without exception in a *jiriki* direction—this, out of reaction against the sentimental excesses that have come to afflict much of Christian thought— therefore it is well to be warned that such a reaction, however understandable, can also, if too one-sided, become sentimental in its turn: we are thinking especially of a neo-Buddhist pharisaism which is for ever giving thanks that it is not as that miserable theistic publican; a dose of *tariki* might, for these people, prove beneficial. It is in fact unnecessary for piety to become sentimentalized even though an element of feeling necessarily enters into its make-up, if only because man has been made with feelings among other things and these must, just like other things, have their place and use in spiritual life, otherwise they will surely run to seed; religion demands the whole man, without omission. Likewise intellectuality need not become supercilious and indeed cannot be so while remaining true to itself, for such is only a mental counterfeit, a gnostic pretension inhibiting true intelligence, beside which even a little sentimentality in a devotional life otherwise genuine, though not a desirable feature in itself, probably—nay, certainly—represents a less repellent evil.

A recent experience will provide one last illustration to the argument: the author was listening to a lecture by a distinguished Japanese spokesman of *jiriki* under its form of Zen Buddhism in which the distinction between the two possible religious attitudes was well brought out, with passing allusion to Meister Eckhart and the Sufis; after which the lecturer passed on to describe in a vivid way the training of a Zen disciple in Japan, from his first day on, showing also the ideals this discipline was trying to express. When the lecture was over, the author went up and put this question to the speaker: "In the earlier part of your talk you mentioned the difference between 'own power' and 'other power'—is it not correct to describe them as two sides of the same coin, inseparably linked to one another?" To which answer was given: "Of course, that is self-evident, for ours is a doctrine of non-duality in which all such oppositions have no place."

Truly said! But one asks oneself whether this necessarily would be self-evident to members of an audience conditioned both historically and by their education to think always in terms of "either . . . or" with hardly an inkling that their most cherished antitheses could disappear under the light shed from a more universal principle. Eastern exponents, heirs to a different tradition, when they come over here, are inclined to overlook this difficulty and it might be more prudent, in most cases, for them to call people's attention deliberately to the fact that to follow a *jiriki* path does not, whatever appearances may suggest to the contrary, invalidate the latent presence of *tariki* or vice versa. What needs above all to be shown, if a non-dualistic doctrine is to be successfully put over and, still more, applied, is that oppositions do retain their validity at one level, that of their relative truth, but forfeit it at a higher (or more interior) level. Two-less Knowledge (*advaita*) consists in embracing both these views in a simultaneous synthesis, not in pretending to suppress one term in favor of another, thinking thus to master the opposition: that is but a "monistic" parody of *advaita* (to which the misnomer of monism is often carelessly applied), hence the need to combat this error as in the present instance.

As a fitting conclusion to this discussion and also by way of ending on a note of traditional authority superior to any expressed opinions of one's own, a quotation is offered from the sayings of a great Saint and exponent of *tariki,* Honen, patriarch of the *Jodo* school, in which he synthesizes all the chief points of view embraced by the Buddhist tradition, thus showing that in their finality they are one and only, a lesson for all concerned: this quotation is taken from *Honen, the Buddhist Saint, His Life and Teaching,* as translated by Rev. H. H. Coates and Rev. Ryugaku Ishizuka (Kyoto, 1949) and reads as follows:

> Now we find in the many teachings the great Master (Buddha) himself promulgated during his lifetime, all the principles for which the eight Buddhist sects, the esoteric and exoteric and the Greater and the lesser Vehicles stand, as well as those elementary doctrines suited to the capacity of the immature, together with those intended for people able to grasp reality itself. Since then there have been various expositions and commentaries on them such as we now have, with their multitude of diverse interpretations. Some expound the principle of the utter emptiness of all things. Some bring us to the very heart of reality, while others set up the theory that there are five fundamental distinctions in the natures of sentient beings, and still others reason that the Buddha-nature is found in them all. Every one of these sects claims that it has reached finality in its world view, and so they keep contending with one another, each

persisting in saying that its own is the most profound and is absolutely right. Now the fact is that what they all say is exactly what the Sutras and Sastras say, and corresponds to the golden words of Nyorai himself, who, according to men's varying capacity, taught them at one time one thing and at another time another, as circumstances required. So it is hard now to say which is profound and which is shallow, or to distinguish their comparative value, for they are all equally taught, and we must not go to either extreme in our interpretation. If we but attend to our religious practices as the Sutras teach, they will all help us to pass safely over the sea of birth and death to the other shore. If we act according to the Law, we shall attain Enlightenment. Those who go on vainly disputing as to whether a color has a light or dark shade, are like deaf men talking about the quality of a man's voice whether it is good or bad. The one thing to do is to put the principles into practice, because they all teach the way of deliverance from the dread bondage.

Origin and outcome of initiation, shown as the Buddha Dorje Chang

Waiting for the arrival of the head abbot, Punakha, Bhutan

Appendix II
Discovering the Interior Life[1]

When the Venerable Lama asked me to stand in for him at this conference, I confess to having felt some dismay at the prospect of replacing one whose whole training, from early childhood, was conditioned by the aim of developing the interior life to the fullest possible extent. Schooled in the tradition of Tibetan Buddhism under its most contemplative form, your chosen lecturer was well qualified to discourse on the means whereby a human soul may be opened to its own latent possibilities of illumination—to the "Kingdom of Heaven that is within you," to quote the phrase used by Christ Himself. It is a real pity that a conjunction of unforeseen causes prevented him from attending your meeting, but this could not be helped; he wishes me to say how sorry he is to have disappointed you. He had, however, told me something about the line he intended to take when addressing you, and this evidently has been some guidance to me. I can only express the hope that what I am going to say ties up sufficiently with the specific question raised in your conference prospectus, namely how to help the young people placed under your care to form themselves in the love and

---

[1] A talk given at a conference of Catholic religious headmistresses in January, 1968. The Venerable Lama Trungpa, who was to have delivered the lecture, being prevented from keeping the appointment, asked the present author to act in his stead. Given the nature of the audience, no attempt was made to stick to a Buddhist terminology; Pali and Sanskrit words have been replaced by expressions more familiar to Christians. Both sources have been freely drawn on in the shape of quotations and other illustrative material. Emphasis all along has been less on antithesis than on intelligible dialogue.

knowledge of the Lord in a manner that will be not merely conceptual but also effective.

This in fact is a question that concerns us one and all, be we young or old, clever or simple, European or Asian, religious or lay; quite simply, the supplying of an answer to this question is the purpose of religion under all its forms. Buddhism expresses this truth by saying that for any human enterprise to be brought to proper fulfillment, wisdom and method must operate together, as one conjoint principle. They must keep in step with one another; otherwise the enterprise will be frustrated as a result of its own inherent unbalance. The Tibetans convey this lesson by the following parable: Two men were both trying to get to the City of Nirvana, but neither of them could make much headway because the one was blind while the other was lame, so they decided to join forces. The lame man climbed on the blind man's back and pointed out the way (this is wisdom) while the man who had sound legs (this is method) carried his companion along the road. This sets the pattern of every spiritual life; all the rest is but a matter of variable circumstance and detail.

The same idea is expressed traditionally by saying that method and wisdom are husband and wife, who may never be divorced. In the Buddhist iconographical symbolism method is always depicted as a male figure, wisdom by a female. When the two appear together on the same icon, they are usually shown in conjugal embrace, a fact that in the past has often been misinterpreted in an obscene sense by uninformed European observers. Had they but known it, it was their own minds that were thus affected, since these particular icons illustrating what might be called the "mystical marriage of wisdom and method" are regarded by Buddhists as conveying a message of austerest purity; to suspect anything different would, for them, savor of blasphemy.

It is noteworthy that though method is represented as playing the male part in the divine alchemy, that is to say in the process of transmuting the lead of our creatural ignorance into the gold of the saving enlightenment, it is wisdom, female counterpart of method, who will first be encountered by the human aspirant, and the reason for this is evident. There must be some kind of initial vision of the truth, a first glimpse of wisdom, before any man will feel impelled to alter the direction of his life by turning his back on the world and its manifold allurements in order to seek God. This change of direction, which the word "conversion" by its etymology expresses, itself implies an initial grace thanks to which one suddenly becomes aware of the futility of one's present state and, by the same token, becomes aware of the possibility of reaching a better and happier state. This grace, the gift of faith, marks the first awakening of wisdom in the soul; automatically it will give rise to the question "What must I do (or avoid) in order to reach a goal I now discern in the dim distance? What road am I to follow?" This very word "what" implies a prayer for method; all the prescriptions, positive or negative, of religion can in fact be grouped under one or other of our two main headings. Its doctrinal formulations indicating what is to be realized and which correspond to wisdom under various aspects, whereas the ritual, moral, and artistic equipment provided by religion may properly be grouped under the heading of "methodic supports" at various levels. The supreme instrument of method is the life of prayer, taken in the widest sense; Buddhists would rather say "the practice of meditation," a matter of terminology that indicates a certain difference of viewpoint but certainly not any essential incompatibility.

In this same connection it should be pointed out that from a Buddhist standpoint a too preponderantly abstract presentation of theological truth is dangerous inasmuch as this can easily degenerate into mere philosophizing, into a mental art for art's sake. A theology offered without its con-current means of active verification in the soul, that is to say as an isolated wisdom, will at best lead the mind into an intellectual dead end; at worst, it will engender its own opposite, since typically the world's heresies have all arisen from an unbalanced presentation of some truth or other. Error—a failure in respect of wisdom—will always imply a parallel failure in respect of method and vice versa. One cannot afford to forget for a minute the essential interdependence of the two great spiritual factors. The great value of tradition is that it serves to maintain the polar balance between theory and practice, between wisdom and its effective realization, through calling into play the appropriate spiritual means. If wisdom is by definition concerned with *knowing*, method for its part is concerned with *being*. In fact, one can only really claim to know something by being that thing; to mistake a merely mental appreciation for knowledge is the classical trap of the philosophers. Realization can be said to take place at the moment when being and knowing coincide.

If one were called upon to describe the process of spiritual regeneration or enlightenment as a whole, one could perhaps best qualify it in terms of a circuit, with wisdom calling forth its appropriate method at each stage of the way, with the result that this same wisdom will become integrated in the soul as a henceforth inalienable element of one's being. The way starts from wisdom and ends in wisdom. Buddhism by its own showing offers itself as a series of methods calculated to lead suffering beings more or less directly to enlightenment; this is Buddhism's specific "note."

To give the parallel version: Christ offers Himself to men both as "Light"—another name for wisdom—and as "the Way." "I am the Way." He could equally well have said, "I am the Means." The prayer "Light up our way, O Lord!" sums up man's most essential needs. What we call the interior life is but an answer to that prayer.

Before entering on a discussion of method under its more technical aspects, it would be well to give our attention briefly to two important conditions attaching to any form of contemplative discipline if it is to be fruitful. The first of these conditions relates to the attitude a man should take up versus nature and the things of nature, whereof he himself is one thing among others; the second relates to what may be called "the mythological mantle of truth," this being one among several means whereby divine wisdom has chosen to reveal its secrets in intelligible form, either in certain parts of Holy Scripture or else through the medium of a traditional folklore, for both these ways of conveying certain truths have been in evidence throughout the world. If our own rationalistic education has rendered us largely impervious to this mode of communication, then it is important for us to reanimate the missing faculty, since a mind that has become closed in this respect will certainly be gravely hampered in its discovery of the life within.

To take the question of man's place in nature first of all: Quite obviously mankind, in order to exist, are compelled to draw on the things around them for their sustenance and in various other ways. As far as that goes, man does not differ greatly from the cow or the tiger or any other living thing, except that his ingenuity in procuring what he wants exceeds theirs, and so do his appetites, a fact that, religiously speaking, is hardly a cause for self-satisfaction; rather should it be deemed a cause for self-questioning.

To suggest, as has been far too commonly the case, that the right to use the fruits of this world's garden, as recorded in Genesis, can be equated with permission to indulge an irresponsible and limitless cupidity, destructiveness, and even cruelty toward our nonhuman fellow creatures is an insult to the Creator, first because it makes nonsense of the statement that "God hateth nothing of what He has made" and second because it restricts the idea of the usefulness of things to their material possibilities alone, and even to only a part of these. Their illuminative uses, as signs or reminders of God's merciful presence, are ignored. The beauty of animals and plants, for instance, and the intrinsic qualities that make of each created thing a unique and irreplaceable witness to one or other divine aspect—all this is food for the intellect, chosen instrument of intuitive contemplation wherewith man is enabled to behold mysteries far beyond the reach of his discursive reason. It is this transcendent faculty, which since Adam's fall has been as if asleep, that needs reawakening in such a way as to allow all our other faculties of perception and action to group themselves harmoniously around it: The word "Buddha," which means "the wake," testifies to this crowning need. For Buddhists, goodness is first of all *intelligent*, since it leads to God. Sin, on the other hand, is stupid; it proceeds from ignorance and leads back to ignorance, and its mere "badness" pales beside its principal disadvantage, which is to thicken the veil between ourselves and the Divine. Buddhism always tends to see in sin a greater or lesser degree of incompetence and in virtue a proof of skill. A Buddhist would readily agree with the statement that Christian "love," that which makes a man yearn to know God and experience His constant presence already here in this world, is firstly and lastly an activity of awareness. As for the love of neighbor, in which Buddhism includes all that shares in man's capacity to suffer—itself a consequence of separation from the divine center—this is both a logical and indispensable condition of deliverance from suffering through a clear discerning of its root cause; Christ's words "Inasmuch as ye have done so to the least of these, ye have done it unto Me" will always find a ready echo in any Buddhist heart.

A compassionate attitude in both thought and practice toward all that lives is one of the keys of a true contemplation. It is preceded in a Buddhist religious training by intense meditation on the theme of the *impermanence*, including suffering and death, that man and all other creatures have to share. This thought is inculcated early in the Buddhist child; such a remark as "Look at that horrid moth, let's kill it" would be quite unthinkable in a Buddhist home. In Tibet, to swear at a horse or a mule, let alone to beat it, was a thing unknown. Wild animals and birds were mostly half-tame because they had so little cause to fear their human neighbors, and their peaceful proximity was in fact a particularly powerful factor in molding the spiritual outlook of the people at large—an object lesson in what Eden must have felt like for Adam.

Let me quote you one passage from the writings of a great saint which perfectly sums up the attitude I have just been describing:

> What is a charitable heart? It is a heart aflame with charity for the whole of Creation, for men, for birds, for beasts, for devils, for all creatures. He who has this heart will be unable to remember or see a creature without his eyes filling with tears because of the compassion that grips his heart; and that heart is softened and cannot endure to see even a slight pain inflicted on a creature or to hear of it through others; this is why such a man does not cease praying also for animals, for the enemies of the Truth, for those who do evil to him, so that they may be protected and purified; he even prays for reptiles, moved by an infinite pity which is awakened in the heart of those who assimilate themselves to God.

Surely a world so schooled would be a world far less contentious and destructive than the one we know. But now I must make a confession, since I have been playing something of a spiritual practical joke on you all, if such an expression be not far-fetched! The quotation I have just read out to you does indeed well express the Buddhist spirit, but it is in fact taken from a Christian saint, Isaac the Syrian. The Desert Fathers, the Celtic hermits, and Saint Francis all represent a similar trend. Contemplation of the divine mysteries and a fellowship with nature go hand in hand; this is the point I have been trying to make. And now for the second condition alluded to above, the function of "mythological communication." This need not occupy us long, yet some mention of the subject is indispensable.

Latterly a widespread movement has made itself felt in the Christian West the aim of which, as its supporters put it, is to "demythologize" the church's teachings. This is a most sinister development, one fraught with peril both to faith and to the object of faith, which is none other than truth. This anti-mythological bias proceeds from two evident causes: first, a feeling of defeatism versus modern science, its discoveries and its gibes, and second, an inability to see that it is quite in the nature of things for revelation to use various means of communicating its message, traditions with a mythological form exemplifying one kind of means among others and indispensable in their own place. Every religion contains this element to some extent, and in certain religions—Hinduism, for instance—this enters in very largely, as I was myself able to observe when living in the hills of North Bengal. My gardener, for instance, had a strongly developed sense of the omnipresence of God of which the evidence, for him, was for the most part vehicled by scriptural narratives of a mythological and therefore also timeless character; historical considerations hardly entered in.

Like Christianity and Islam, Buddhism has a strongly affirmed historical framework. The life of the founder can be timed and featured, and its episodes provide the prototype whereon a man's spiritual life is to be modeled. However, even in these traditions there are to be found other concordant ways of conveying the saving message, and the respective Scriptures all include portions that are ascribable neither to the historical unfolding of the religion in question nor to its purely doctrinal side; they narrate mythological happenings which, to be understood, have to be read not physically but metaphysically. This does not mean, of course, that these stories are of human invention and therefore lacking in truth—indeed quite the contrary. Their place in the corpus of revealed truth is guaranteed by the fact that certain lessons can best be conveyed by this means and thanks to the very fact that they take one into a metaphysical dimension that is as real today as yesterday and will remain equally so tomorrow.

The Old Testament, in particular, is rich in this kind of ever-actual narrative; a mind that can respond aright to such a teaching has to be free of a certain self-imprisonment in time and space. Many people are apt to confuse the miraculous with the mythological, which is wrong inasmuch as a miracle, whenever it occurs, belongs by definition to the order of historical happenings; a miracle is an exceptional manifestation in this world of an influence of a transcendent order on a particular occasion. Those who say they wish to remove the mythological element from the church's inheritance may not admit, even to themselves, that after mythology miracles will be their next target; a false mental association of these two elements will nevertheless make this likely. Where possible, miraculous happenings will be explained away, as by saying of the Virgin Birth that the mother of Jesus was so pure a soul that her purity was "tantamount to virginity" or some such thing. I fully expect this to happen—if this warning proves to have been needless, so much the better! Common prudence, however, requires us to be prepared for this and other similar attempts, for pointers in this direction are now too many to be overlooked by anyone who is not blind.

In the case of happenings that could properly be qualified as pertaining to a sacred mythology, such as the story of the Ark or the Tower of Babel, those who wish to discredit them start off from an assumption that such happenings are either historical or else mere fiction; they can discern no other choice. What they fail to see is that even if these stories be accepted as literal fact, as was the case with our ancestors, this in no wise deprives the stories of their power to convey truth. Where a genuine myth is concerned, its illuminative effectiveness operates outside the alternative "belief or disbelief"; whosoever cannot receive it thus will fail to understand it.

Let the two aforementioned examples from the old Hebrew mythology tell us what they can. First, the Ark. From its description in Genesis 11, complete with measurements given in cubits, it is obvious that a person in the Middle Ages, for instance, had he felt so minded, could easily have found out that a vessel of that size could not possibly have accommodated all the known kinds of animals, let alone the food needed to keep them and also Noah's family alive for forty days or more. Since there is not the slightest reason for supposing that people were more stupid then than nowadays, and good reason for believing the contrary, one has to explain their apparent lack of interest in certain questions of probability or otherwise by the fact that, for them, the dimension of sacred happenings was accepted as a whole, for what it plainly told them; its intrinsic truth shone too brightly to require corroborating through a meticulous canvassing of details. The medieval mind, for all the presence there of human defects as well as virtues, was a *whole* mind, and so was its view of the cosmos; the Gospel references to receiving the truth "as a little child" well describe this attitude. For such a mentality the story of the Ark retains all its intrinsic validity quite apart from any possibility that at a certain moment in time an extensive flood might in fact have overwhelmed part of the inhabited world and thus given rise, in retrospect, to this marvelous story. Its lesson is for all time, for the flood (or its equivalent) is always on the point of overwhelming some section of humanity—today it might well be humanity as a whole that is thus threatened—and escape from the disaster is always by way of an ark of sorts to which only those who fear the Lord can gain admission, because this very fear spells intelligence. The fate of those who become oblivious of God (they may appear to be quite kindly people) is always to be drowned in the consequences of their own forgetfulness.

The Tower of Babel is another such universal myth, also peculiarly applicable to our own time, as it happens. Here again, it is irrelevant whether some ruler in ancient Mesopotamia may or may not have inaugurated an ambitious project of constructing an edifice bigger than ever before and describable as "reaching to heaven." The Empire State Building in New York almost answers to that description, especially on days when the top is swathed in cloud while the street below is clear—in this respect it can emulate many a natural hill. All this remains beside the point, however, because the spirit of Babel is something that is repeating itself continually in human history, in the form of megalomaniac plans wherein man sees himself as the "conqueror of nature" and as the arch-planner who can manipulate the future at his own sweet pleasure. The day some Russian or American spaceman first sets foot upon the moon you can be sure that the world will be treated to a babel of blasphemous boasting exceeding all that has been heard hitherto; for the "confusion of tongues" one has but to substitute "confusion of minds" and the Bible story will be lived over again with almost literal similarity.

It is moreover noticeable that those who have taken part in recent cosmonautical exploits have been alike in one thing, namely that their comments relayed from the heights of space have been of a uniformly abysmal triviality that contrasts disconcertingly with the supposed greatness of their achievement, let alone with the courage these people undoubtedly have shown. This is the story of Babel repeating itself with a vengeance! Who then shall say that this story has lost its relevance for us moderns and should now be "demythologized" into oblivion?

As you doubtless are expecting, the latter part of this discussion will contain some reference to the question of "method" in its positive sense of aiding concentration or, to give it also its negative sense, of overcoming distraction. Needless to say, this is where the Venerable Lama will be most sadly missed by us today, for though still young he has already had a wide experience of handling this matter of practical training in the contemplative art, both in relation to the ever-varying

253

needs of individual disciples and, at a more external level, when offering general guidance to groups. Though I cannot hope to emulate him in this respect, I can at least suggest that considerable profit may be derived through reading his book *Born in Tibet*. Though this is presented as a personal account of the lama's early life and training leading gradually to his adventurous escape with a band of refugees in 1959, the book episodically contains much that throws light on the power of a steady contemplation to regulate action even under the utmost stress of danger and hardship—a lesson to our contemporary activists. Whoever will but read between the lines will find in this book much that speaks to his condition.

Since we are on the subject of books, I take this opportunity of drawing your attention to another book by a contemporary Catholic author, Dom Aelred Graham, an English Benedictine who spent many years in America as director of a large boys' school. As a result of experience in the practice of meditation in company with some Buddhist friends, Dom Aelred wrote a book[2] to show how certain current Buddhist techniques might be adapted advantageously for Christian use, with the aim of deepening the contemplative awareness of Christians at a time when the pull is mostly in the opposite direction. As you see, his motives and your own are much the same in this respect.

With much sagacity, Dom Aelred Graham has arranged his material according to the plan that is traditional in the Buddhist East; that is to say, he has presented it under the twofold heading of theory or wisdom and of practice or method whereby that same wisdom may be experienced in one's inmost being—the only way to know, as has been said already. Every initiatic teaching, in Tibet or Japan, has always rested on the authority of a particular *sutra* or group of *sutras*, that is to say, on certain inspired treatises or selected portions

---

[2] *Zen Catholicism* (New York: Harcourt, Brace & World, Inc., 1963).

of the Scriptures related directly to the method in question and from which the method itself draws its technical apparatus in appropriate form; normally these *sutras* would be memorized before embarking on the corresponding course of meditation. In Dom Aelred's book this wisdom function is filled by a quite remarkable series of quotations mostly drawn from Saint Thomas Aquinas and disposed in such a way that the subsequent comments about ways and means will at once be recognizable as "enactments" (if one may so use the word) of the truths expressed specifically by those quotations. I feel sure that this book will be helpful to many of you here.

Incidentally, in a talk on this same subject given by Dom Aelred Graham to the Anglican Congregation of Saint John the Divine in Boston he mentioned one fact that will surely interest you greatly. In his school, quite unprompted by himself, a number of the boys came and asked to be allowed to join in a session of what they called "Catholic Zen meditation" each Sunday for half an hour of their free time. Dom Aelred said this had been one of the most moving experiences of his life at the school. What this shows above all is that the young, given the right example exerted through the presence of a revered teacher even more than through any spoken exhortation, may well discover in themselves that very possibility of contemplation that provides faith with its inward dimension and with an unshakable defense. This does not mean, of course, that the spoken or written word has ceased to count, where these profound matters are concerned; what it means is that wherever wisdom at any degree is content to shine with its own light, by an "activity of presence," its communication will be both more clear and more far-reaching.

To return to Buddhists and their practices: Certain methods of inducing a habit of attention or "mindfulness," as it is most commonly called, have been in current use since the beginning, whereof an example is the practice of watching the alternate incoming and outgoing breaths over a longer or shorter period; this method remains classical where beginners are concerned, and it has many variants. Similarly in Hinduism exercises in breath control are in common use, as also a whole body of quasi-gymnastic movements and posturings whereby rhythm and poise are promoted in body and mind together. A number of instructors in these methods have found their way to the West, many of whom, however, offer them as a means of promoting bodily and psychic health apart from any religious purpose. Whatever benefits may accrue from such a restricted application of these methods, the results will always suffer from a taint of profanation, as indeed happens with many things familiar to us today—tobacco smoking, for instance, started as the profanation of a sacramental rite of the American Indians which the white settlers in America prostituted to a mere luxury of the senses. Carried out under proper direction, however, this kind of physical or psychological adjunct to meditation can have great uses, provided the indispensable link with a traditional wisdom is maintained from start to finish.

It is not, however, about this kind of method that I wish to speak today, not being expert in this field. Nor is there much point in discoursing on some of the more elaborate meditative schemes belonging to the Tantric form of spirituality, as found in India and Tibet, for the simple reason that these methods require conditions such as would not easily be realizable in a Western framework, save by exception. I do not think these methods would easily transpose into a Christian medium just as they stand, though theoretically the possibility of adaptation in certain cases need not be excluded altogether. What can be said, however, in a more general way is that in a time of growing alienation and disbelief apparatus of a very complex kind hardly fits the need, which calls for a discipline that is at once "central," that is to say expressive of the most central truths of the tradition, and at the same time extremely concise as to the instruments it sets in motion, thus allowing of their methodic exercise under all kinds of circumstances, be it even the most unfavorable.

Such an instrument is typically represented by the invocation of a sacred name (the Indian *japa*) or else of a short formula in which a sacred name is found enshrined. All the great traditions are agreed in saying that this way of concentrating attention and pervading a person's whole being with continual reminders of God is a spiritual means particularly suited to the needs of the Dark Age, when religion is at a low ebb and the forces of godless subversion seem to be a mounting tide. In Buddhist Japan, for instance, this method is associated with the school known as Jodo, or "Pure Land," in which the name of the Buddha Amitabha (meaning "Infinite Light") is the invocatory means provided. In Tibetan Buddhism a similar means exists in the form of the six-syllabled phrase *Om mani padme hum,* of which the manifold and complex mystical correspondences have caused it to be described as "the quintessence of the wisdom of all the Buddhas"; but time does not allow of more than a bare mention of the sacred formula in question. In the Islamic tradition the name of God (in Arabic *Allah*) is recognized as the spiritual means *par excellence.* Its invocation, in the Sufi confraternities that exist for the sole purpose of fostering the inward life, is known as *dhikr,* remembrance; the Sufi initiations, instituted for this purpose of bringing about the "divine encounter" in the heart all trace back their lineage to the Prophet himself.

Perhaps some inkling of how an invocatory method is intended to operate in the soul may be afforded by recalling the words of a lama whom I met near Shigatse in Tibet when I was staying in the district in 1947. After describing some other methods of a more specialized kind, he offered the following advice: "If a man has been given a particular task to accomplish, this should be carried out with diligence according to the needs of the moment. This having been done, one's remaining time should be filled up with the invocation, leaving no gaps."

Thinking afterward about that lama's advice, it came into my mind that here was a case for applying the lesson of the Gospel story about the man whom an unclean spirit had just quitted. The text goes on to relate how this unclean spirit wandered away through dry places vainly seeking rest until it began to feel homesick for its previous haunt within the man, so it came back there to find the place empty and nicely tidied up—the text says "swept and garnished"—as if awaiting a new occupant. Then that evil spirit proceeded to recruit seven more wickeder than itself, and they all came to dwell there so that the last state of that man was worse than the first.

Here we have a perfect picture of the process of distraction in the mind. If one distracting thought be expelled, a horde of other distracting thoughts will crowd in to fill the vacant place, for willpower alone will not suffice to fight them off. What is needed is a wholesome presence that will leave no room for anything else of a harmful kind. This presence is the Name and its continual invocation. So long as the Name is there, no unclean spirit can gain access to that soul; let this state become an established habit of unbroken attention, and the agents of distraction will give up the struggle, leaving the man in peace.

After what has been said about the Oriental religions, it will be no cause of surprise to find an analogous spiritual method in the Christian tradition itself; indeed it could scarcely be otherwise, since such a way corresponds to a basic human need, outside all questions of religious form. In fact a quintessential formula of the kind referred to above exists in the churches of the Eastern rite under the name of the Jesus Prayer, being invoked there in much the same way as in the traditions of the farther East and giving rise to a whole spiritual method that goes under the name of Hesychasm, from the Greek word *hesychia*, meaning "tranquility," that peace in Christ that is the recompense of saints in this world and the next.

Probably a good many of those here present will have read a small book published under its English title of *The Way of a Pilgrim,* its author being an unidentified Russian of the mid-nineteenth century. At that time the Jesus Prayer and its invocation was the lamp lighting up the way of salvation for many pious men and women in both Russia and the Balkan countries. Monastic centers or hermitages where eminent masters of this spiritual art were known to reside attracted a continuous stream of pilgrims drawn from all sections of the population. Such a master was called *geron* in Greek and *staretz* in Russian, both of which mean "old man." The "Elder" Zosima, in Dostoevsky's *Brothers Karamazov,* is a somewhat fanciful portrait of such a master. The most famous center where the Hesychast methods were practiced and taught was the Holy Mountain of Athos, having been so since Byzantine times; but the roots of this form of Christian yoga, as it may well be called, can be traced much further back, to the hermit communities of the Desert Fathers in Egypt and other parts of the Christian East.

In the eighteenth century a specially selected collection of Greek texts from the Fathers was compiled and first printed in Venice under the name of *Philokalia,* its purpose being to provide the appropriate sapiential foundation for those following the Hesychast way. This collection was soon translated into Russian, being also slightly modified in the process. Two sizable volumes of extracts from this book exist in English, translated by E. Kadloubovsky and G. E. H. Palmer. I recommend this book to your notice with all my heart.

The Jesus Prayer itself consists of a single sentence, which runs as follows: "Lord Jesus Christ, Son of God, have mercy on me" (or "on us" or "on me a sinner," since all three variants exist). Quite evidently, this formula sums up the essentials of the Christ-given wisdom in relation to human need; as a Buddhist would say, this is an *upaya,* or spiritual means, of the greatest efficacy and power. It is equally evident that as far as the prayer itself goes, it is accessible and appropriate to every baptized person as such; moreover its conciseness makes it suitable for all possible occasions—even in the presence of scoffers and persecutors it can be pronounced unobtrusively, just as it also lends itself to being whispered by the dying with their last conscious breath.

Seeing that the Jesus Prayer belongs historically to Eastern Christianity, it may be asked by some whether its transplantation to the West at this late hour would be entirely appropriate, using it of course in its Latin translation of *Domine Jesu Christe Fili Dei miserere nobis*. Could not the rosary, as an existing Western form, fill the same purpose? This is a question I do not feel prepared to answer outright. All one can say is that "invocation," in the methodic sense given to its practice in the East, seems to require a maximum of concentration in the form so used, so that a more extended formula, though not inferior *per se* since it relates to the same wisdom, may not in practice lend itself quite so well to the purpose the invocation is intended to foster. According to one spiritual master, the natural equivalent for a Western follower of the method might well be either *Christe eleison* (which in effect is a compressed form of the Jesus Prayer) or else simply the twofold name *Jesu-Maria*, whereof the concentration of both light and power is too evident to require comment. Another point to note in this connection, one that has an important "technical" bearing on this whole method, is that the less the formula used lends itself to rational analysis, the better will it match that inward synthesis of which it is destined to become the operative support. It is the holy name, sonorous presence of the divine grace enshrined in the formula, that is both the source of its power to illuminate and a sharp sword to cut off ignorance and distraction at the root. The name when treasured in the heart may be likened to a spark of that same uncreated light that shone into the faces of the three Apostles on Mount Tabor and out of which, as the Hesychast tradition itself teaches, the crowns of God's saints both here and hereafter are made.

In point of fact, a number of Catholics known to the writer have long been using one of the above forms of invocation, and there is no reason why others should not follow their example, if so minded. In Greece and Russia the Jesus Prayer can be invoked on a rosary or else aloud or silently according to circumstances; with those in whom the invocation becomes fully operative, the formula begins to repeat itself spontaneously in the heart, by night as well as day. Christian saints have testified to this fact, and so have Hindu, Buddhist, and Muslim saints who have followed corresponding methods; in every case it is a divine name that is at the center of the process, being first the apparent object of invocation and then becoming its subject, until finally the subject-object distinction disappears altogether. This, as Buddhists would say, is the consummation of the marriage of wisdom and method in the heart—but here words fail entirely, and only silence remains to express this supreme experience.

One question relating to the invocation is likely to be put by some; those who have written from actual knowledge in this connection have been almost unanimous in emphasizing the need to practice this method under direction of a spiritual master who has himself proceeded far along this way. As in the case of those following one of the Indian forms of yoga, an intending Hesychast disciple is warned of dangers that might arise from an unguided use of a spiritual instrument of such great inherent potency, for instance through the development of unusual psychic powers whereby attention might be diverted from "the one thing needful" to the ego of the person himself, as proud possessor of the powers in question; this is always a danger, especially when a man is passing from the elementary to the more advanced stages of a spiritual training, when the bodily faculties have been considerably disciplined but the far more elusive psychic faculties are still half out of control. For this reason, it is far better to work under direction of a qualified master who thus becomes, for the disciple, the earthly representative of Christ in relation to the method and should, as has been said again and again, be treated as if it were the Savior Himself who was imparting the instruction. Given this need for qualified direction, it may well be asked where today is such direction to be sought? For it is in no wise to be supposed that qualification for this spiritual office somehow goes with the priestly office, the latter being sacrificial and ritual but not *per se* connected with the initiatic function of a "director of souls." If the sacerdotal office represents the organized side of the tradition, the office of spiritual master represents "the spirit that bloweth where it listeth"; if the spiritual master happens to be a priest and monk (as in fact has usually been the case in practice), this must nevertheless be accounted an "accident" in respect of his special vocation.

When I was preparing this talk, I often put to myself the question "What shall I answer if I am asked where qualified guidance may be found by a Christian seeker today?" This is admittedly a difficult question, but in fact, the Hesychast Fathers had already foreseen this contingency long ago, for after dwelling at length on the imperative need to find a master and put oneself under his direction, they add that if despite all efforts no master is found, the aspirant is not to despair but is to practice the Jesus Prayer with fear and love, instructing himself where possible through reading. As they say, he must throw himself confidently upon the mercy of Christ the Lord, imploring him to be his instructor, and if the aspiration be a genuine one, surely God's grace will come to the man's aid. One is never justified, however discouraged one may feel, in behaving like the man in the parable who only received one talent; one cannot compel the grace of God, but one can always keep oneself in the disposition of responding to it if and when it chooses to manifest itself.

Properly speaking, it is the interior life itself that chooses the man, not the contrary—let this also be remembered. To wait upon the Lord by day and by night is already to be well on the way. There is no time or place where man is left devoid of all spiritual opportunity, unless it be that he himself refuses or ignores the divine mercy that surrounds him.

Orthodox Monastery on Mount Athos, Greece

His Holiness Sri Chandrasekharendra Saraswati Swamigal, the 68th Acharya of Kanchi Kamakoti Peetam

Appendix III
A Buddhist Garland for the Jagadguru

It was with not a little surprise, coupled with a strong sense of occasion, that I read the letter inviting me to contribute to the Souvenir collection marking the 76th birthday of His Holiness of Kanchi, an auspicious occasion indeed! The contribution is made with all the greater willingness since its author is a Buddhist by traditional participation and intends to speak from that angle.

But is this proper, some may ask, for, how can a professing Buddhist presume to write in honor of one who bears Sri Sankaracharya's august title, associated as this has been in the past with the turning back of Buddhism in India? Is not such a person disqualified from doing so, or alternatively, is he not in a sense betraying the tradition of the Lord Buddha to which he himself is dharmically attached? In either case such an action is blameworthy, so these critics will argue.

To which I will answer that not only is it proper for a Buddhist to act in this manner now, but also that there is a particular value in his doing so, both for his own sake and also for the sake of others as much as he will be enabled thereby to bring out certain aspects of truth too often overlooked.

First of all, it is important to point out, quoting one whose name is well known among the friends of Kanchi Kamakoti, namely, Frithjof Schuon, that the inhibitive part played by the Adi Sankaracharya versus the Buddhist of his time in no wise implies an inability on his part to grasp the essence of Buddha's teaching at its own level. The Master of *Advaita Vedanta* quite obviously was capable of situating any knowledge regardless of the formal limits attaching to its dialectical expression. It was indeed no accident that certain Hindus belonging to other schools accused him of uttering a doctrine that was but a disguised form of Buddhism; however outrageous such a statement may appear at first sight, it does nevertheless harbor a truth pertaining to more than those who offered the above criticism. This interior view of the matter, discoverable "beyond forms," does not affect the nature of Sri Sankaracharya's specific function of appointed restorer and illuminator of the Hindu Dharma. In discharging this function, as Frithjof Schuon has also pointed out, the great Vedantic sage had no particular call to spare another traditional form which, though essentially true, did not fit in with the characteristic exigencies of Hinduism. Had Buddhism done so, it would have become yet another Hindu *darsana*, but such in fact was not its dharmic destiny.

All this is perfectly intelligible to a Buddhist viewing the matter in a spirit of non-attachment, just as, on the other hand, a Hindu similarly motivated is able to see that the Lord Buddha did not set out to "reform" Hinduism and that his teaching represented a spontaneous manifestation of the Spirit at that "cyclic moment" which rendered it opportune. There could be no question here of human contrivance.

Judging after the event, it is also evident that the Buddhist revelation was, among other things, a means of rendering the Indian wisdom accessible to non-Indian races to whose mentality this presentation was perfectly suited. The marvelous flowering of the *Mahayana* in China, Japan, and Tibet is a living proof that such was the case; for this result to become possible, however, a certain departure from the specifically Hindu norms was necessary. All this goes to show that such a conflict does not only have a negative function, it also has a providential, therefore positive, function in regard to those sections of humanity respectively concerned in it.

There is no occasion now to recapitulate the arguments formerly put forward by the sages and saints who acted as spokesmen of the two traditions in the course of their debates with one another. Some of the arguments bore fruit in ways that much exceeded their temporary purpose, as when Sri Sankaracharya used his controversy with the Buddhists as a means of giving point to his masterly exposition of the doctrine of *Atma*, by which jnanically-minded men are still illuminated today just as they were in his own time. We can all thank God that this same light still shines in Kanchi Kamakoti and that the voice of Dharma has never been silenced in that hallowed place.

By way of special tribute on this joyful occasion of the 76th birthday of His Holiness of Kanchi the present writer wishes to draw attention to a formula belonging to the Semitic wisdom, as illustrating in a most remarkable way the metaphysical reciprocity between the Vedantic teaching about the Self and the Buddhist theory of *anatma* which many people have regarded as marking irreconcilable positions. This formula is the Shahadah or "Testimony" of Islam in which the Advaitic doctrine is summed up with miraculous conciseness. A moment's glance will show that the Arabic words *La ilaha illa'Llah*: "There is no divinity (or reality, or self) outside the divinity (or Reality, or Self)" enshrines at one and the same time the truth of the Buddhist *anatma* and the Vedantic *Atma*; like Buddhism it "annihilates" any belief in the reality of the world and its contents in order to make way for the only intrinsic Reality, the Divine Suchness of Self. Need anything be added to prove that Vedanta and Buddhism have a common link between them? To look in the mirror of a tradition other than one's own tradition with all the greater certainty!

On the auspicious day of Vaisaka Anuraadha this garland is laid, in deepest reverence, at the lotus feet of His Holiness the Jagadguru of Kanchi Kamakoti Pitha by the hand of Munishastra Dhara.

Biographical Notes

MARCO PALLIS was born of Greek parents in Liverpool, England in 1895, received his education at Harrow and Liverpool University, and served in the British army during the Great War. He was widely respected as a teacher and writer of religious and metaphysical works, and was also a gifted musician and composer, as well as a mountaineer. His Himalayan travels led to his adoption of Tibetan Buddhism and in 1947 he visited Tibet itself. His other writings include the best-selling classic *Peaks and Lamas,* a unique blend of travelogue, botanical lore, and discursive essays on Tibetan civilization, and *A Buddhist Spectrum: Contributions to Buddhist-Christian Dialogue,* a compendium of his writings that originally appeared in the British journal *Studies in Comparative Religion.* Macro Pallis died in 1989.

JOSEPH A. FITZGERALD studied Comparative Religion at Indiana University, where he also earned a Doctor of Jurisprudence degree. He is a senior editor at World Wisdom and a professional writer. For twenty years, he has traveled extensively throughout the Buddhist world, including visits to Bhutan, Mongolia, Cambodia, Burma, Thailand, Indonesia, Nepal, and India, as well as three trips to Japan. He previously edited *Honen the Buddhist Saint: Essential Writings and Official Biography.* He lives with his wife in Bloomington, Indiana.

HARRY OLDMEADOW is Coordinator of Philosophy and Religious Studies in the Department of Arts, La Trobe University, Bendigo, Australia. He studied history, politics, and literature at the Australian National University, obtaining a First Class Honors degree in history. In 1980 he completed a Masters dissertation on the work of the renowned perennialist author Frithjof Schuon and the other principal traditionalist writers. This study was awarded the University of Sydney Medal for excellence in research and was eventually published under the title *Traditionalism: Religion in the Light of the Perennial Philosophy*. His other works include *Journeys East:20th Century Western Encounters with Eastern Religious Traditions*, *The Betrayal of Tradition: Essays on the Spiritual Crisis of Modernity*, *Light from the East: Eastern Wisdom for the Modern West*, and *A Christian Pilgrim in India: The Spiritual Journey of Swami Abhishiktananda (Henri Le Saux)*. He currently resides with his wife and younger son on a small property outside Bendigo.

PAUL GOBLE was born in England, and studied at the Central School of Art in London. He has written and illustrated over 28 children's books that retell ancient stories and legends of the Native Americans. His illustrations accurately depict Native American clothing, customs, and surroundings in brilliant color and detail. His many awards as an author and illustrator include the prestigious Caldecott Medal. He and his wife live in Rapid City, South Dakota.

Index of
Significant Foreign Terms

For a glossary of all key foreign words used in books published by World Wisdom, including metaphysical terms in English, consult: www.DictionaryofSpiritualTerms.org. This on-line Dictionary of Spiritual Terms provides extensive definitions, examples and related terms in other languages.

Photo Credits

Shree Shree Anandamayee Sangha: 58; British Museum: 233; Buddhist Society: *xxii*; Joseph A. Fitzgerald: *vi, xi, xxi, xxxi,* 27, 78, 120, 225, 242; Audrey Harris: 150; Kanchi Kamakoti Peetam: 264; Wolf Hegner: 234; Cauthra Mulock: 108; R. C. Nicholson: *ii, xxxii,* 130; M. H. Robins: *xxii*; Vladimír Sís and Josef Vaniš: *xii,* 28; Spink & Sons Ltd.: 172; Victoria and Albert Museum: 241; unknown: 130, 192

Other Titles on Buddhism by World Wisdom

The Buddha Eye: An Anthology of the Kyoto School and Its Contemporaries
edited by Frederick Franck, 2004

A Buddhist Spectrum: Contributions to Buddhist-Christian Dialogue
by Marco Pallis, 2004

The Essential Shinran: The Path of True Entrusting
edited by Alfred Bloom, 2007

The Golden Age of Zen: Zen Masters of the T'ang Dynasty
by John C.H. Wu, 2004

Honen the Buddhist Saint: Essential Writings and Official Biography
edited by Joseph A. Fitzgerald, 2006

The Laughing Buddha of Tofukuji: The Life of Zen Master Keido Fukushima
by Ishwar Harris, 2004

Living in Amida's Universal Vow: Essays in Shin Buddhism
edited by Alfred Bloom, 2004

Naturalness: A Classic of Shin Buddhism
by Kenryo Kanamatsu, 2002

*Samdhong Rinpoche: Uncompromising Truth for a
Compromised World: Tibetan Buddhism and Today's World*
edited by Donovan Roebert, 2006

Treasures of Buddhism
by Frithjof Schuon, 1993

Zen Buddhism: A History, Vol. 1: India and China
by Heinrich Dumoulin, 2005

Zen Buddhism: A History, Vol. 2: Japan
by Heinrich Dumoulin, 2005